MARY ELLEN MILLER was educated at the universities of Princeton and Yale, receiving her PhD in History of Art from Yale, where she is Sterling Professor of the History of Art. Professor Miller has worked extensively in Central America, particularly Mexico, Guatemala, Belize, and Honduras, where she has carried out research in Maya art, architecture, and culture. She has written many articles on Mesoamerican art for learned journals, and her book with Linda Schele, *The Blood of Kings* (1986), is considered a landmark in Maya studies. She is also the author of *Maya Art and Architecture* (1999) and, with Karl Taube, *The Gods and Symbols of Ancient Mexico and the Maya* (1993). She served as guest curator of 'The Courtly Art of the Ancient Maya' exhibition in 2004 at the National Gallery of Art in Washington, DC, and wrote the accompanying book with Simon Martin. She has recently completed *The Spectacle of the Late Maya Court: Reflections on the Paintings of Bonampak* with Claudia Brittenham.

Thames & Hudson world of art

This famous series provides the widest available range of illustrated books on art in all its aspects.

To find out about all our publications, including other titles in the World of Art series, please visit **thamesandhudsonusa.com**.

WITHDRAWN

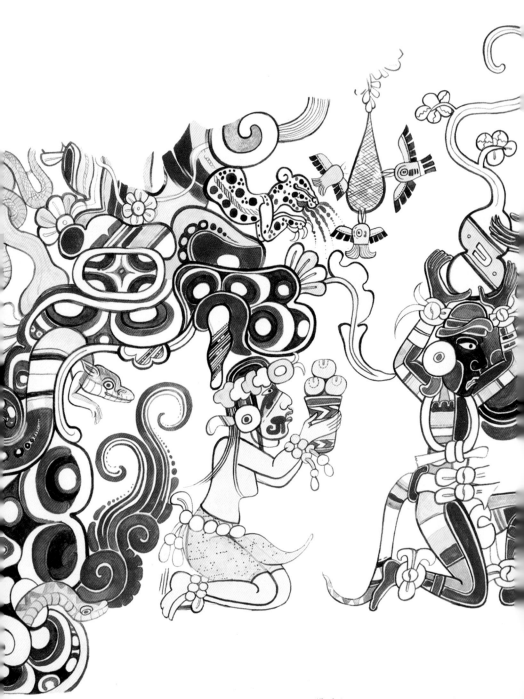

08.11.12

Mary Ellen Miller

The Art of Mesoamerica

from Olmec to Aztec

Fifth edition

250 illustrations, 185 in color

 Thames & Hudson world of art

Pronunciations and spellings of Mesoamerican names require some attention. In the sixteenth century, the letter x in the Spanish alphabet was pronounced like the phoneme sh in English today. In general, names in native Mesoamerican languages with this consonant require the sh sound – as in Yaxchilan, for example. Most Mayan cs, regardless of the following vowel, are hard. When u precedes another vowel, the resulting sound is similar to a w, as in Nahuatl. Spanish words ordinarily have a stress on the final syllable unless they end in a vowel, n, or s (when preceded by an n or a vowel) – in which case the penultimate syllable is stressed. Most words in the language of the Aztecs, Nahuatl, take the emphasis on the penultimate syllable. Words in Mayan languages are not strongly accented. Accents are generally used in this work only where they occur on names in Spanish (e.g. José). In general, place names used here are the standard ones found on maps published by national governments, although accents have been dropped where they would not be used in native pronunciation.

1 Astonishing in the complexity that they reveal at an exceptionally early date of c. 100 BC, the Maya paintings of San Bartolo depict the Maize God (right), accepting a gourd from a kneeling attendant; a female attendant kneels at left, within a cave mouth, probably relating the story of the annual rebirth of maize. The artists show mastery of pigments, binders, and compositional order. Reconstruction by Heather Hurst.

The Art of Mesoamerica © 1986, 1996, 2001, 2006 and 2012
Thames & Hudson Ltd, London

First published in 1986 in paperback in the United States of America by Thames & Hudson Inc., 500 Fifth Avenue, New York, New York 10110

thamesandhudsonusa.com

Fifth edition 2012
Reprinted 2015

Library of Congress Catalog Card Number 2011945985

ISBN 978-0-500-20414-6

Printed and bound in China through Asia Pacific Offset Ltd

Contents

		CENTRAL MEXICO	OAXACA	GULF COAST	WEST MEXICO	MAYA HIGHLANDS/ PACIFIC COAST	LOWLAND MAYA South	LOWLAND MAYA North
1519	LATE POSTCLASSIC	*Aztecs* Tenochtitlan Tlaxcala	Mixtec independent kingdoms	Totonacs *Cempoala*	Tarascans	Maya independent city-states *Mixco Viejo, Iximche, Utatlan*	Tayasal (Itza)	Tulum *Santa Rita*
1200		*Toltecs* Tula		Huastecs				Mayapan
	EARLY POSTCLASSIC		Mitla Yagul					Chichen Itza
	TERMINAL CLASSIC	Xochicalco					Tepeu Late Classic Maya	Puuc and Central Yucatan
900		Cacaxtla		Classic Veracruz				
	LATE CLASSIC	*Teotihuacán Phases I–IV*	Monte Alban IIIb	*El Tajín*				
600				*Remojadas*		Cotzumalhuapa		
			Monte Alban IIIa	Cerro de las Mesas		Kaminaljuyu	Tzakol: Early Classic Maya	
	EARLY CLASSIC				Ixtlan del Río	Escuintla		Oxkintok
300	PROTO CLASSIC		Monte Alban II					
AD BC	LATE FORMATIVE			Tres Zapotes	Chupicuaro	Izapa, Kaminaljuyu, Takalik Abaj	Cerros El Mirador San Bartolo	
		Cuicuilco			Colima			
300			Dainzu	La Venta				
			Monte Alban I					
600	MIDDLE FORMATIVE	Tlatilco		*Olmecs*				
900	EARLY FORMATIVE			San Lorenzo				
1200					Teopante-cuanitlan Xochipala Capacha	Ocos		
1500	ARCHAIC							

Preface

As I have written and rewritten this book for over twenty-five years, I have learned not to get too comfortable with one set of interpretations, nor with a chronology, nor even a geography. *The Art of Mesoamerica* now starts earlier, with radiocarbon dating that reveals use of Mesoamerica's signature material, jade, back to 1800 BC in the tropical forest of the Gulf Coast. Its end is signaled with the Spanish invasion of 1519, but the manipulation of Mesoamerica's precious materials – whether feathers or pigments or obsidian – does not cease abruptly, like the drop of a curtain, and the negotiations of the sixteenth century can be understood to be a part of the process of Mesoamerican art-making rather than a coda. New discoveries continue to change the contours of study and knowledge, and the very fact that the single largest Aztec monolith ever to be found would come to light in 2006 alerts us to the fact that future discoveries await.

The end of the twentieth century and the beginning of the twenty-first have been rife with raw, new discoveries, from Olmec heads that have rolled out of ravines along the Gulf Coast to the opening of some of the wealthiest tombs that the Maya interred deep within massive pyramids. *National Geographic* magazine continues to provide insightful coverage of archaeology, although its focus on the excavations it supports directly can result in less attention to Mexico than to excavations elsewhere. *Arqueologia Mexicana*, on the other hand, stays atop both the latest discoveries within Mexico and considerations of materials known for centuries, providing both breaking news and satisfying digestion of familiar works. News of discoveries travels faster than ever before: for nearly two decades students and scholars have followed hieroglyphic decipherments and conference proceedings with the Aztlan network, the Foundation for Mesoamerican Studies, Inc (FAMSI) website, and mesoweb.com, but high-quality photographs and video postings can take the interested observer from armchair to fieldwork with unprecedented ease. At the same time that new information proliferates – and with generally improved Wikipedia entries that detail site walkthroughs or lives of archaeologists – the latest technology often results in homogenized, simplified readings and interpretations, repeated from one web posting to another.

Recent exhibitions continue to bring new discoveries and scholarly interpretations to a broader audience. The vast Aztec exhibition that came to New York's Guggenheim Museum in 2004 studded the central spiral staircase of that museum with serpents,

This mask was placed over the face of the woman now known as the 'Red Queen,' whose funerary pyramid was roughly contemporaneous with that of King Pakal, in the adjacent building at Palenque. Geologists have found raw malachite, the material thinned to form the tesserae of the mask, only in northern Mexico.

shells and warriors in ways that surely would have appealed to the museum's architect, Frank Lloyd Wright, who took much from the ancient Mexican past. *Courtly Art of the Ancient Maya* and *Lords of Creation* brought new Maya discoveries and notions of a courtly kingship to major American cities in 2004; *The Fiery Pool* added the dimension of the Maya sea in 2010–11. The Art Institute of Chicago's *Hero, Hawk, and Open Hand* of 2004 helped promote thinking about Mississippian cultures in North America, and their connections to those of Mesoamerica, and *El Vuelo de las Imágenes* ('The Flight of Images') at the Museo de Arte Nacional in Mexico City in 2011 tracked the trajectory of finely crafted works of feathers throughout the Colonial era. Recent exhibitions sponsored by the Museo Nacional de Antropologia, with stunning catalogs, have resulted in long queues of visitors.

At the same time that many native languages can be considered 'endangered' and at risk of ceasing to be spoken, others now play a role in the United States. Some open-air markets in California are punctuated by the glottal stops of Mixtec; I have heard Nahuatl spoken in New Haven supermarkets. New Nahuatl words, particularly names of foodstuffs, continue to migrate into common parlance: *chipotle* now seems as familiar a word in English as do tomato and avocado.

Although administration has taken more and more of my time away from the classroom in the past few years, I have nevertheless continued to collaborate with colleagues – and my work with Stephen Houston, Michael Coe, Claudia Brittenham, Megan O'Neil, Matthew Robb, Barbara Mundy, Diana Magaloni, Dennis Carr, and Khristaan Villela has been particularly rewarding. The work of Jorge Gomez Tejada, Jennifer Josten, Sara Ryu, and Sarah Hetherington, PhD students at Yale, has continued to push boundaries, disciplinary and otherwise, and we've learned from one another, especially on site in Mexico. I am grateful to have had the opportunity to present the 2010 A. W. Mellon lectures at the National Gallery of Art, which gave me the opportunity to synthesize my thinking in fresh ways.

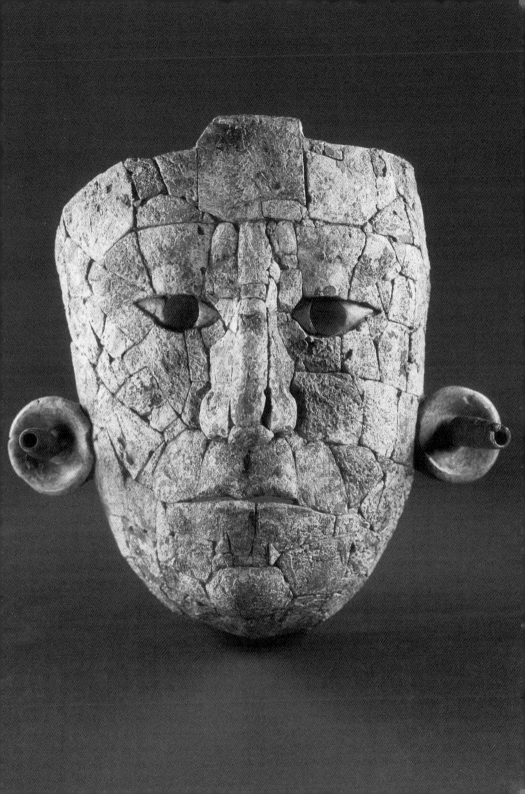

Chapter 1   Introduction

At the time of the Spanish invasion, the Aztec ruler Motecuhzoma II kept tax rolls that show tribute paid from regions far to the north and south, from the limits of the barbarian ('Chichimec') north to the rich, cacao-producing coast of modern Guatemala. If we extend these limits across their respective lines of latitude, 14 to 21 degrees north, we define Mesoamerica, a cultural region united by use of the ritual 260-day calendar and a locus of New World high civilizations for over 3,000 years, from 1500 BC until the arrival of the Spanish. Although the Caribbean, lower Central America, northern Mexico, and the United States Southwest all had contact with Mesoamerica, these connections waxed and waned over time to a greater degree than the internal connections among Mesoamericans. Nevertheless, these more distant contacts were important, introducing both goldworking from the south and turquoise material from the north.

These borders of Mesoamerica, like the terminology itself, are the constructions of twentieth-century archaeology and anthropology. Some recent discoveries illustrate the porosity of any limits. In 2009 archaeologists in the United States Southwest discovered the remains of chocolate in a vessel from the Chaco Canyon cultures in New Mexico and recognized that the distinctive tall black and white cylinders had their roots in the black and white cylinder vessels for chocolate [3, 4] common to the Maya. In that same era, neighbors to the south in lower Central America emulated Maya polychrome ceramics in shape, color, and deployment of figures, often bordered with rim patterns based in Maya texts, but perhaps only signifying the value of text without being text. It would be Malintzin, a bilingual woman (more commonly known as Malinche), who would both guide and advise Hernando Cortés, especially as she gained fluency in Spanish, but Cortés and his men brought with them from Cuba a woman from Jamaica who was able to understand the Mayan speakers of Yucatan. There was more knowledge of the world beyond Mesoamerica's traditional boundaries than is commonly acknowledged, connections underpinned by long-distance trade by land and sea.

Despite its narrow latitudinal range, Mesoamerica is a place of great climatic and topographic diversity, depending on both

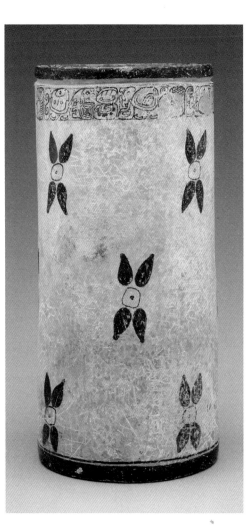
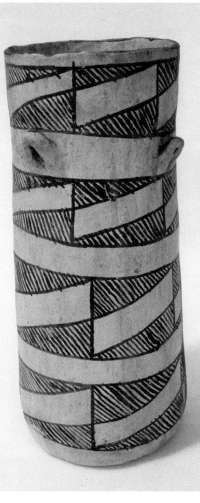

3, 4 The Maya formed tapered cylinders for the serving of frothy cacao for elite consumption, as confirmed by both texts and residues. Recent studies of eleventh-century vessels from Pueblo Bonito, Chaco Canyon, New Mexico, also reveal the persistent theobromine of chocolate, confirming the long-distance trade from Mexico's tropical regions to the arid US Southwest. Yet more astonishing for the study of art is that the form, size, and slip patterning at Chaco emulates a Maya model.

altitude and rainfall. The tribute paid to Motecuhzoma II ranged from jaguars to eagles, and from exotic bird feathers to gold and jade treasure, materials and resources found in greatly varying ecological zones. The high, cool valleys contrast sharply with the steamy lowland jungles, and then as now the valleys attracted dense populations. Certain critical resources, such as obsidian, the 'steel' of the New World, were found only in the highlands; cacao and cotton grew in moist, tropical regions. Trade in these goods brought highland and lowland Mesoamerica into constant contact.

Among the greatest civilizations to thrive in Mesoamerica were the Olmec, Maya, and Aztec, although as we shall see, the less-familiar Teotihuacan and Oaxaca cultures achieved pinnacles of sophistication too. Most of these were located either in the highlands or lowlands, although the Maya inhabited both. The earliest civilization, that of the Olmecs, rose along the rivers of the tropical Gulf Coast. Most Maya development also took place in the lowlands, under tropical conditions ranging from rainforest to scrub jungle in Yucatan, Chiapas, Guatemala, and Belize. The ancient cities of Tula and Teotihuacan, as well as Tenochtitlan, Motecuhzoma's city, were located at high altitudes, and the center of highland life was the Valley of Mexico. Modern Mexico City is built on top of the Aztec capital, and so the Valley of Mexico still dominates Mesoamerica as it did in antiquity.

Despite the periodic presentation of data that humans first arrived in the New World as early as 40,000 years ago, most scientists believe that modern humans came to the Americas across a land passage at times of low sea level from Asia to Alaska starting roughly 17,000 years ago. Arriving by foot but in waves, humans brought no domestic animal other than the dog, eliminating, on the one hand, reservoirs for disease, and on the other, sources of protein and subjects to enhance human labor. At least some peoples had probably arrived within the boundaries of Mesoamerica by 10,000 BC, and waves of migration of widely different language groups drove more newcomers from north to south right up until the Spanish invasion. These waves affected the political geography of Mesoamerica, for each succeeding movement of peoples required re-adjustment on the part of the others. For instance, some think that Nahua speakers were late arrivals, entering the Valley of Mexico at the fall of Teotihuacan in the seventh century AD and perhaps in part responsible for that city's decline. These Nahua speakers soon dominated the highlands, developing first as Toltecs and later as what we know as Aztecs. Yet the extremely important people of Teotihuacan remain of unknown ethnicity. Were they also Nahua speakers?

Little that is of interest to the history of art remains of the earliest colonizers of the New World. Fine projectile points, such as the Folsom, were crafted almost 10,000 years ago, and village life thrived throughout Mesoamerica by the second millennium BC. Only with the rise of Olmec civilization around 1500 BC, however, did art and architecture appear which combined ideological complexity, craft, and permanence.

Compared with the Old World, the Mesoamerican high civilizations seem to have lagged behind technologically: the wheel

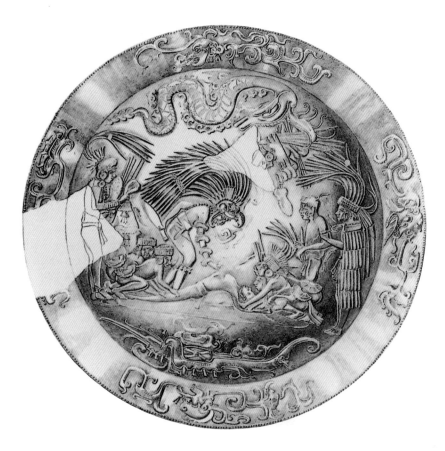

5 Early underwater archaeologists dredged up gold repoussé disks from the Sacred Cenote, Chichen Itza, and, like the paintings in ill. 206, they show Central Mexican warriors gaining dominion over their enemies. The graceful human proportions and foreshortening suggest Maya facture.

was never used for anything other than miniatures, and obsidian tools and weapons served in place of wrought metal ones. Absence of a draft animal may explain why the wheel and its critical component, the axle, were never developed; even in the Andes, the llama served as a pack animal but will not pull a cart. Wheels but not axles turn up on toys in Central Mexico and in Veracruz, never making the leap to the pulley, potter's wheel, or even a human-propelled vehicle like a rickshaw or wheelbarrow. Obsidian, though easily chipped, in fact makes such a sharp instrument that it has been returned to use by modern opthalmic surgeons! New World technology did, in any case, develop slowly. Metallurgy, for example, was first used in the ancient Andes about 3000 BC, and metalworking techniques were gradually passed north, traveling up through Central America and arriving in Mesoamerica about AD 800 [5]. Even then, however, metals did not replace stone and obsidian functional objects, and precious metals

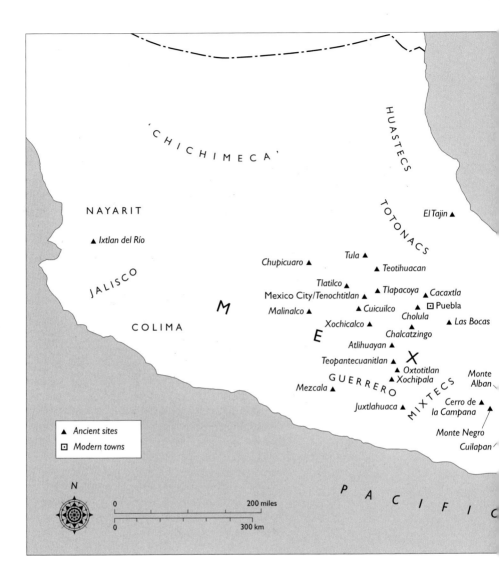

'CHICHIMECA'

HUASTECS

NAYARIT

TOTONACS

El Tajin ▲

▲ Ixtlan del Río

JALISCO

M

COLIMA

E

X

GUERRERO

Mezcala ▲

Juxtlahuaca ▲

MIXTECS

Chupicuaro ▲

Tula ▲

▲ Teotihuacan

Tlatilco ▲

Mexico City/Tenochtitlan ▲ ▲ Tlapacoya ▲ Cacaxtla

Malinalco ▲   ▲ Cuicuilco   ▲ ▣ Puebla

Xochicalco ▲   Cholula   ▲ Las Bocas

Chalcatzingo
▲
Atlihuayan ▲

Teopantecuanitlan ▲ ▲ Oxtotitlan
         ▲ Xochipala   Monte
                          Alban

Cerro de ▲
la Campana

Monte Negro

Cuilapan

PACIFIC

▲ Ancient sites
▣ Modern towns

N

0 _____ 200 miles
0 _____ 300 km

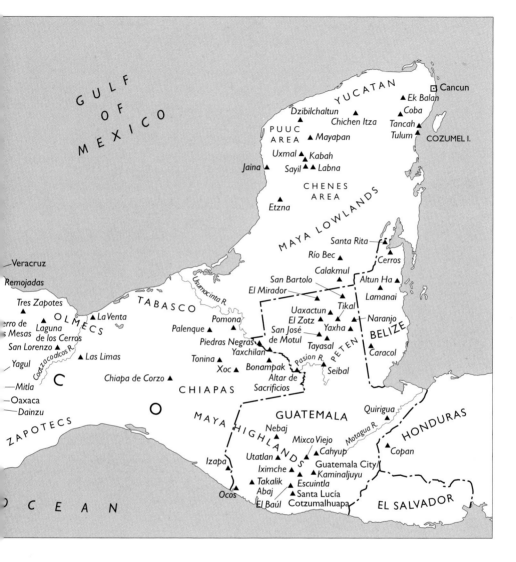

6 Mesoamerica, showing sites
mentioned in the text.

Map labels:

GULF OF MEXICO

YUCATAN

Cancun
Ek Balan
Coba
Dzibilchaltun
Chichen Itza
Tancah
PUUC AREA
Mayapan
Tulum
COZUMEL I.
Uxmal
Kabah
Jaina
Sayil
Labna
CHENES AREA
Etzna
MAYA LOWLANDS
Santa Rita
Río Bec
Cerros
Calakmul
Altun Ha
San Bartolo
El Mirador
Lamanai
Veracruz
Remojadas
Uaxactun
Tikal
Tres Zapotes
Pomona
El Zotz
Yaxha
Naranjo
erro de s Mesas
Laguna de los Cerros
La Venta
OLMECS
Palenque
San José de Motul
BELIZE
San Lorenzo
Piedras Negras
Tayasal
TABASCO
Usumacinta R.
Yaxchilan
Caracol
Yagul
Las Limas
Tonina
PETEN
Mitla
Xoc
Bonampak
Seibal
Oaxaca
Chiapa de Corzo
Altar de Sacrificios
Pasion R.
Dainzu
CHIAPAS
Quirigua
ZAPOTECS
MAYA HIGHLANDS
GUATEMALA
Motagua R.
HONDURAS
Nebaj
Mixco Viejo
Izapa
Cahyup
Copan
Utatlan
Iximche
Guatemala City
Takalik Abaj
Escuintla
Kaminaljuyu
Ocos
Santa Lucía Cotzumalhuapa
EL SALVADOR
El Baúl
OCEAN

Coatzacoalcos R.

15

were worked instead into luxury goods: jewelry, masks, and headdress elements – although gold never completely replaced jade as the most precious material. Cortés's men quickly learned that the people of Mesoamerica valued greenstones more than any other material, and gold was willingly traded for green glass beads. Throughout Mesoamerican history, the finest objects were worked from jade and other green materials, such as feathers. What has come to be called 'Motecuhzoma's headdress,' for example, was made of 450 long, green quetzal feathers, blue cotinga and pink flamingo plumes and studded with jade disks, and tiny hollow gold beads [238]. Dozens of fine masks of precious greenstones, including malachite, have been excavated in the past few years, at Palenque, Teotihuacan, and Calakmul.

We know of the extreme importance of woven cloth to the ancient Andes, and the key role of cloth's early invention there, where it predated fired ceramics. Was it equally central to Mesoamerica? No single item was more widely demanded in tribute at the time of the Spanish invasion, whether plain white weave or fancy and colorful brocade or embroidery, along with finished dresses and full warrior suits, but almost nothing survives of prehispanic textiles today. A weaver sees the entire pattern unfold in her mind (and by and large, the weaver on the backstrap loom was and is female), the part standing in for the whole, key to successful abbreviation of iconography, as demonstrated early on by the Olmecs. Working with wefts and warps gives the maker an understanding of right angles, helping establish principles of grid and symmetry. Textile makers would have mastered the skills necessary to dye threads – particularly challenging for cotton – with indigo and cochineal. The first complex and widely shared religious symbol system, that of the Olmecs, could be reduced to 'plectogenic' designs, that is to say those that could conform to the constraints of weaving, which may have supported the dissemination of a belief system.

Long before the emergence of high civilization in Mesoamerica, humans had domesticated maize, manioc (cassava), beans, squash, tomatoes, avocados, sunflowers, sweet potatoes, and chili peppers; they learned to harvest wild cacao pods for chocolate and the pods of a certain wild orchid for vanilla, and they kept stingless honey bees in hollow tree trunks. They discovered wild cotton and learned to spin and weave. Even in Olmec times, surpluses made it possible to develop full-time specialists devoted to the arts, especially art and architecture [7]. By the first millennium AD, these crops supported rising populations which in turn required the development of high-yield agriculture, including terraces, ridged fields, and raised fields. Not only were there full-time craftspeople and artisans but also astronomers to chart the movements of the heavens and poets to tell the stories of gods and heroes. By AD 100, the Maya and perhaps others had put into a use a calendar of interlocking cycles as accurate as any known today – and certainly more accurate than the Julian calendar used by Cortés and his men [39]. Powerful lords commissioned monumental city plans that transformed natural geography with vast pyramids and ranging palaces, frequently with rich burials, caches, or offerings within that testify both to the value of such materials and the personal power to remove such works from circulation.

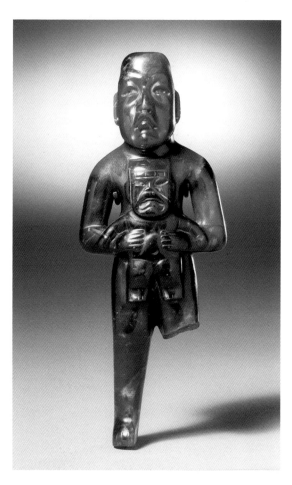

7 Olmec artisans selected translucent blue-green jade for this sober rendering of the adult who holds the Rain God, carved with babylike features.

Because of its realistic system of human proportions and complex hieroglyphic writing, Maya art long seemed a reflection of a pinnacle of civilization, and by 1950, most students of its art called its florescence between AD 300 and 900 the Classic [8]. Preclassic and Postclassic were the terminology then assigned to the predecessors and successors of the Classic Maya. Despite the suggestion of value that these terms bear and repeated efforts to replace them with such conventions as those used in the Andes (e.g. 'Late Intermediate Period'), these terms survive, although the

8 With his elegant proportions, the Maize God of Structure 22 from Copan models an ideal human form. Local volcanic rock lent itself to three-dimensional forms.

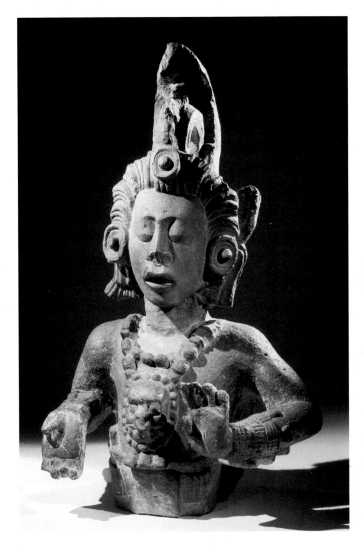

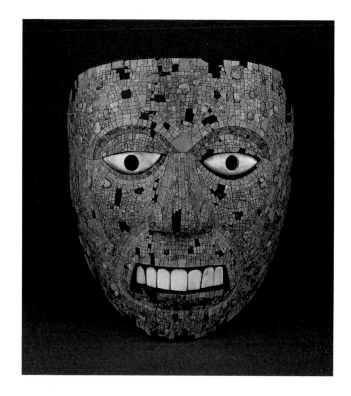

9 Brilliant turquoise tesserae cover a wooden support and yield a dramatic face of an Aztec god; pieces of shell form skeletalized teeth. This mask may once have served as part of a full deity suit used to adorn a stone or wood mannequin.

Preclassic is often referred to today as the Formative. Formative, Classic, and Postclassic should now be considered chronological markers, not descriptive terms, and wherever possible dates will simply be referred to by century, rather than period terms. The Olmecs flourished first, with signs of the first complex culture in the rainforest emerging after 1500 BC. So-called Classic cultures are harder both to define and to align, with the fits and starts of Maya civilization before the time of Julius Caesar and the burning of Teotihuacan now pushed back into the seventh century AD. Cities in Veracruz and Oaxaca persisted after the collapse of most Maya southern lowland centers c. AD 800. Strangely enough, the years 900–1325 remain the murkiest in Mesoamerican cultural history, both enlightened and confused by ethnohistory and seen through the lens of the Aztecs who ruled supreme at the time of the Spanish invasion [9]. Although an earlier generation of scholars insisted on reading Precolumbian cultural extinction within a generation of the Spanish victory over the Aztecs in 1521, both new materials and new interpretations can now cast light on the complexities of the Nahua-Christian world in the sixteenth century.

Not all the art and architecture of ancient Mesoamerica was lost from view as culture succeeded culture. Teotihuacan in the Valley of Mexico was visited regularly by Motecuhzoma II as a place of pilgrimage, and Western visitors have traveled there since the Conquest. Indeed the question of the recovery and understanding of the past preoccupied the Aztecs as much as it does archaeologists today (even if in a different way) – as recent excavations in the sacred precinct of Tenochtitlan have shown. Objects and treasures were uncovered by the Aztecs and brought to Tenochtitlan from throughout the realm, often with little appreciation of their original significance. These objects were then deposited in caches, leaving yet greater archaeological and chronological puzzles for modern humanity.

Sources record that Motecuhzoma II's grandfather, Motecuhzoma I, sent out wise men to seek the origins of the Aztecs, but no answers were found. In turn, the Spanish wondered whether these new people were truly human at all. Did they, so it was asked, derive from the same creation in the Garden of Eden as they themselves did? Explanations were sought for the isolation of a New World race: were the Amerindians a Lost Tribe of Israel or refugees from Atlantis? Did they, as Father José de Acosta suggested in the late sixteenth century, enter the New World by a land bridge from Asia?

Even after it was accepted in the nineteenth century that Mesoamerica was populated by the means Father Acosta had suggested, Mesoamerica continued to be identified as the recipient of culture from the Old World. Egypt, Phoenicia, China, and Africa have all been cited at one time or another as probable sources, usually on the basis of nothing more than vague resemblances. For example, the distinctive scrollwork of El Tajin has often been associated with the scroll designs made in China in the late Zhou dynasty. In Mesoamerica, the origin and use of the double scrolls are linked to the game played with a rubber ball. Rubber (as well as the game it gave rise to) is native to the New World. The Zhou dynasty ended in 256 BC, long before the advent of the Classic era in Mesoamerica. Based on an interpretation of Olmec colossal heads, Afro-centrists have recently made broad and unfounded claims that Mesoamerican civilization depends on African contact. It is worth noting that useful technologies – just what one would imagine would be most likely to be exchanged – were generally not shared between Old and New Worlds. Powerful though such suggestions may be, one must also note that these claims are made by those unwilling to accept the modern Mesoamerican peasant as the descendant of creators of high culture. Although the question of contact remains unanswered in all its details, by and large it will be assumed here that ideas, inventions, and civilizations arose independently in the New World.

The systematic recovery of ancient Mesoamerica by modern man did not begin until almost 300 years after the Spanish invasion. Starting at the end of the eighteenth century and continuing up to the present, explorers have searched for the ruins of ancient Mesoamerica. With the progress of time, archaeologists have unearthed civilizations increasingly remote in age. It is as if for each century logged in the modern era an earlier stratum of antiquity has been revealed. Nineteenth-century explorers, particularly John Lloyd Stephens and Frederick Catherwood, came upon Maya cities in the jungle, as well as evidence of other Classic cultures [10]. Twentieth-century research revealed a much earlier high civilization, the Olmec. It now scarcely seems possible that the frontiers of early Mesoamerican civilization can be pushed back any further in time, although new work – such as in Oaxaca – will continue to fill in details of the picture.

The process of discovery often shapes what we know about the history of Mesoamerican art. New finds are just as often made accidentally as intentionally. In 1971, for instance, workers installing Sound and Light equipment under the Pyramid of the Sun at Teotihuacan stumbled upon a remarkable cave within the structure; this chance discovery has done as much for our understanding of the pyramid as any systematic study. Archaeology has its own fashions too: the isolation of new sites may be the prime goal in one decade, the excavation of pyramids the focus in the next; in a third decade, outlying structures rather than principal buildings may absorb archaeologists' energies. Nor should one forget that excavators are vulnerable to local interests. At one point, reconstruction of pyramids to attract tourism may be desired; at another, archaeologists may be precluded from working at what has already become a tourist attraction. Modern construction often determines which ancient sites can be excavated. In Mexico City, for example, the building of the subway initiated the excavations there and renewed interest in the old Aztec capital.

The study of Mesoamerican art is not based exclusively on archaeology. Much useful information about the native

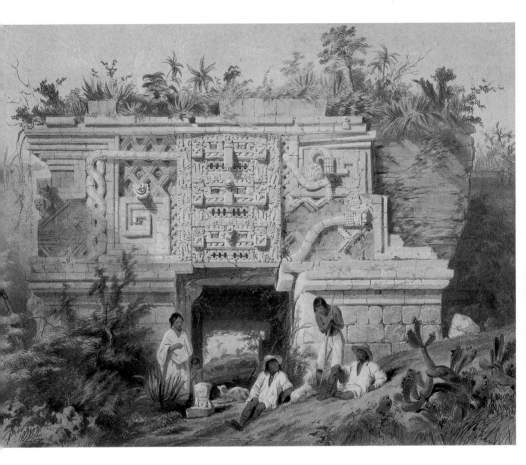

10 Despite the romantic foliage and setting Frederick Catherwood recorded the West Building of the Nunnery at Uxmal with remarkable accuracy in the 1840s. He also made some of the earliest surviving renderings of the Maya people of the region.

populations was written down in the sixteenth century, particularly in Central Mexico, and it can help us unravel the Precolumbian past. Although there are many sources, the single most important one to the art historian is Bernardino de Sahagún's *General History of the Things of New Spain*. A Franciscan friar, Sahagún recorded for posterity many aspects of prehispanic life in his encyclopedia of twelve books, including history, ideology, and cosmogony, as well as detailed information on the materials and methods of the skilled native craftsmen. Furthermore, traditional ways of life survive among the native peoples of Mesoamerica, and scholars have increasingly found that modern practice and belief can decode the past. Remarkably, some scholars have even turned this process around, teaching ancient writing to modern peoples who may use it to articulate identity in the twenty-first century.

During the past forty years, scholars have also made great progress in the decipherment and interpretation of ancient Mesoamerican writing systems, a breakthrough that has transformed our understanding of the Precolumbian mind. Maya inscriptions, for example – long thought to record only calendrical information and astrological incantations – can now be read, and we find that most glorify family and ancestry by displaying the right of individual sovereigns to rule. The carvings can thus be seen as portraits, public records of dynastic power. Although scholars long believed that Mesoamerican artists did not sign their works, David Stuart's 1986 decipherment of the Maya glyphs for 'scribe' and 'to write' opened a window on Maya practice, where at least one painter of ceramic vessels was the son of a Naranjo king. Now the names of known Maya painters and sculptors – all male – exceed most other ancient traditions. Knowledge of the minor arts has also come in large part through an active art market. Thousands more small-scale objects are known now than in the twentieth century, although at a terrible cost to the ancient ruins from which they have been plundered.

What kind of antiquity did ancient Mesoamerican peoples see for themselves? When they looked up at the heavens, they saw a great serpent spanning the cosmos, forming the great white road that we understand to be the Milky Way. Serpents, particularly plumed ones, brought bounty and culture to earth, a notion made manifest in architecture, where plumed serpents flow down balustrades. Ancient Mesoamericans also linked stars together to form constellations, with rare examples like the Scorpion common to both Old and New Worlds. Among these constellations are three bright stars (we know them as Alnitak, Saiph, and Rigel and see them in the the constellation we call Orion) that form the hearthstones set in heaven's home by ancient gods as the founding act of civilization, when humans took up permanent residence and began to form villages. When Motecuhzoma reviewed his tribute list, he would have known that every home would have such a hearth – as indeed do many today. In a very general sense, the story of Mesoamerica's art begins with this permanency – and remarkably, with permanency in one of the least probable locations, the tropical rainforest of the Gulf Coast.

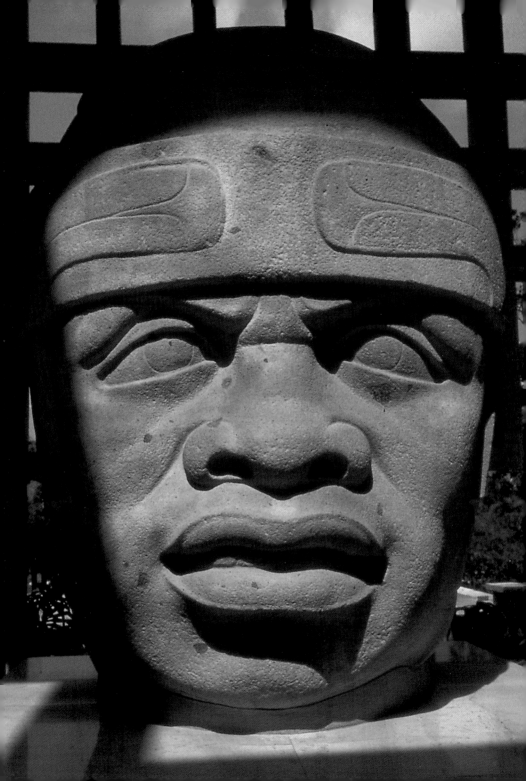

Chapter 2   The Olmecs

By 1500 BC, population growth, competition, and a successful agricultural base gave rise along the Gulf Coast to the complex culture now called Olmec. A misnomer, 'Olmec' derives from Olmeca-Xicalanca, the name of the successful Gulf Coast polyglot traders of the Conquest era, rather than the Mixe or Zoque speakers that most linguists believe began to establish a formal order of artistic expression back at the hazy origins of Mesoamerican civilization. The ethnic identity of Olmec peoples themselves remains unknown.

These early Olmecs established major centers along the rich riverine lowlands of the modern Mexican states of Veracruz and Tabasco, particularly at the sites of San Lorenzo, La Venta, Laguna de los Cerros, and Tres Zapotes, or what is called the 'heartland' of Olmec culture. At distant Teopantecuanitlan, Guerrero, Olmecs established a sacred precinct, the first such monumental evidence of the Olmecs in the highlands. But, as we shall see, the Olmecs had an advanced social and economic system, with networks for commerce extending far to the west and south. The fertile Gulf plain probably allowed for an agricultural surplus, controlled by only a handful of individuals. From the art and architecture of their ceremonial centers (we know too little about Olmec domestic life to call their sites 'cities'), it is clear that social stratification was sufficiently advanced for a major emphasis to fall upon the monumental record of specific individuals, particularly in the form of colossal heads.

Long before radiocarbon dating could testify to the antiquity of this culture, archaeologists and art historians had become aware of the powerful physiognomy of Olmec art through individual objects. Some identified this Olmec culture as the oldest of Mesoamerican civilizations, perhaps a 'mother culture,' from which all others derived, an increasingly viable understanding of the critical role played by these shadowy figures of Mesoamerica's distant past. Eventually, much to the chagrin of Mayanists, who wanted the ancient Maya to hold this position, the antiquity of Olmec culture was confirmed. Today – and it seems as though further validation of this turns up in the archaeological record with astonishing alacrity – most of the elements of Mesoamerican

11 Discovered in 1970, San Lorenzo Colossal Head 8 (Monument 61) reveals a powerful physiognomy. The count of colossal heads at San Lorenzo now stands at ten, more than any other site.

art and architecture can be seen to have an Olmec origin: rubber balls and ballcourts, pyramid building, bilaterally symmetrical plans, jadeworking, mirror-making, and an interest in human portraiture. Even the attention to the human head may show Mesoamerican understanding of the concentration of human sentience, especially the soul, in the gray matter of the brain. One of the most fundamental of Mesoamerican gods, the Maize God, survives from Olmec times. And recently scholars have argued that the mixed writing system of logographs and phonetic signs that is most fully exploited by the Maya may have its earliest logographic expression by 900 BC, on the work known as the Cascajal Block.

One of the first important Olmec objects to come to modern attention was the Kunz Axe, acquired in the 1860s in Oaxaca and then brought to world attention by the semi-precious gem expert at Tiffany's, in New York, where the carving still remains at the

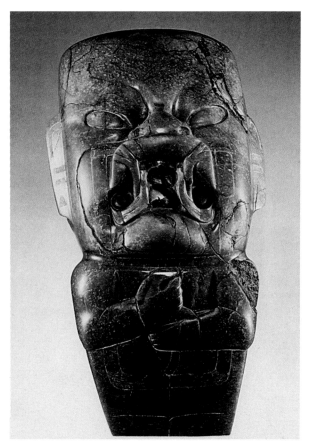

12 The largest known example of its kind, the Kunz Axe is a jadeite effigy 'were-jaguar' which grasps a miniature axe in its hands. Pieces of the precious greenstone have been cut away from the back of the figure. Middle Formative.

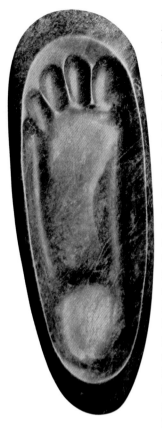

13 Dozens of ceremonial jade celts of early date – perhaps going back to 1600 BC – have been discovered at El Manati. This winsome footprint in axe form was found there, along with the wooden figures in ill. 16.

American Museum of Natural History [12]. The object takes the form of a celt, or axe head, although of course it never functioned as such. It was clearly neither Aztec nor Maya: in fact, it had no features that could be linked with known Mesoamerican cultures, yet it had surely been made in Mesoamerica in antiquity. The axe exhibits many qualities of the style we now call Olmec: precious blue-green translucent jade, worked to reveal a figure in both two and three dimensions. Using tools only made of jade, and perhaps using jade powder as an abrasive, an ancient artisan sawed the block of jadeite into the rough axe form, and then drilled it sharply at the corners of the mouth and eyes – the drill holes can still be seen at the corners of the mouth. More than half the celt is devoted to the creature's face – the open, toothless mouth, and closely set, slanting eyes which have often been likened to the face of a howling human infant. The viewer's attention first focuses on the open mouth, and then the more subtle qualities of the rest of the creature's body become evident. His hands are worked in lower relief, and in them he grasps a miniature version of himself. Feet and toes are indicated only by incision, and incision also marks the face, ears, and upper body, perhaps to suggest tattooing, ear ornaments, and a tunic. For over two millennia the large, precious Kunz Axe was presumably kept as a treasure or heirloom. Sections were periodically cut from its rear, each slice perhaps carrying something of the power and magic of the whole. It was not until 1955, after several seasons of excavation at La Venta had produced many fine jade objects and a convincing series of radiocarbon dates in the first millennium BC, that objects such as the Kunz Axe were at last understood by scholars to embody the principles of the first great art style of Mesoamerica [12, 13].

Early students of the Olmec style noticed a repeated pattern of imagery on the carved stone objects. Many 'howling baby' faces were found, and other faces seemed to combine human and jaguar features in a sort of 'were-jaguar.' Today, while the presence of jaguar imagery is still acknowledged, scholars have discovered that aspects of many other tropical rainforest fauna can be identified in the carvings. The caiman (a kind of crocodile), harpy eagle, toad, jaguar, and snake all appear in the Olmec supernatural repertoire. The sharp cleft in the forehead of many Olmec supernatural beings may be associated with the naturally indented heads of jaguars or toads, or it may simply indicate the human fontanel. It could also indicate emergence from the earth, especially as seen in the head of the Maize God, from whose cleft emerges the tender

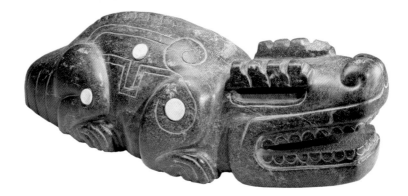

14 The Olmec dragon is a
composite being based on the
tropical crocodile, but with both
sky and terrestrial aspects. Flame
eyebrows, perhaps related to the
crested feathers of the raptorial
harpy eagle, indicate its movement
across the sky.

15 Olmec artisans fitted carved
basalt drain sections together to
channel water through the vast
manmade mound of San Lorenzo.
A sculpture of the rain god,
Monument 52, marked where
water entered at the top; water
poured into a duck-shaped
fountain far below.

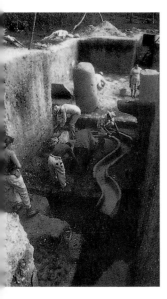

maize plant. The Olmec mastered the concept of *pars pro toto*, in which the depiction of one part can stand in for the whole. The 'paw-wing' motif, for example, can be shown to be an element of the Olmec dragon, as can 'flame eyebrows' – and each can signal to the viewer the larger supernatural being [14]. This intricate symbolic code appears to have been in use from the first appearance of the Olmecs, and to have been employed consistently for a thousand years.

San Lorenzo

The earliest known Olmec center was probably the great earthen platform at San Lorenzo Tenochtitlan, where careful testing by Michael Coe and Richard Diehl in the late 1960s revealed that the entire complex was manmade, honeycombed with drainage systems, and perhaps planned in a zoomorphic shape [15]. The elaboration of the drains themselves was remarkable: Monument 52, for example, a sculpture of a crouching Olmec rain god, was hollowed on its back to guide copious waterflow that eventually poured out into a recarved duck at the base of the massive structure, forming a duck fountain. Freestanding architectural forms were limited to lowlying mounds, possibly including an early ballcourt of two parallel structures, the acropolis, and the Red Palace, the single greatest of all structures at San Lorenzo, recognized today by the floors painted red with hematite and the rooms for craft specialization.

Coe and Diehl found dozens of partly destroyed sculptures interred along the ridged western edge of the site. For years, this destruction seemed inexplicable – many of the defacements required essentially as much energy as the original carving effort itself. Some of this destruction may have been ritual killing – Monument 34 was systematically decapitated and placed on a red gravel floor and covered with at least 6 ft 7 in (2 m) of specially prepared limestone fill. But the concentration of fragments and broken pieces offers another possibility: this location may have been where monuments of one generation were recycled into the sculptures of a new order. The Olmec imported every scrap of basalt to San Lorenzo, and such a precious – not to mention heavy – material, brought at great human cost (surely transported on rafts for as much of the trip as possible) from Cerro Cintepec in the Tuxtla Mountains, almost 60 miles (100 km) away as the crow flies, would have been reused and recycled at a specialized workshop. When the end of San Lorenzo came in 900 BC or so, sculptors simply abandoned many broken sculptures *in situ*.

Early Olmec sculptors mastered the human form by 1500 BC. Archaeologists have now discovered wooden Olmec sculptures in the swampy bogs at El Manati [16], along with deposits of rubber balls and polished plain jadeite celts. Rather than exhibiting hesitant engagement with the human form, the artist shows, even in these earliest works, mastery of the human face. Carved atop a plain wooden staff that could have been dressed and adorned, each El Manati figure seemingly renders individual physiognomy, and collectively, they may have once formed a tableau.

What are we to make of these early works, that emerge so fully developed and three-dimensional? Many of the earliest sculptures from around the world exhibit somewhat abstract or conventionalized characteristics. We can compare these Olmec sculptures with the Altamira or Lascaux cave paintings, where the first renderings are among the most powerful evocations of hunters and their prey known, executed with vividly accurate depictions of natural forms. Yet at the same time, the Olmec did indeed master abstraction and imbued special materials with power, especially the smooth axe-shaped celts that may have been understood as the permanent compression of everything green and blue: sky and water, quetzal feathers and maize. There is no single evolutionary stream that Mesoamerican art follows, and the complexity of its pathways characterizes it right up until the Spanish invasion. Even the Olmec practice of recycling and reusing materials can be seen in later works.

Ten colossal heads formed from basalt boulders have now been found at San Lorenzo, and they take the mastery of the human face, seen at El Manati, to new levels [11]. Among the most commanding of faces is the one seen on Colossal Head 5, probably a depiction of a second-millennium BC ruler of the site [17]. Like small-scale works such as the Kunz Axe, the features of the

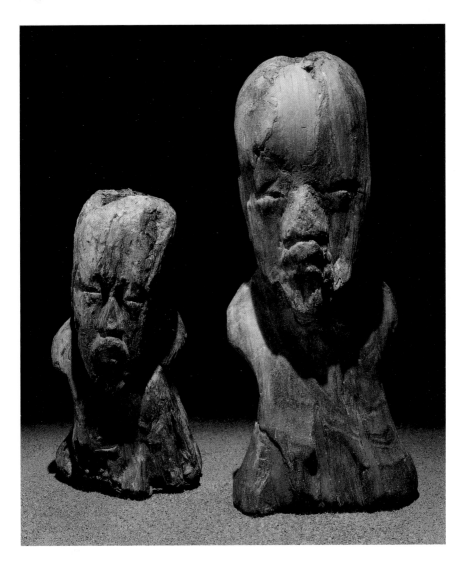

16 At El Manati, archaeologist Ponciano Ortíz discovered caches of wooden sculptures formed from tropical hardwoods that have survived deep in swampy muck. Many may have served as staffs.

colossal head were drilled, giving emphasis to the deep-set eyes, nostrils, and strong, slightly asymmetrical mouth. Eight round dimpled pits were bored into the head, and the prominent ones on chin, lip, and cheekbone do not detract from the stern gaze. Jaguar paws are shown draped over the figure's forehead, and perhaps the individual wore the feline pelt as a lineage title or symbol of office. (Much later, in Mixtec manuscripts and Maya inscriptions, many lords are named with a jaguar title.)

Not only were there workshops to recarve and resize Olmec sculptures, but Olmec sculptors remade even their largest pieces

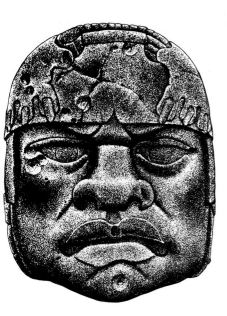

and converted huge thrones (often called 'altars') into colossal heads. San Lorenzo Colossal Head 7 retains the remnants of a deeply carved niche on the side of its head; Monument 14 once served as a throne, but was smashed almost beyond recognition, perhaps on its way to taking the shape of a colossal head. One can imagine a scenario in which the throne serves the living king, only to be converted into his essence, his head, upon his death. Mesoamerican peoples believed that all experience and emotion, along with the soul, resided in the head alone. The ten colossal heads themselves are of greatly varying size: they may have been posthumous records of the great kings who had led them – and the defacement, cuts, and other markings on the heads themselves may also alert us to the transience of mortal power.

Above:
17 Colossal Head 5, San Lorenzo. Jaguar paws, perhaps emblematic of family lineage, drape across the head and brow of this early Olmec ruler. Early Formative.

Right:
18 In 1994, Ann Cyphers Guillen discovered San Lorenzo Colossal Head 10 in a ravine at the site's edge. The distinctive helmet and chin line distinguish this 8-ton portrait (compare ills 11, 17).

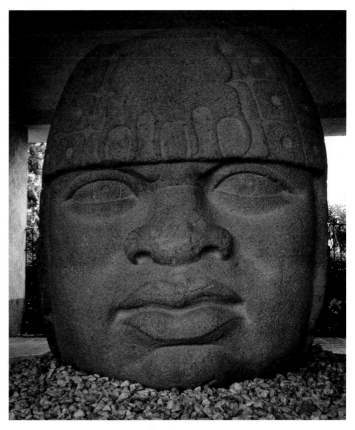

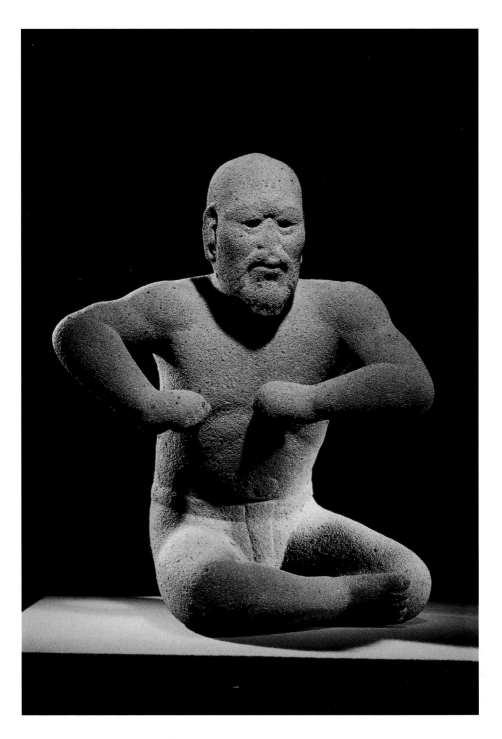

Monument 34 from San Lorenzo, buried so carefully at the site, also reveals the strong three-dimensional qualities of early Olmec art. Perishable and movable arms were once attached to the torso, and it is easy to imagine the torsion of the figure, from the tense, compact, lower body to the moving arms. The tucked right foot is like a coiled spring, about to be released. Special attention has been given to costume detail, and knots in particular are carefully drawn. The figure wears a concave disk as a pectoral decoration, which probably represents a concave mirror of the sort recovered from Olmec contexts. Magnetic materials appealed to the Olmecs, and they worked ilmenite and magnetite into dark, shiny disks. Indeed, such objects were highly prized throughout Mesoamerican history. The polished surface not only showed one's reflection, but it also cast light; the bearer is revealed to be not only a lord but also a priest and diviner.

The 'Wrestler', discovered in the early twentieth century near what is now the town of Antonio Plaza, Veracruz, and used for over a decade to prop up a chicken coop, has three-dimensional qualities similar to those of Monument 34 and other early Olmec art, although its size and scale may also link it to the later sculptures of La Venta, where it is much like a niche figure [19]. The human figure is completely released from the stone in contrast to much Mesoamerican sculpture. The artist must have intended it to be viewed from all sides. The long diagonal line of the figure's back and shoulders is as beautiful and commanding as the frontal view. The beard and mustache, as well as the look of deep concentration, reveal a masterly portrait, one whose individuality would be enhanced by long-lost perishable attire and ornament. Although some have attacked it as a mid-twentieth-century forgery, many other scholars in the United States and Mexico, including this author, have vigorously argued for its authenticity.

In her work at San Lorenzo, Ann Cyphers Guillen has brought remarkable works to world attention, not only colossal heads but also a number of sculptures from nearby Loma de Zapote. Two identical figures kneel, the weight shifted forward as each grasps a short, thick staff in front of him [20, 21]. Crinkled paper headdress elements fall across their ears, giving a false impression of Egyptian headdresses – folded paper headdress elements are typical of Mesoamerican rain gods, who received offerings of rubber sap on strips of folded paper. When burned, these folded bits of paper yielded black, acrid clouds of smoke to propitiate rain. A small museum on-site features these twin sculptures, which face a pair

19 Long known as the 'Wrestler,' this dynamic male figure has the powerful upper body physique of a swimmer. The sculptor turns the arms clockwise and the legs counterclockwise.

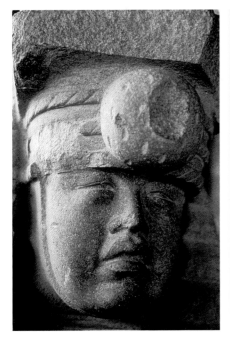
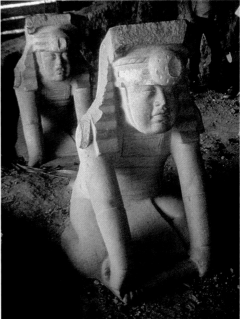

20, 21 The discovery of two nearly identical Early Formative sculptures near San Lorenzo has prompted some scholars to propose that they represent the Hero Twins, known in later times as Maya culture heroes. Some viewers have wished to read an Egyptian origin into their stylized head regalia. But the pleated side accoutrements are the folded paper adornments associated with Mesoamerican rain gods, right up until the Spanish invasion. Early Formative.

of carved felines, all of whom seem to be in an original location. Such an assemblage may have brought a religious narrative to life – here, one thinks of the Maya cultural heroes, the Hero Twins, whose story may have been permanently conveyed in a tableau visible from the river below.

Some features of Mesoamerican art and materials come into coherent focus for the first time at San Lorenzo. Remarkable trade routes brought precious materials from distant realms: mica, jade, and serpentine were all desired, but porters carried ilmenite to San Lorenzo by the ton, probably for on-site manufacture. Rubber and feathers may have been principal exports. Local builders used local rock and clays, but elite status depended on imports, a lasting aspect of Mesoamerican elite economy. What is also clear is that a systematic destruction of San Lorenzo took place about 900 BC, and a new center of Olmec civilization was established at La Venta.

La Venta

La Venta occupied a small, swampy island in the Tonala River, where oil derricks have now finally been removed and the site opened for tourism, including a museum that features many new discoveries at the site. During the 400- or 500-year occupation of the site, both monumental architecture and earthworks of colored clays and imported stones were completed [22]. The most important structure is a large pyramid toward the end of the northern axis, in the form of what has been called a 'fluted cupcake.' This impressive mound may have been intended to echo the shape of a Central Mexican volcano, or it may simply be the eroded remains of a pyramidal platform – the first of a long series in Mesoamerican history – designed to raise a perishable shrine above the plaza level. In the 1950s the excavators discovered fine burials under other structures at La Venta, but they failed to penetrate this main mound, which may yet hold the tomb of an individual whose portrait appears as one of the four colossal La Venta heads. Parallel mounds lead north from the pyramid to a sunken courtyard flanked by massive basalt columns. Great basalt sarcophagi were found buried in the court. A smaller stepped pyramid with a single staircase then ends the axis to the north.

Most – although not all – offerings follow the bilateral symmetry reflected on the surface, creating a dynamic link between what is hidden and what is seen – as archaeologist Robert Heizer discovered in the 1950s. Although contemporary artist Michael Heizer has resisted any attempt to interpret influence on his works from his father's archaeological excavations, knowledge of the latter is useful when looking at his contemporary desert projects of artificial earthen strata. Vast deposits of serpentine, granite, and jade celts were laid out and buried at the entrance to the sunken northern court. Some of the slabs formed mosaic masks, such as the one illustrated here, a

22 Reconstruction of the major mound cluster at La Venta. The ceremonial center extends north from the 'fluted cupcake.' Ancient Olmecs placed structures and offerings in bilateral symmetry either side of the north-south axis, in the section of the site known as Complex A.

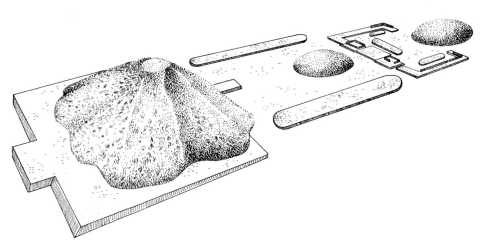

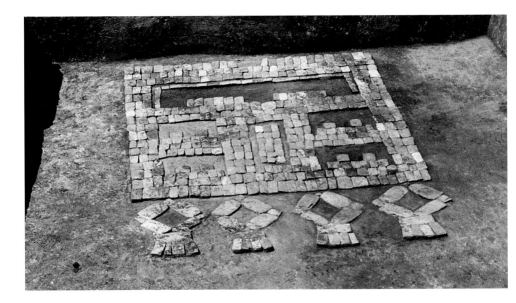

Above:
23 Made of large serpentine blocks, this abstract mosaic mask was systematically buried under cubic tons of colored clays and slabs of plain, imported rock at La Venta. Tassels decorate the chin, and a cleft marks the top of the head. Middle Formative.

Opposite:
24 Giant talons mark the helmet of Colossal Head I at La Venta, as if to show both blessing and authority embodied by this ancient ruler. The raw stone came from the distant Tuxtla Mountains; a massive sculpture of this sort underscored the power of local elites to 'move mountains.'

cleft-headed monster [23]. Few of these constructions were meant to be seen, and most were buried immediately after they had been created. Such works show the relation of art to architecture for the Olmecs, and the interest in process over product. We can think of these works as a sort of 'hidden' architecture.

The whole of La Venta was laid out on a specific axis, eight degrees west of north, establishing some principles of architectural planning that were repeated many times in the history of Mesoamerica: ceremonial cores laid out along astronomically determined axes; concern for natural topography – a sort of geomancy – which may have inspired the erection or overall orientation of individual structures (as for instance the 'fluted cupcake'). The plaza, a 'negative space' seen in the sunken court of La Venta, was as significant as the structure or 'mass' that defined it. The process of interring works of art may also have been as important as their execution. But above all the visual emphasis fell on the pyramid.

The four colossal heads of La Venta were set like sentinels guarding the ceremonial core. Heads 2, 3, and 4 all stood at the north end of the complex, in front of A-2, while Head I [24] was set just south of the 'fluted cupcake.' All faced outward. If erected during the reign of a ruler, such heads would have been effective images of royal power; if erected posthumously, fearsome memorials. The La Venta heads are somewhat broader and

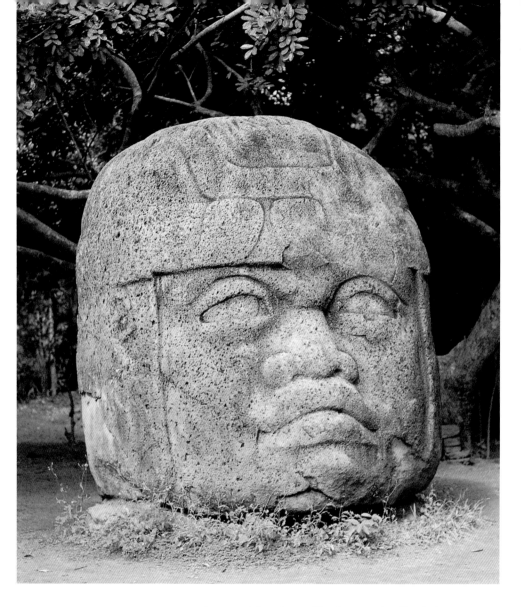

squatter in general than those of San Lorenzo, but like the latter they suggest a series of powerful men who held absolute sway over the populace.

Other sculptural types are known from La Venta, including the so-called altars and stelae. Through time, the monuments of La Venta became increasingly two-dimensional and specific in terms of setting, costume, and ritual paraphernalia. These developments suggest a growing preoccupation with the trappings of the ruler.

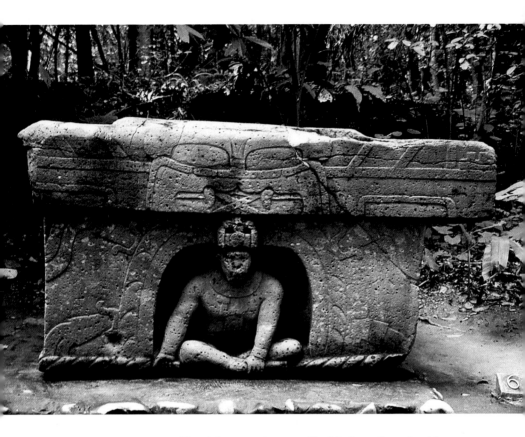

Above:
25 Altar 4, La Venta. An Olmec ruler emerges from the mouth of a schematic cave at the front of the stone. Such 'altars' may also have been thrones from which the reigning lord would have presided. Middle Formative.

Opposite:
26 Altar 5, La Venta. Badly battered, the massive sculptured throne may have been abandoned while being recarved into a colossal head.

Altar 4 shows a ruler carved in rich three-dimensional form seated within a niche or cave, holding a rope wrapped round the perimeter of the stone which binds two-dimensional captives in profile to the lord on the front [25]. The lord's power is emphasized by his action, the grasping of the rope, and by the technique, which subordinates the two-dimensional figures. Such monuments almost certainly served as thrones; the painted figure at Oxtotitlan (see below, [37]), for instance, is represented sitting on a throne similar to Altar 4, and Altar 4 may once have been decorated in the brilliant colors of the painting. The surface of the monument is carved with a jaguar pelt, a royal cushion on the seat of power.

Altar 5 may emphasize a different aspect of Olmec rulership. As on Altar 4, a highly three-dimensional figure, about life-size, emerges from a niche on the front of the monument, while two-dimensional figures are shown on the sides [26]. The central figure in this instance, however, holds out an infant, who lies limp in his lap. The

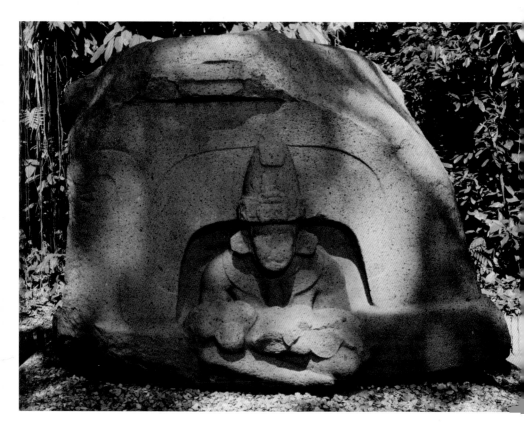

Las Limas figure [29] is also of an adult and infant, although there the child is clearly supernatural. The representation on Altar 5 may reflect a concern with legitimate descent, and perhaps the ruler is displaying an heir, as in some Maya paintings and carvings. The subsidiary figures on the sides of Altar 5 are also adults and infants, humans who hold rambunctious Olmec supernatural children.

On Stela 3, two men face one another while small figures, perhaps deities or ancestors, hover above [27]. The man at left carries a baton, and the one at right wears what appears to be a beard, winning for this monument the nickname 'Uncle Sam.' Indeterminate shapes, perhaps architecture or landscape, appear behind the two men, thus suggesting that the setting for a particular event is being recorded, not just historical figures. This is a new preoccupation at La Venta, one not emphasized at San Lorenzo, and it may be an indicator of concern for historical records. Even the notion of carving an upright finished stone slab, or stela, is new, introduced here for the first time.

Offering 4, excavated at a corner of the basalt courtyard at La Venta, may record history in a different fashion, as well as in a different medium: jade and serpentine, which, carved into sinewy figures, reveal Olmec mastery of the material [28]. The hardest rock commonly found in the Mesoamerican world, jade found its keenest masters among the Olmecs. Six celts and fifteen jade and serpentine figurines were specifically set out in Offering 4 so that the one figure made from a base stone – granite – faced the group made from precious stones. The celts placed behind recall the

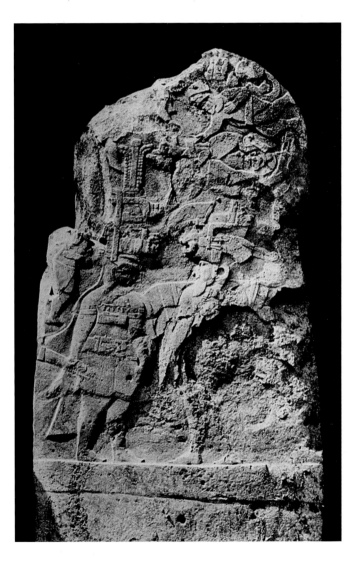

Right:
27 Stela 3, La Venta. Two Olmec lords meet in front of a schematically rendered cave. The beard and towering headdress of the figure at right has earned this monument the nickname of 'Uncle Sam.' The figure on the right has been recarved. Middle Formative.

Opposite:
28 Offering 4, La Venta. Like the monumental deposits (ill. 23), Offering 4 was buried after being laid out in just this configuration. The single figure of granite, facing out with celts behind him, is studied by those made of precious greenstone. Middle Formative.

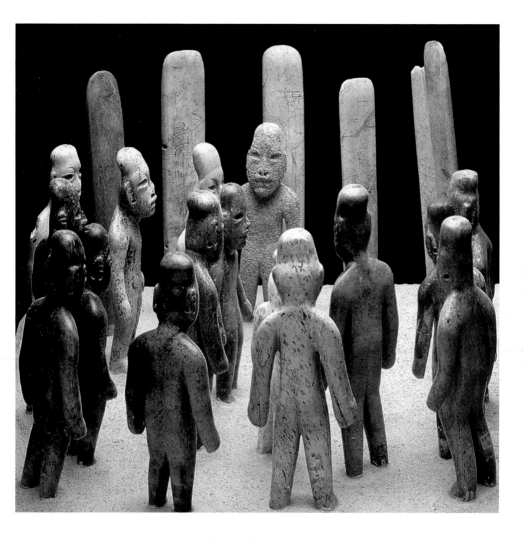

columns of the La Venta sunken court where this offering was laid, and it is entirely possible that the scene recreates an action against the lone figure that once occurred within inches of its small-scale, tableau-like memorial. About a century after its interment, this offering was uncovered and then reburied, as if an important event needed to be reconfirmed. The later exhumation was made with precision, indicating that records were kept, even if through oral tradition. In this respect we see that burial did not equal object death or loss but rather transformation into words and memories. Other individual, sinewy jades – warm, plastic, and almost feline in their posture – have been found, and were among the objects that

41

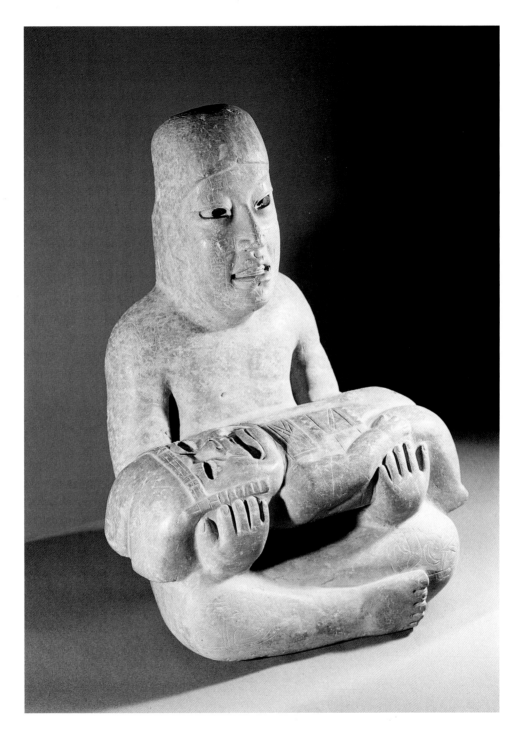

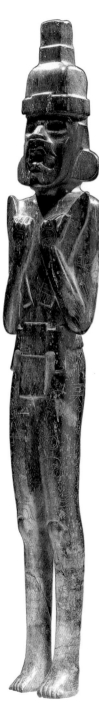

attracted the attention of collectors early in this century [30, 31, 32]. It is likely that they came from similar groupings elsewhere. The recently excavated assemblages at El Manati and Loma de Zapote now make it possible to imagine that many Olmec sculptures were parts of tableaux. The desire to retain configurations may also have contributed to the push for two-dimensionality over time, with the greater permanency of adjacencies possible.

Of all Olmec greenstone sculptures, the largest and most beautiful is the Las Limas figure [29]. When it was discovered in 1965, villagers considered it a miraculous madonna, and it was brought to the church of Las Limas. The sculpture, however, is no Christian mother and child. A youth, neither specifically male nor female, holds an infant in its lap, a reference, perhaps, to legitimate descent. The infant has the monstrous face of the Olmec rain deity, and the knees, shoulders, and face of the larger individual are incised with the faces of other supernaturals. This incision may reflect the tradition of body paint, which may have been Mesoamerica's first art form.

Left:
30 Over 2 ft (65 cm) in height, this scepter in human form himself holds two scepters to the chest. His body is carpeted with exquisite incision that is symmetrical but distinct on his right and left sides.

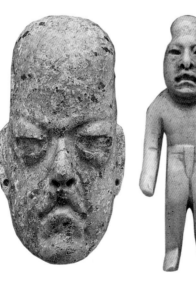

31 Despite the diminutive scale, this small head – and the tiny figure of ill. 32 – shares both technical qualities and a sense of monumentality with the massive Olmec works, translated to small and fine greenstone.

32 Olmec shamans may have wrapped this tiny pale jade figure in cloth and adornments and kept it in a sacred bundle.

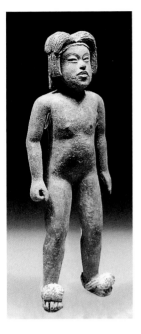

Exceptional in their size, the Kunz Axe and Las Limas figure have opened a window on the larger tradition of precious greenstones among the Olmec. On the one hand, the axe form seems to have lent itself to the notion of the royal scepter, powerful both as a handsome shaft of jade and with fine-grained incision that can only be interpreted under close study; on the other, the forms and ideology – say, of the adult holding the infant – could be expanded when made of coarse stone and miniaturized, as the handheld object.

The Olmec Frontier

Scholars of the Olmec early in the twentieth century had pondered the relationship of the Gulf Coast sites to isolated objects that turned up in Guerrero, Chiapas, and in Central Mexico. The Olmec search for precious jade and other raw materials was clear enough, as was the widespread presence of Olmec materials in the highlands. Olmec ceramics, for example, have survived poorly, if at all, in the petroleum-rich soil of Veracruz, while they are found in abundance in the highlands, although often in association with more obviously local materials. Now, since the discovery in 1983 of the site of Teopantecuanitlan, it is clear that at least some Olmecs considered Guerrero home.

At Xochipala, Guerrero, solid, life-like figurines had emerged as an indigenous tradition by 1500 BC. Expressive gestures, naturalistic forms of hair, breasts, and plastic arms and legs, make the early and rare Xochipala figures among the finest ceramic works of the ancient New World [33]. Many of the figures, both male and female, are naked, and they may once have been dressed with jewelry and perishable garments.

33 A ceramic figure of unspecified gender from Xochipala. The detailed sandals provide clues of the fancy but perishable raiment the figure once wore. Early Formative.

34 Framing a sunken courtyard at Teopantecuanitlan, four nearly identical sculptures feature the Olmec Maize God. Although 400 miles (650 km) from the Olmec heartland, these sculptures nevertheless convey standard Olmec imagery. Early Formative.

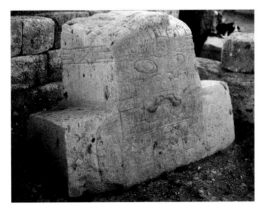

Such local traditions may have made the region attractive to the Olmecs, for just across the Mezcala River from Xochipala lies Teopantecuanitlan, which thrived from 1400 BC to 600 BC, with the greatest construction from 1200 to 800 BC. During that brief period, Olmec lords constructed a monumental sunken court lined with green travertine rock, and marked by unusual T-shaped sculptures on west and east sides [34]. These sculptures feature Olmec Maize Gods, who define the four corners of the universe. In later Maya ideology, the Maize God is reborn in a ballcourt: at Teopantecuanitlan, as if to indicate such belief, a ballcourt occupies much of the sunken patio. Nearby, archaeologists have recovered what is the smallest of known colossal heads.

Could the Olmecs have initiated their culture in this cool highland setting? As much as the thought has been appealing to those who struggle with the concept of tropical rainforest as the source of civilization in Mesoamerica, the earliest – and throughout time, the most diverse – evidence for the Olmecs all resides in the tropics. As remarkable as they are, the Teopantecuanitlan patio sculptures exhibit a uniformity unknown at the Gulf Coast sites.

At Tlatilco, on the outskirts of modern Mexico City, a rich cemetery revealed a figurine cult perhaps dedicated to fertility. Swelling breasts and thighs were emphasized, as well as narrow waists. The hair and face received great attention, and these figurines are often known as 'pretty ladies.' Others are grotesques, and their split 'Janus'-like faces appealed to artists of the early twentieth century.

The Tlatilco 'pretty ladies' were found in association with large Olmec-style ceramic figures, known also from Las Bocas, Atlihuayan, Tlapacoya, and other places in Central Mexico – incomplete ones have been discovered at coastal sites too. The fine-grained, plastic white kaolin of Las Bocas may have freed its artists to produce the finest of these figures. Although many of the sculptures seem to be babies, the loose, hanging flesh also suggests age, perhaps not unlike late medieval representations of the Christ child, where both age and infancy are portrayed. The hollow figure from the Metropolitan Museum sucks his thumb [35]; his hair is groomed in the shape of a helmet. A red cross-bands-and-wing motif runs down this baby's back, perhaps made by a rocker stamp. Similar motifs carved on ceramic vessels, such as the hand-paw-wing, are repetitions of the constant Olmec symbolic system, coded references to particular deities, and are

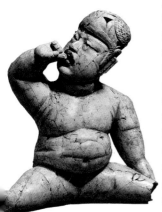

35 A hollow 'baby' ceramic figure from Las Bocas. A rocker-stamp motif associated with an Olmec deity runs down its spine. Early/Middle Formative.

suggestive of writing. Other pots were worked as three-dimensional animal effigies, particularly of fish and ducks. Rocker stamps may have been widely used to paint the human body.

Another important class of Olmec works of art was identified in the 1930s at Chalcatzingo, Morelos. Here strange figures and fantastic creatures were carved in three distinct groups on the surface of a great natural rock formation, an igneous plug that marks a pass through the eastern end of the modern state of Morelos and access to the rich Valley of Puebla. The most striking of these carvings is known locally as 'El Rey,' a representation of an enthroned ruler (probably female, given the skirt the figure wears) [36]. This may be an Olmec overlord or governor, who could well reflect the extent to which power was imposed by the Olmecs in this frontier region, far from the Gulf Coast and the heartland of their civilization. She sits within a section of a cave or niche, like that depicted three-dimensionally on Altar 4, La Venta. In the petroglyph, the cave lies within a schematic landscape where phallic raindrops fall on young maize plants. Petroglyph 4, on the other hand, shows large felines attacking human figures with supernatural characteristics. The foreshortened human forms suggest that their outlines might first have been traced from cast human shadows. The petroglyphs at Chalcatzingo are remarkably varied: some portray warring Olmecs, others simple natural motifs, such as squash plants.

The earliest Mesoamerican paintings survive only in caves, their condition and presentation not unlike Paleolithic cave art in France, although not on the same magnificent scale, and not, lamentably, from such an early date. Fine examples have been found at Oxtotitlan and Juxtlahuaca caves in Guerrero. One from Juxtlahuaca shows what may be the mating of a human male with a female jaguar, perhaps the source of the race of 'were-jaguars' so common in Olmec imagery. A badly battered sculpture from the Olmec heartland also shows such mating, but in that instance a human female and a male jaguar are represented.

A large painting at Oxtotitlan, set 33 ft (10 m) over the entrance to the cave, depicts an Olmec lord wearing a green bird suit, cut away in X-ray fashion so that we see his face and limbs [37]. The bird's eye was probably

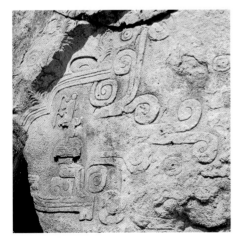

36 Petroglyph 1, Chalcatzingo. Set within a cave mouth in a schematic landscape where maize flourishes, an Olmec ruler, probably a woman, sits on a throne. Middle Formative.

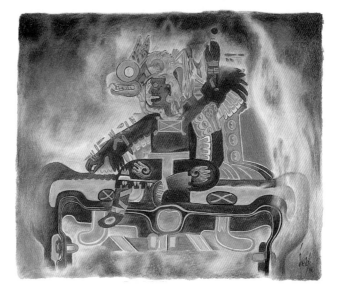

37 Painting at cave entrance, Oxtotitlan. The ruler's face can be seen in X-ray fashion, within a great bird hood. The painting is large, 12 ft 6 in x 8 ft (3.8 x 2.5 m). Early or Middle Formative.

38 Carved on a rock outcropping along a mountain pass, this Olmec figure carries a flowering bundle, perhaps signaling the agricultural wealth and potential he carries with him to others who would make the journey.

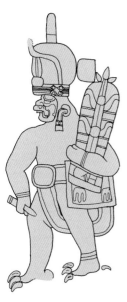

inlaid with a precious material, and the lord sports a jade noseplug. His throne resembles Altar 4 at La Venta. The palette of these early Olmec paintings was broad, including bright greens and reds, although simpler black-on-white paintings have also been found. A bird deity plays an important role in the Late Preclassic and among the Maya more broadly; this may be one of its earliest depictions, impersonated by a ruler or embodied by a shaman, flying out of the cave. Years later, a powerful goddess at Teotihuacan will wear this green owl to symbolize her powers.

Far to the south, at Copan, Honduras, kings were buried with Olmec pomp, including jade celts, jade necklaces, and vessels worked with Olmec symbols. Also distant from the heartland, at Xoc, Chiapas, an Olmec petroglyph was discovered depicting a male Olmec carrying a great burden [38]. One wonders what this lord bore in his bundle: could it have held cult objects, perhaps even a sculpture like the Kunz Axe? A maize plant in full tassel is drawn over the bundle's exterior, revealing the significance of the plant to Olmec ideology. Whatever the content of the bundle, the very presence of Olmecs far and wide raises perplexing questions. But with contacts from Honduras to Guerrero, the Olmecs came close to defining the geographic boundaries of Mesoamerica.

At the beginning of the Late Formative, around 400 BC, the once-thriving Olmec culture weakened and collapsed for reasons that are still unknown. The first of the great Mesoamerican civilizations to rise, flourish, and fall, it influenced all the civilizations that were to follow.

Chapter 3   The Late Formative

The Olmecs continued to hold sway in some areas into the Late Formative, but the great center of La Venta followed its predecessor San Lorenzo into eclipse and oblivion by 400 BC. Olmec contacts with distant regions apparently broke down; the ceramics of Central Mexico, for example, were no longer infused with the symbolism of elite Olmec culture. Of the major Olmec sites known today, only Tres Zapotes enjoyed sustained occupation and development during Late Formative times (that is, 400 BC–100 BC and continuing on for perhaps 200 years more). Yet there was a minor florescence of Olmec culture in highland Guatemala at this time, and several smaller but still colossal heads were made. Even more surprisingly, perhaps, it was at just this point that early Mesoamericans made their most lasting contribution to New World high civilization: the creation of sophisticated writing and calendrical systems. The very disorder of the period may have fostered the development of a uniform symbolic system. What linguists call 'incipient writing' appears at many locations, although with concentrations in the Olmec region, even in the Middle Formative. Our understanding of the writing begins to develop with the Late Formative manifestation.

The disintegration of Olmec long-distance trade routes probably made it possible for strong regional and ethnic styles of art and architecture to develop under independent local elites, perhaps as early as Middle Formative times. It was in this era that the Zapotecs first flourished at Monte Alban, Oaxaca, subsequently their capital for 1,500 years. In West Mexico, the shaft tombs of local elites were filled with fine ceramics. Among the Maya, the first cities of the Peten were built, along with substantial seacoast settlements. In recent years, stunning works have come to light from the most ancient Maya cities, where sophisticated paintings reveal a fully developed religious narrative in place no later than 100 BC.

What made all this growth possible? The end of the first millennium BC brought swift changes to ancient Mesoamerica – volcanic eruptions would annihilate habitation and agriculture in one area for a generation. But more importantly, intensive agriculture took root elsewhere. Although maize agriculture had been a part of the Olmec florescence, archaeologists do not know when corn *masa* prepared with ash or lime took off as a foodstuff. When prepared this way, maize is far more than a useful carbohydrate: the alkaline materials enrich the amino acids in maize, releasing proteins and making it the key building block of the Mesoamerican diet. The corn *masa* of the tortilla and tamale made it possible for populations to grow and for city life to emerge. These foods remain at the heart of Mexican and Guatemalan diets today, particularly among indigenous people, but they are readily available in supermarkets around the world as well.

Writing and calendrical systems

The roots of all Mesoamerican calendrical systems – highly varied though they subsequently became – lie in the Late Formative era. Two such means of recording time, the 260-day calendar and the 365-day calendar, evolved at the very beginning of the period and were generally used simultaneously. In terms of intellectual achievement, however, the most important system was a slightly later development, the continuous record called the Long Count, used in conjunction with the 260- and 365-day calendars. An appreciation of the intricacies of all three systems as they appear in ancient inscriptions is necessary, not only to help us date monuments, but also to understand the concepts of time and thought expressed in Mesoamerican art and architecture.

The 260-day cycle is the oldest and most important calendar in Mesoamerica. Stone monuments in Oaxaca indicate its use as early as the sixth century BC when Zapotecs began to chart achievements publicly, and it is still employed in Guatemala today for ritual divining. Indeed, use of the 260-day calendar effectively defined the limits of high civilization in ancient Mesoamerica and provided an aspect of cultural unity. Yet its origins remain obscure. Some have noted that 260 days is the period of time that elapses between solar zenith passages (when the sun lies directly overhead at noon) at a latitude of 15 degrees north – the latitude along which the important sites of Izapa and Copan lie. Zenith passage is a relatively easy phenomenon to observe in the tropics, but it seems an unlikely basis for a calendar first recorded to the north of the 15-degree latitude. A much more fundamental unit of 260 days in the human life cycle is the length of gestation, from first missed menstrual flow to birth. Mesoamerican peoples were named for the day of their birth in this calendar and were

39 All Mesoamerica observed the 52-year cycle, created by the intermeshing of the 260-day calendar (left) and the 365-day calendar (right). It is drawn here as a system of interlocking cog wheels and follows standard Maya notation, although the days and months had different names and symbols in each culture.

The 260-day calendar was perhaps the most basic to Mesoamericans. It is the first one for which written records survive, and it is the one still in use today among some Highland Maya. It is composed of twenty day names (outer wheel) and thirteen day numbers (inner wheel), both of which rotate endlessly. It takes 260 days for all the combinations to occur.

The 365-day calendar is composed of eighteen months, each of which has only twenty days, numbered 0–19 or 1–20, depending on the region, and the five unlucky days (known as Uayeb among the Maya). In this larger wheel, the end of the month of Cumku and the five unlucky days (the Aztec called them nemontemi, or 'nameless' days are shown – other month glyphs are at right.

Here, 13 Ahau (left) and 18 Cumku interlock. It will take 52 x 365 days (in other words, 52 years) before the cycles will all reach this point again. This is the calendar round.

perceived as having completed a 260-day round at birth. Midwives, rather than agriculturalists, may have launched this calendar.

The 260-day calendar was not subdivided into weeks or months as our year is, but into a round of twenty different day names. Counting systems around the world on the whole use a base of either 10 or 20 depending upon whether fingers or fingers and toes are used, and throughout Mesoamerica the base was vigesimal rather than decimal. But the twenty day names were also associated with a cycle of thirteen day numbers, which ran at the same time. Each day, therefore, had one of twenty day names and one of thirteen day numbers, so the cycle would take 260 days to complete.

This cycle always had its own name in various Mesoamerican languages: the Aztecs, for example, called it the *tonalpohualli*, and the written version of the cycle – the fundamental tool of the diviner – was called the *tonalamatl* (*amatl*, or *amate* in modern Spanish, refers to the fig paper on which such a manuscript was often written). The 260-day system is the 'almanac' of Mesoamerican calendrical cycles.

A child was named for the day on which he was born in this cycle – 13 Monkey, for example, in the *tonalpohualli* – and the diviner or calendar priest was consulted to study the augury both for that day and for the period of thirteen days within which it fell. According to the Aztecs, some entire such periods were afflicted by either certain shortcomings or gifts. Those born under the period of 1 Death, for example, would suffer drunkenness. To try to alter the prediction, a naming ceremony was often held on a more auspicious day.

In conjunction with the almanac a 365-day calendar was used. This corresponded roughly with the true solar year, and was divided into eighteen 'months' of twenty days each, plus five 'nameless' days at the end of the year. Each group of twenty days had its own month name, and was linked with a number from 1 to 20 or 0 to 19, depending on the region. Each year took a name, usually the day name and number of the day in the 260-day calendar that coincided with the 360th day of the solar calendar. Because of the nature of the calculation, only four days can be 'yearbearers.' These four day names were paired with coefficients 1 to 13, yielding a 52-year cycle [39]. There is no evidence that the approximate solar year was ever corrected in the calendar to allow for the extra days that accumulate in the true tropical year, but the Maya calendar priests at Piedras Negras noted true

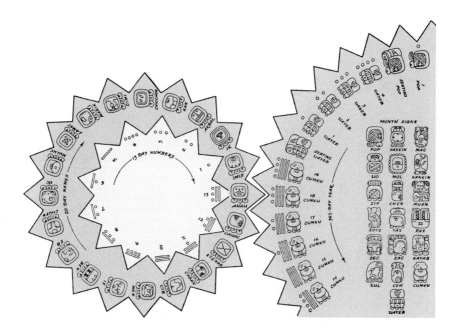

tropical anniversaries in their records. Without the addition of leap days, the 365-day calendar wandered, eventually passing from one season to the next, and requiring movable agricultural feasts.

When the 260-day calendar and 365-day calendar were set in motion, it took exactly 52 years of 365 days for a given day to recur. This period of 52 years is called a calendar round, and we may liken it to a century in our own system. The end of this 52-year cycle was widely celebrated, particularly by the Aztecs, who held a New Fire ceremony at its completion. The five nameless days which preceded the end of the cycle were especially dangerous: the gods might choose that moment to end life on earth. Certain behavior was required: all pots had to be smashed, pregnant women kept indoors, and fires doused. At midnight before the first day of the new year, a sacrificial victim had his heart ripped out, and there, in his open chest, a flame was started with a fire drill. The burst of light assured the light of the morning sun and the opening of a new 52-year cycle.

The calendrical systems described so far were based on relatively short periods of time that could be easily related to human experience. It is true that the completion of an entire round of 52 years by any individual would have meant a very long life in Mesoamerica, or anywhere, but it was possible to survive to this age, barring death in infancy, war, or pregnancy.

40 The Maya used three basic symbols in their numbering system: a dot for one (a), a bar for five (b), and to represent the null cipher similar to our zero a Maltese cross (d) on stone monuments and a stylized shell (e) in the codices. The number six, for example, was made up of a dot and a bar combined (c) – the space either side of the dot being filled by so-called 'spaceholders' which are not counted.

As well as this standard notation, the Maya sometimes introduced a head or full figure as variant: the number nine, for instance, in its common form (f) also appeared as the head in (g) or the full figure in (h).

Over longer periods of time, dates in the calendar round may have been difficult to order chronologically, since any given year name recurred once every 52 years. The use of the last two digits of our year calendar produces a similar effect: is '49 a reference to the California Gold Rush or the beheading of Charles I? At some point during the Late Formative, perhaps to eliminate just such ambiguity in historical records, another calendrical system, the Long Count, was introduced, and it was perfected by the Maya in Classic times.

Long count dates record the complete number of days elapsed since a starting point corresponding to a date in 3114 BC in our calendar – hence the alternative modern name, Initial Series dates. The Maya later held that the 'zero' date fell within an era of divine activity, as does the zero date of our current calendrical system. But even this zero starting point was no blank slate but rather the end of a previous grand cycle. For the Maya, the initial day of the calendar, 4 Ajaw 8 Cumku, was also the last day of the old cycle. On this day, the gods set three hearthstones of creation in place, giving rise to the era of civilization, the Maya believed.

In the Long Count, time was normally recorded in periods of 400 years, 20 years, years, 20 days, and days – i.e. to five places running from largest to smallest, much as we record our years to four places, e.g. 2007. The Mayan date 9.10.0.0.0, for example, records the day 22 January, 663. In the vigesimal (rather than decimal) system the places 'fill' at 20, although in the 'years' space, second from right, the count fills at 18, noting a calculating period of 360 days. Most dates inscribed archaeologically begin with the coefficient 9, referring to the 400 years (of 360 days each) from AD 435 to 830. After 13 periods of 400 years, a new grand cycle begins, and the next is due to start on 23 December, 2012.

The achievement of the Long Count was the ability to pinpoint events in time without ambiguity. Particularly for the Maya, this very record was a focus of artistic achievement, and Maya artists transformed what could have been simple notations into beautiful works of calligraphy. Although other cultures must have known of the inscribing of these initial dates with their formulaic notations of time, only in the late Olmec culture and among the Maya did the practice take root.

Long Count dates can be easily read. They were always placed at the beginning of inscriptions and recorded in a system of bar-and-dot numeration, in which the bar equals five dots [40]. The development of the null cipher, a placeholder similar to our zero,

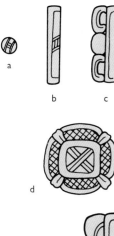

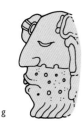

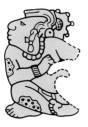

a

b

c

d

e

f

g

h

was a crucial step forward intellectually. In the history of mankind, it was achieved only in the Indo-Arabic and Mesoamerican numerical systems. The Maya generally represented this symbol as a Maltese cross, perhaps derived from the human body with all four limbs outstretched, indicating the twenty digits. In Postclassic manuscripts a shell is used for the null cipher, and in Maya inscriptions a head or full-figure variant could be substituted. With place notation of this sort, Mesoamericans could have also kept track of large numbers of things, whether cacao beans or warriors, and added, subtracted, and multiplied them. It's worth noting here that the Roman system of numeration was inherently limiting to the sorts of calculations and accounting possible.

The earliest known Long Count date is 36 BC, recorded on Stela 2 at Chiapa de Corzo. The cessation of the system in the tenth century (AD 909 at Tonina is the last date known) generally marks the close of the Classic era. The *katun* (the period of twenty years) count persisted up to the sixteenth century, thus allowing a correlation to be established between the Mesoamerican and European systems.

The importance of this accurate calendar to the art historian and archaeologist should not be underestimated: when inscriptions are present, the calendrics precisely document Maya chronology in a way not known elsewhere in the New World. A subtle difference of style between monuments, for instance, can be shown to reflect a ten-year difference in their erection, and this knowledge can be used subsequently to date monuments and ceramics without such calendrical inscriptions, even those outside the Maya area.

The Maya recorded hundreds of dates, generally of the first millennium of our era, but on occasion they reckoned mythological dates deep into the past and future. In some inscriptions, calendrical information can occupy a third to a half of the glyphs. For years, scholars made progress in deciphering only the calendrical content of Maya writing. This led some of them, particularly Sir Eric Thompson, to posit that the writings were purely calendrical, glorifications of the passage of time itself. The same thinking prompted the notion that the human figures carved on Maya monuments must have been anonymous calendar priests. But, as we shall see, Thompson's hypothesis and its corollary that the Maya were a pacific people, their lives overseen by astronomer priests, were abandoned as scholars determined the meaning of non-calendrical inscriptions.

Non-calendrical writing first appeared during Late Formative times, both in association with and independent of calendrical statements. Glyphs occur with human figures, perhaps as names or events, and in long passages. Little progress has so far been made in reading these non-calendrical Late Formative glyphs. Some of the earliest Maya inscriptions, however, are recarved Olmec objects, as if an Olmec heirloom were later worked with a new owner's name. A fine Olmec greenstone pectoral now at Dumbarton Oaks, for example, was incised with a long Maya text, perhaps at the end of the Late Formative.

The mid-1980s recovery of a huge carved stela from La Mojarra, Veracruz, in the region thought of as the Olmec 'heartland,' has revealed previously unknown sophistication and skill in early writing [41]. Two Long Count dates run in columns at the center of the monument, recording dates in AD 143 and 156. Other signs and their syntax can be recognized, but not 'read.'

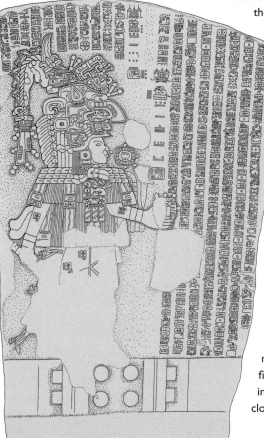

Adorned in the headdress of the Principal Bird Deity, the standing lord wears regalia that the Classic Maya would subsequently emulate, including the celt assemblage on his chest.

When John Lloyd Stephens visited the Maya area in 1839, he found inscriptions that he believed represented a single system used from Copan in the south to Chichen Itza in the north. Writing in the era of the Rosetta Stone's decoding, Stephens felt sure a scholar would one day read names and places of the ancient Maya kings. About 120 years later, and 80 years after Long Count dates were first cracked, two breakthroughs began to fulfill his prophecy. They also began to explain just why the Maya (and probably the Olmecs and Zapotecs before them) were so absorbed in chronological reckonings: they needed a means to fix historical information firmly in time. Heinrich Berlin first noticed in 1958 that a particular glyphic compound closed many Maya texts, yet the main element

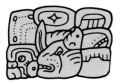

a

b

c

d

e

f

of this cluster varied from site to site. It quickly became evident that these glyphic compounds must refer either to place or family, if not both. (Similarly the name York, for example, refers to both a lineage and a place in England.) These glyphs have now been identified for most Maya sites with inscriptions [42]. The text of Naranjo Stela 24, for example, includes two different 'emblems,' as Berlin called them. One might suspect trade, warfare, alliance, or marriage as the motivation for such an inscription, and in fact the hefty woman depicted on the monument was a foreigner who married into the Naranjo dynasty. Both the emblem of Naranjo and that of her place of origin appear in the text.

At about the same time that Berlin was working on emblems, Tatiana Proskouriakoff explained how the pattern of dates at Piedras Negras implied their historical nature. She hypothesized verbs – to do with birth, accession, capture, and death, among other things – and names – 'Bird Jaguar' and 'Shield Jaguar' at Yaxchilan, for example. She also showed the importance of royal women, and documented a 'female indicator' glyph.

A look at Yaxchilan Lintel 8 shows why she began to suspect that such inscriptions had historical content [43]. A skull within a beaded cartouche is inscribed on the thigh of the captive at right: this same glyph appears as the fourth glyph in the text above, left. The first two glyphs yield a date in AD 755; given modern Maya syntax and the frequency of the third glyph in passages associated with armed men and captives, Proskouriakoff then hypothesized that the third glyph was a verb, probably meaning 'to capture,' since that activity is depicted. To the right, the text continues. The last glyph could already be identified as a Yaxchilan emblem (cf. ill. 42d); the glyph preceding it is a jaguar head with a small bird superfixed. Based on its frequency in texts dating from about AD 750 to 770, Proskouriakoff proposed this glyph to be the ruler's name in that era, and she called him 'Bird Jaguar.' Thus, if we ignore the caption material that appears in the middle of the scene, the text might be paraphrased: 'On 7 Imix 14 Tzek [in AD 755] was captured Jeweled Skull by Lord Bird Jaguar, of the Yaxchilan lineage.'

By this time studies had also been completed by Yuri Knorosov in St. Petersburg, who was able to show the phonetic values of many glyphic elements. Unlike Proskouriakoff or Berlin, who worked with Classic inscriptions, Knorosov took the sixteenth-century manuscript of Diego de Landa, bishop of Mérida, and the three Postclassic Maya manuscripts surviving in Europe as his

43 Lintel 8, Yaxchilan. Bird Jaguar, at right, captures 'Jeweled Skull,' whose name is emblazoned on his thigh and at the bottom of the column of glyphs at left. Bird Jaguar's name is the second in the column of glyphs at far right, and it is followed by the Yaxchilan emblem glyph (cf. ill. 42d). AD 755

focus of study. Landa had asked an educated Maya source to write Maya characters beside the letters of the Spanish alphabet. In this way, some thirty-odd Maya glyphs had been written down. Knorosov used these to begin to determine the phonetic value of the texts.

The capture glyph in the passage decoded by Proskouriakoff was one to which Knorosov had already turned his attention. He read the three elements of the third glyph of the column at right as *chu-ca-ah*, or *chucah*, literally the third person of the verb 'to capture' in many Maya languages today. With the publication of Proskouriakoff's work, the phonetic interpretations of Knorosov began to gain acceptance.

Scholars had long noted the use of Maya symbols in iconography – even before the decipherment took place that would demonstrate that they are, in fact, writing. In their recent work, Andrea Stone and Marc Zender have compiled an index of Maya visual and textual signs, assessing the close connection between the aesthetic units that make up Maya glyphs and art. For example, as David Stuart first demonstrated, on a panel from Emiliano Zapata [44], the glyph for yellow labels the 'yellow stone' that the seated lord carves; the words 'yellow stone' appear directly overhead in the inscribed passage. Maya glyphs were the foundation of the ancient viewer's cultural literacy, which spanned image and text.

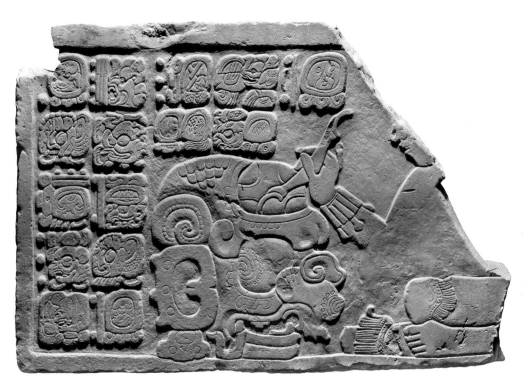

44 After a Palenque king died in 702, a neighboring lord took up a tool to carve a 'yellow [the word yellow is embedded in the forehead] stone [the monstrous head is the word for stone],' as the text also records.

Modern initial understandings of the nature of the Maya script changed the way scholars perceived the ancient Maya. The first group of glyphs deciphered showed them to have been territorial; the next stressed the role of individuals and their quest for power at various Maya cities. With a few strokes of the pen, the notion of a peaceful Maya had become obsolete and insupportable. As a result, scholars began to seek evidence for similar cultural patterns through Mesoamerica, and the impetus to decipher other scripts gained renewed energy.

The Zapotec writing system was also used to record names and places. Names were indicated by their position in the 260-day calendar, and the places recorded were those conquered by the successful lords of Monte Alban. Javier Urcid has identified several missing elements of the calendar, and the script may have been more complete than scholars previously assumed.

By means of logographic manuscripts, the Mixtec of the Postclassic (probably earlier as well, but the manuscripts no longer exist) recorded their genealogical histories. Names are either the calendrical day names or logographs (that is, word pictures) which first appear attached physically to given individuals. Events are

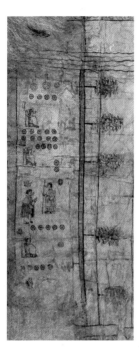

symbolized by widely understood signs: an umbilical cord denotes birth, a couple seated on a reed mat marks marriage. With this kind of record, the reader must provide the words to a story for which places, dates, events, and persons are specifically indicated.

Among the Aztecs, dates and logographic writing also prevailed. Writing was used by individuals for divining manuscripts and genealogies and by the state for keeping track of the tribute collected from the whole of Mesoamerica. At the time of the Conquest, Aztec writing had developed substantial phoneticism, which continued to develop under Spanish rule, even as Nahuatl scribes adopted the Roman alphabet. New situations may have driven linguistic developments: a map at Yale's Beinecke Library, for example, features phonetic names for local lords, including the image of a banner, PAN, against a background of salt, or IZTA, yielding Estéban, as Gordon Whittaker has shown [45]. Multiple female landowners tagged by the Aztec glyph of twisted cords, or 'ma,' indicating the Christian name Maria. Effective as these scripts were, no other script replicated the sounds of speech in written form the way Maya writing did. The elegant poetry recited by Aztec nobility was not written down until the introduction of the Roman alphabet, although a guide with cues could have existed.

45 Aztec rulers, or *tlatoque* (plural of *tlatoani*, literally 'speaker') line the left side of an Early Colonial land map in Yale's Beinecke Library, c. 1565. Viceroy José Maria Velasco (ruled 1550–64) appears midway, the authority of the Spanish Crown depicted by the diadem overhead. He faces an indigenous judge, Estéban de Guzmán, who ruled during a three-year interregnum of the *tlatoque*.

Late Formative Art and Architecture

Late Formative planners moved vast quantities of stone and earth and redesigned natural earth formations to establish places of devotion and commerce across Mesoamerica. At the same time certain sculptural types that developed at La Venta, such as the stela, began to appear in disparate locations, yet consistently adopting proportions that favored human representations.

Monte Alban

The most spectacular early development in Oaxaca took place at Monte Alban. The city was founded at the beginning of the Late Formative, presumably as the Zapotec capital. A mountainous outcrop overlooking three important valleys of central Oaxaca was reworked into a great manmade acropolis. In the first era of occupation, a main axis running roughly north-south was established and at least some structures were erected to define the main plaza as the ritual core.

Monte Alban has no natural source of water, and one might legitimately surmise that it took an advanced social organization to sustain a community so high above the fertile valleys. Various ideas have been put forward to explain the selection of this remote mountain for settled life, and all depend upon the most important early temple there, the Temple of the Danzantes, and the nature of its reliefs.

While some scholars have imagined Monte Alban as a site of pacific unification, others have seen in its early writing and art patterns of conquest and domination more typical of Mesoamerica.

The Danzantes, or 'dancers,' were so named in the nineteenth century because of their free, loose postures. In Late Formative times, over 300 individual slabs were carved with these figures, and about 140 were incorporated into the Temple of the Danzantes [46]. About the same number were set into Mound J [47], a slightly later structure, and others were reused in later contexts. In the Temple of the Danzantes, the slabs are set so that some face out, away from the main plaza, while others line a narrow passageway and yet others flank the main façade. Some, particularly those considered 'swimmers,' form a flight of stairs. No single figure is arranged with regard to another, insofar as can be determined now.

Each slab is different in its imagery, but all were worked in a simple incised technique with little relief. One assumes that the carver simply followed a charcoal sketch made directly on the stone. Most bodies are shown frontally or in three-quarter view, while the heads are in profile. All are male. Hands and feet hang limp. The closed eyes of most figures indicate that they are dead. Although some retain a necklace or an earplug, they are all naked, normally an indication of humiliation in Mesoamerica. Scroll motifs

46 Danzantes at Monte Alban. These limp, mutilated figures, long thought to be 'dancing,' may be sacrificed captives of war. Monte Alban I.

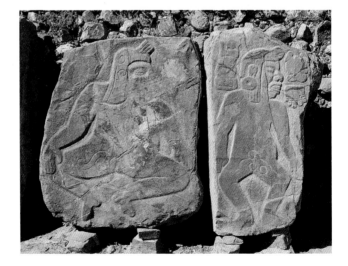

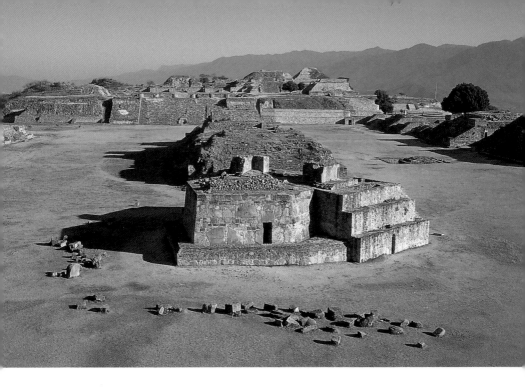

47 Mound J, Monte Alban. From the south, the dramatic, arrowlike positioning of the structure can be seen. Monte Alban II.

streaming from the groin no doubt reveal an ancient pattern of genital mutilation in Oaxaca. A few are accompanied by glyphic cartouches, probably names.

In all likelihood, these slabs show the victims of war. To Richard Blanton, who has studied early settlement both in the valleys and on Monte Alban, the Temple of the Danzantes suggests a war memorial, erected at the beginning of Monte Alban's growth, to commemorate the end of divisive strife among the three valleys. Prisoner galleries, however, occur in later art, particularly among the Maya, and in general they indicate a different sort of memorial. The north wall of Room 2 of the Bonampak paintings, for example, shows a group of tortured captives at the feet of victorious warriors on a flight of stairs. If we were to repopulate the 'swimmer' staircase of the Temple of the Danzantes, we would have a similar scene. In the later Maya cases, it is clear that the captives were displayed to proclaim the prowess of the victors, not to discourage the horrors of war. In accordance with Mesoamerican patterns, the message conveyed at Monte Alban is likely to have emphasized the power held by those who dominated the valley.

Somewhat later, probably after 200 BC, the Zapotecs erected Mound J in the center of the plaza at Monte Alban. By this time the

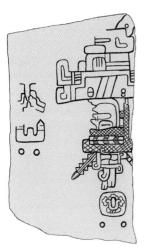

48 Incised on a slab from Mound J, this glyph for 'hill,' indicating a placename, includes the upside-down head of a lord, probably recording his defeat.

Overleaf:
49 Hands outstretched, this large hollow tomb figure from Monte Alban II discouraged anyone seeking to violate the space of the dead.

50 Masters of large-scale ceramic modeling, Zapotec clay sculptors conceived here of a supernatural puma. The scarf around the neck probably indicates a sacrificial ritual.

51 An early Monte Alban king was buried with this jade bat assemblage. He probably once wore it on his chest, like the lord of La Mojarra (cf. ill. 41), or as a belt adornment, as demonstrated by later Maya lords (cf. ills. 122, 124). Monte Alban II.

symmetrical guide lines of the plaza had been laid out; but Mound J was set prominently off axis and given unusual form. The structure looks like an arrow pointing to the southwest, yet its unusual configuration cannot be observed from the north or east. From the northeast, the building shows only a wall of steps, flanked by broad balustrades. The pointed head of the building is honeycombed with tunnels that are vaulted with stone slabs slanted to touch one another, creating a visual pointed archway but with no structural strength. Both these odd tunnels and the unusual shape of the structure itself have given rise to the idea that Mound J may have had an astronomical function. Recent studies have borne this out. Some 31 miles (50 km) to the east, at Cabellito Blanco, a structure nearly identical to Mound J has been found. At zenith passage both mounds point to particularly bright stars. Mound J, then, is one of the first buildings in Mesoamerica that we can consider a giant chronographic marker. Its purpose was to acknowledge the passage of time, and – interestingly enough – it appears about the same time as the proliferation of the written calendrical system.

The evolution of the writing system is also evident in Mound J [47]. Carved slabs, technically similar to those of the Temple of the Danzantes, were set along the façade, the projectile wall, and within the tunnels. On these slabs, although the genital mutilation persists, the figures show more costume details. The writing too is far more elaborate; it seems to record battles with dates and placenames, as distinct from the more general record of conquest shown previously on the Danzantes temple. A rough incision, probably following a charcoal sketch, characterizes the Mound J carvings, and is characteristic of a lapidary style common at the time. On several, a human head is shown upside-down under a placename, indicating conquest, and the accompanying glyphs suggest a date in the 52-year calendar [48].

Monte Alban was very much the main center in Oaxaca during the Late Formative, but it was not unique. To the southeast, at Dainzu, another great mountainous outcrop was the focus of occupation. In this instance, the main architecture arose on the valley floor, and a large temple structure there had inset carved slabs technically similar to the Danzantes. Individuals with masks or helmets, perhaps ballplayers, form the majority of the representations. Above, on the peak itself, steps and chambers were carved from the living rock, and the site may have functioned as a religious shrine.

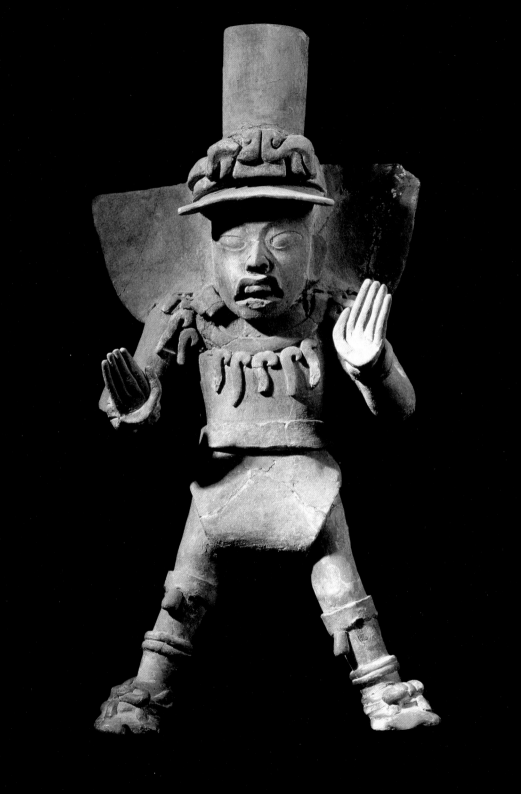

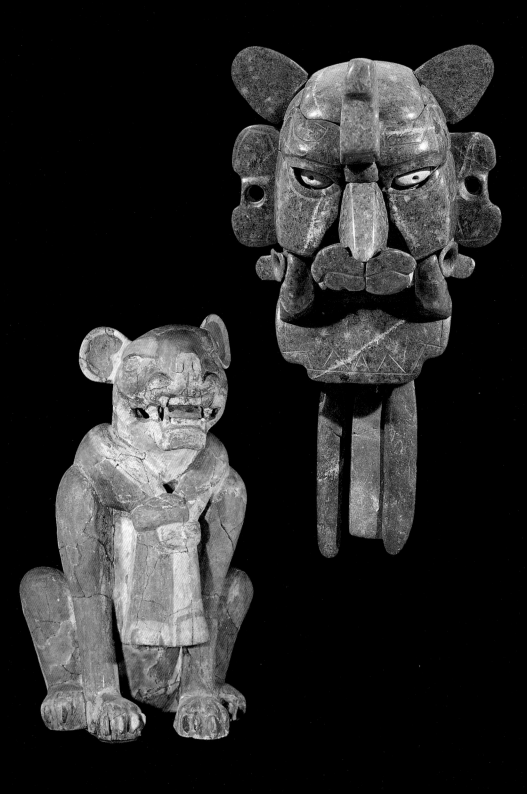

The careful excavation of the tombs at Monte Alban produced a dependable chronological sequence long before radiocarbon testing could provide a second check. The two earliest periods are known as Monte Alban I and Monte Alban II. Ceramics show the most periodization; other architectural innovations of the Late Formative, such as the construction of masonry ballcourts or the use of columns, show a steady development into later forms.

Most of the tomb goods from Monte Alban I were simple offerings of gray-colored ceramics. Strong affinity with Olmec conventions of physiognomy can be seen in the earliest effigy pots, the best of which come from Monte Negro, also in the modern state of Oaxaca. Slightly slanted eyes and a strongly downturned mouth are typical of these early wares. By Monte Alban II, the technical qualities that characterize later Monte Alban tomb offerings are evident, although stylistically distinct. Many large full-figure hollow effigy sculptures were made in animal and human forms. Technically, large ceramic figures may have derived from Olmec precedents, but the imagery is particular to Oaxaca.

A carefully formed large standing figure of this period holds his hands out as if to warn away tomb robbers, and Alfonso Caso found these figures at tomb entrances [49]. Life-size hollow pumas and jaguars wear scarves and adornments, indicating their supernatural qualities [50]: surely such guardians acted to deter potential violators of these entries to the underworld! But the figures represented encompass a wide range of human expression. The Scribe of Cuilapan, with his slight asymmetry, uneven shoulders, and partly opened mouth, seems simply to capture a portrait of a contemplative young man.

Fine pieces of Olmec jade, among them the Kunz Axe [12] have been collected in Oaxaca, perhaps treasures originally held by early Zapotecs. By Monte Alban II, the Zapotecs themselves were skilled lapidaries. One of the most splendid of their works of this time is the jade leaf-nose bat belt assemblage [51]. This object would have been worn at the waist or chest, the three shiny jade plaques dangling. (The Leiden Plaque was once part of such an assemblage made by the Maya.)

West Mexico

The history of ancient West Mexico is in many ways one of separate development from the rest of Mesoamerica. There is, for example, no evidence that the Mesoamerican calendrical systems were known or used. The relationship of the region to the high civilizations also remains obscure: neither the art nor the architecture indicate direct contact. Moreover there is no clear florescence of culture during one era, and it seems likely that the political developments of the Olmecs or the Aztecs barely touched the region.

This does not mean, however, that the works of art produced there lacked subtlety or craftsmanship. Far from it. West Mexican ceramic figures and groups – almost all of which have no archaeological provenance – are among the most directly appealing of all Mesoamerican artworks. Charmed by their apparent lack of elite symbolism, the modern artist Diego Rivera made a large collection of them – now in the Anahuacalli Museum in Mexico City – and regularly incorporated images based on their styles in his murals. Needless to say, this demand for West Mexican ceramic sculptures has not only promoted the looting of ancient tombs but also nurtured an industry of modern forgeries and pastiches. Peter Furst linked the modern shamanistic practices of the Huichol to West Mexican ceramics, infusing them with specific ritual meanings, and bringing these sculptures into the greater Mesoamerican tradition.

For the sake of convenience, West Mexican artifacts are grouped here under geographic headings, principally the modern states of Colima, Jalisco, and Nayarit, plus one river, Mezcala. What links these finds together is the context in which they were deposited – the shaft tomb. At anywhere from 3 ft to 19 ft 6 in (1–6 m) below ground level, such tombs consisted of a chamber opening out of a narrow shaft. In the chamber lay multiple burials, often deposited over a considerable period of time. Convincing dates for the tombs are rare, but most belong to the Late Formative, although the chronological span extends from the Early Formative to the Early Classic. The discovery in 1993 of a complete and untouched tomb in Huitzilapa revealed that families used their crypts for generations, adding new bodies and offerings through time. A single chamber held over 300 vessels, including many effigies!

The earliest documented works from West Mexico are from what is known as the Capacha complex, in central Colima. Shaft-tomb goods there have been dated to 1500 BC by radiocarbon techniques. Early vessels include stirrup-spout types remarkably similar to those found in contemporary contexts on the north coast of Peru. Does this imply links between the two areas? On the whole, contact between Mesoamerican and Andean

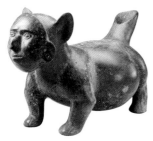

Above:
52 A terracotta dog with human mask, Colima style. Great numbers of native hairless dogs were immortalized in Colima clay sculpture, but the mask of this one makes it an overtly supernatural creature.

civilizations is believed only to have been intermittent, if it occurred at all (the Aztecs, for example, knew nothing of the Incas at the time of the Conquest); but these early vessels may provide evidence for such contact. Crops, weaving and ceramic techniques, as well as elite lore, may have been shared at just this horizon, perhaps via Ecuador. On the other hand, the stirrup-spout jar, a convenient vessel for carrying water without spillage or evaporation, could well have been invented simultaneously in response to similar needs in both areas.

Two principal types of figures have been found in Colima, and they probably reflect a chronological sequence. Flat figures – often considered to be the earlier type – use a slab-and-appliqué technique, with animated postures, and are sometimes grouped together. Better known are the hollow figures of reddish clay, burnished to a high luster, and often spotted with black, white, and gray mineral accretions slowly deposited over the centuries in the tomb. The majority of such figures also double as vessels, whose pouring spouts are usually the tails of the animal effigies. Indigenous hairless dogs were worked in particularly lively forms: playing, sleeping, even nipping one another. Others, such as the dog with a human mask, may have a meaning that goes beyond anecdotal charm [52]. Headrests were made in the form of half-dogs, and the resultant image was of a human head on a dog's back, the dog thus bearing his master into the afterlife. Colima potters formed clay into the shapes of squashes and gourds, the perishable templates for all vessels. Most human figures are males with clubs poised to strike. Like the large felines of Monte Alban II tombs, they may have warded off unwanted visitors, but the single horn protruding from the forehead of many of them has suggested that they might be shamanistic figures for communication between the living and the dead. But these horns may also be the tips of conch shells, worn to signify rulership.

Shaft-tomb deposits from Jalisco are stylistically distinct from other West Mexican ceramics, although not unrelated technically. The potters of this region produced both small solid figures and larger hollow ones. Some of the smaller ones, with pointed heads, and typically showing musicians and performers, have been recovered in lively groupings.

Limited ceremonial architecture has been discovered in West Mexico, although vast adobe mounds have been mapped by Phil Weigand. The most important stone structure is at Ixtlan del Río, Nayarit, where a tiered round platform like a wedding cake came to light. Although the platform may be late in date, other round buildings like it but of perishable materials have been found in West Mexico, and it is a type that seems to have lasted for generations. We should not therefore be surprised to discover that round architectural features often occur in ceremonial groupings of Nayarit figures, and in general, Nayarit ceramics include more architecture than the other regional styles. One of the most common themes is of figures in or near thatched houses, and the groups that show tiny figures underneath houses have been interpreted as funeral scenes related to the act of interment.

Ballcourts also have a prominent place in the group repertoire, and one day actual stone courts may be located in the Nayarit region. The figural scenes at any rate demonstrate the importance of the ballgame at an early date in the area. The court grouping illustrated here shows three or four men in a team, playing with a soccer-sized ball [55]. Dozens of spectators look on: they huddle together under a blanket or gently hug a child in an artistic expression that captures the warmth of everyday life.

The Nayarit potters also made large, hollow figures, often in male-female pairs, which are perhaps marriage portraits interred with the dead [53, 54]. The bright patterning of the ancient textiles worn in Nayarit is recorded in the slip painting of the figures' costumes. The shifts donned by Nayarit men are uncommon in

Above:
53, 54 A male and female couple, Nayarit style. Such male-female pairs, in matching clothing, were frequently placed together in shaft tombs, perhaps to accompany interred married couples. The man at top wears a beaver skin on his head, a pelt still associated with shamanic transformation.

Right:
55 Players in two teams compete on this Nayarit-style clay model of a ballcourt while spectators watch in eager anticipation of the outcome.

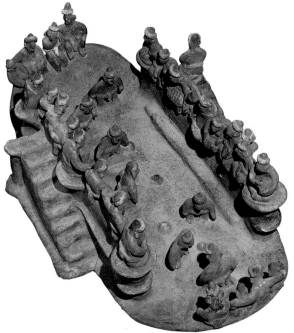

ancient Mesoamerica, and Patricia Anawalt has drawn attention to the presence of this sort of garment in the Andes during the same period, possibly showing contact. The couple in the example here may be of high status, to judge by the elaborate ornaments they wear in ears and nose, and they bear instruments, perhaps to provide musical accompaniment in death.

The drainage of the Mezcala River in West Mexico has yielded a great number of fine stone pieces of unknown date. The Aztecs coveted these serpentine, granite, and cave onyx (the Aztec *tecali*) carvings so much that they demanded them in tribute and interred them in the Templo Mayor in Tenochtitlan. Although the date of these objects has long been the subject of speculation, Louise Paradis has now secured good radiocarbon dates for Mezcala stonework, confirming the early date (*c.* 300 BC) that artists like Miguel Covarrubias long suspected intuitively.

Using string-saw technology, Mezcala artists produced small temple models in abundance [56]. The temple façades they represent are not matched by the architecture so far known from the region, and they suggest a familiarity with developments in Oaxaca. Some of these façades, for instance, resemble those of Mound X at Monte Alban, which dates to the Late Formative, and it is interesting to note that temple models have been recovered from Monte Alban II contexts.

Many functional stone pieces were also made by the Mezcala people: blades, axes, and bowls are known. What makes these materials so attractive to us is their lithic quality. The stone itself was admired by ancient Mezcala craftsmen, and its inherent 'stoniness' appeals to the modern eye.

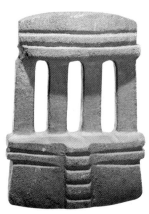

56 Stone temple models, Mezcala style. Miniatures like this may record the perishable temple façades of long-lost architecture.

The Maya region

Exciting new discoveries have begun to make the links between the Olmecs and Maya more evident and more nuanced. During the Middle Formative, the Olmecs had sustained contact with the Pacific coast, and their carvings have been found from Chiapas to El Salvador. During the Late Formative various population centers emerged where art and architecture of an apparently indigenous style were erected, particularly in the Chiapas/Guatemala highlands, at Izapa, Kaminaljuyu, Takalik Abaj, and El Baúl, and by persons who may not all have been ethnically 'Maya.' Excavations in the Central Peten – at Uaxactun and Tikal, the loci of Early Classic florescence – have shown that settlements had been established at both these places by the Late Formative. It was

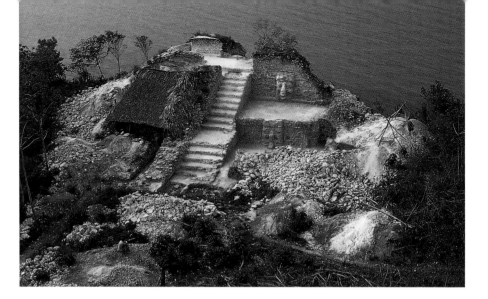

57 At sites across the lowlands, the Maya erected new pyramids with massive stucco decoration. Cerros Structure 5 features huge jaguar heads with solar attributes.

another Peten site, however – El Mirador – which apparently outstripped them in size and importance at this early date. Elsewhere, along the Caribbean coast, Cerros is the best-known site, and paintings of unprecedented complexity have now come to light at San Bartolo, Guatemala, revealing Maya creation accounts from over 3,000 years ago.

Late Formative building materials were often perishable, leaving only large collapsed adobe mounds in the highlands. Moreover, at Kaminaljuyu (with very probably the most substantial highland Late Formative architecture of all), only a handful of structures could be excavated before the modern real estate development of Guatemala City covered the greater part of the ancient ruins. In other locations, later structures still house earlier constructions. Probably the finest of known highland buildings is the great platform E-III-3 at Kaminaljuyu, which covered two rich tombs, in the pattern that later Maya architecture followed.

However, at Cerros, in modern Belize at the mouth of the New River, we see dramatic architectural expressions that participate in the foundations of a new public ideology. About 100 BC there was an unprecedented spurt of building. All previous constructions were razed and new ones, some exceeding 65 ft 6 in (20 m) in height, were built with clean, new rubble cores [57]. At Lamanai, farther up the New River, even taller structures rose to adorn the city. Giant stucco mask façades flanking the stairs are common in these new buildings at Cerros and Lamanai. The masks seem to display a new, codified imagery. *K'in*, or sun, symbols

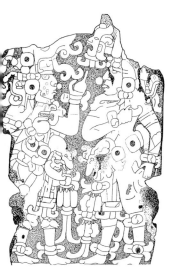

decorate the cheeks of great supernatural faces, in association with jaguar elements. This imagery of the jaguar sun appears along with other concepts emerging at the time and taking the forms in which they would be recognizable for centuries. Notions of sacred mountains became central to Maya pyramids, particularly the idea of what Karl Taube has called 'Flower Mountain,' a place of paradise and emergence. The Plumed Serpent – later known as Quetzalcoatl among the Aztec – must be of great antiquity as well, and is found fully formed among the early Maya, as we shall shortly see. This combined imagery and architecture spread – almost as if it were some new orthodoxy – across the Maya realm, providing an ideological unity that the Maya would solidify through narrative art and writing.

At El Mirador and Nakbe, archaeologists have uncovered vast cities built and abandoned between 600 BC and AD 100, testimony to the authority mustered by early Maya kings, as well as their wealth and power. The powerful ideology that united the Maya first took monumental form, perhaps already shared and transmitted by writing on perishable materials that no longer survive. Some of the largest pyramidal forms ever constructed in ancient America were erected in Late Formative Peten, promoting the shared notions of Flower Mountain, Jaguar Sun, Principal Bird Deity, and the Plumed Serpent. Few carved fragments of stone sculpture have been recovered to date, but at Nakbe, Richard Hansen has uncovered a nearly complete Middle or Late Formative carved stela with two standing figures rendered on it – what may well be the earliest representation of the Hero Twins

58 Stela 1, Nakbe. These two carved figures may be the earliest Maya depiction of the Hero Twins to survive. At left, the figure with jaguar pelage on his cheek may well be Xbalanque, facing his brother Hunahpu. Middle/Late Formative.

59 In this cutaway reconstruction of Structure 1 at San Bartolo, the north wall paintings can be seen as an upper-level frieze within the building. The west wall paintings at the rear of the building have also now been uncovered.

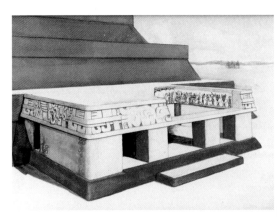

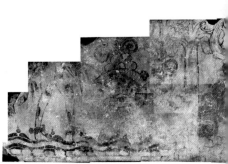

[58]. At El Mirador's demise, when Tikal and Uaxactun were already growing into powerful polities, El Mirador's enemies may have stormed through the center of the declining city, smashing every sign of its former glory.

Now painting can be added to sculpture and architecture of this period. In 2001 in the northeast Peten, archaeologist William Saturno found himself in a looter's tunnel in what is now called San Bartolo Structure 1 (Pinturas), Sub-1 chamber [59]; his flashlight came to rest on two painted figures, just a small part of what was found to be a much larger group of murals. Although these newly discovered works shed light on developments in the Late Formative period, the dramatic paintings at San Bartolo also raise a host of questions. To date, the interior north and west walls have been photographed, reconstructed, and studied; fragments of the other two walls have been found not only in the interior of the structure but deposited in ritual fashion elsewhere at the site, so it may well be unlikely that the entire painting is ever recovered. The paintings wrap around the walls, and the west wall, seen directly through the wide galleried openings on the east side of the building, may well have been the most important [60]. Its prominent scenes of penis bloodletting and jaguar sacrifice make it clear that rituals best known for the later Maya lay at the center of San Bartolo elite practice over 2,000 years ago. The paintings are uniform in style and pigments, arguing for a single phase of painting about 100 BC, although each wall seems to have presented different sacred narratives. Set over halfway up the wall, the paintings ran about 3 ft (1 m) high, and the unusual post and

60 Archaeologist William Saturno directly scanned the west wall paintings of Structure 1 at San Bartolo and stitched them together to reveal a stunning scene of sacrifice.

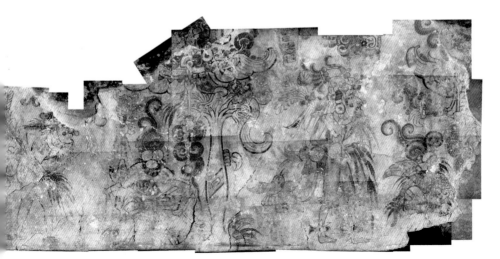

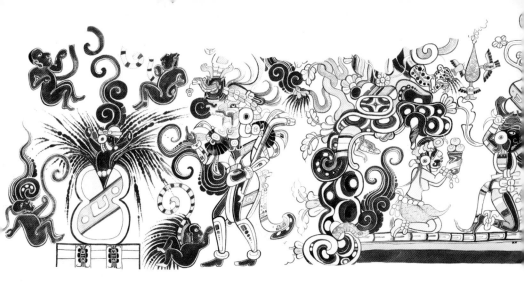

61 An artist's rendering of the north wall paintings at San Bartolo. Four maize maidens attend the Maize God, shown here with a face recalling Olmec models (see also ill. 1). At far left, a gourd splits open, yielding enigmatic babies.

masonry roof may have remained at least partly open to facilitate the process of painting. The figures are about one-third life size.

The north wall reveals two separate mythic scenes [61]. At left, an enthroned gourd bursts open with brilliant streams of blood that the artist has relished feathering across the wall, connecting the central baby with headdress and belt to four naked infants, each with a red umbilicus. Together, the five babies form a quincunx, a common notion of Mesoamerican worldview, in which the four directions join a central axis that links heavens, underworld, and the surface of the earth. Standing just to the right of this scene is a masked standing male figure with an axe, who presumably has just struck the gourd to release the figures.

The preponderance of the north wall – and the section most ballyhooed at the time of the discovery – depicts an only slightly less enigmatic scene [61]. At the center stands the Maize God, a major figure in Maya art and belief, and the model for humanity itself. A seasonal god, he dies only to be reborn and to serve as human sustenance; he is eternally youthful and the ideal of human beauty. Rendered in slim, lanky proportions, and standing taller than any other figure, the red-painted Maize God of San Bartolo has a face of strong Olmec features, an intentional reference by the Maya painter to the antiquity of the deity. As he turns to look over his shoulder, he is attended by three turbaned males and four bare-breasted females – the latter would seem to be his wives, maize goddesses all. The last, at right, wears only a spondylus shell around her waist, a traditional symbol of noble women and sometimes of maidenhood; her body is sheathed in a red painted

72

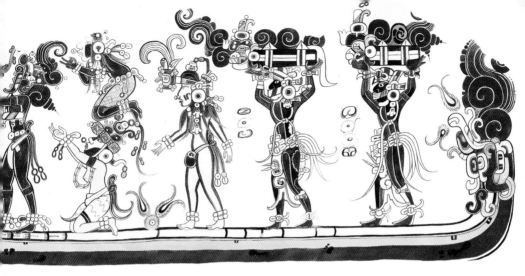

outline and of all the figures depicted, she is the only one to exhibit individual toes. The Maize God himself receives a flowering gourd similar to the one bursting in the adjacent scene; a woman also proffers a vessel filled with tamales. She kneels within the open mouth of Flower Mountain, its cave-like stalactite hanging down just at the back of her head, while a jaguar breathes feathered red streams over her head.

This second scene takes place atop a plumed serpent that runs left to right, or west to east, while footprints – a universal sign of travel, lineage, and directionality in Mesoamerica – travel from right to left across the red and yellow bands of the serpent body. Yellow tufts of feathers cling here and there to the serpent; great red scrolls emanate from its mouth. The figures can be seen to be both atop the serpent and just in front of it. The painter – and although there may have been assistants on the job, there would seem to be one master hand in charge of what has come to light so far – has worked with a consistent palette of yellow, black, cream, and red. Most, but not all features are outlined with a strong black calligraphic line – the red scrolls of blood, breath, and sound stand on their own.

The San Bartolo paintings are important in many respects, but first and foremost, they make it obvious that the heart of the Maya religious narrative – the story of the Maize God – was intact in 100 BC. They reveal a Maya familiarity in some respect with the Olmec that scholars had only guessed at before. Among the Olmecs, for example, cave origins were a common subject, seen in altars, niche settings, and cave depictions; San Bartolo features paired lords within a cave, a subject nearly replicated on the AD 435 Motmot Panel excavated at Copan, Honduras. The San Bartolo paintings also remind the modern-day viewer that painting may well have been the principal medium throughout ancient Mesoamerica, whether on paper, in books, on ceramics, or walls. The San Bartolo paintings are not hesitant first attempts but rather full-blown – dare one say? – masterpieces that speak to a yet deeper background. One can see here that narrative art, with obvious sequence and story, is making not just a debut but a confident appearance. Based on their complexity, so much sculpture of the period now makes more sense, as if an entire underlying stratum has been revealed.

The story of the Maize God goes hand in hand with that of the Hero Twins: they are the Maize God's children and the actors who bring him back to life at the end of the dry season. They are also skilled masters of the ballgame, suggesting that its ritual performance had taken hold as well. As archaeology goes forward, it may well turn out that sculptures and paintings will continue to fill out the picture of vast lowland cities known heretofore largely for their buildings.

In the adjacent Guatemala and Chiapas highlands, new developments – and a shared new ideology – also swept across the region, built in some large part on Olmec forms. Boulder carvings – the ones most likely to have had Olmec precedents – were made at many sites, but other forms, particularly the stela, a late Olmec invention, now paired with an accompanying altar, predominated at Izapa, Kaminaljuyu, and Takalik Abaj.

Later Maya reset the monuments of Izapa, but most of the stelae and altars there were carved during the Late Formative. Many of the altars (perhaps used as thrones by the lords) appear in the shape of large toads and frogs, maybe symbols of the earth. A different segment of the supernatural world from the San Bartolo paintings appears on the Izapa stelae, all part of the shared cosmology that would be recognized by the time of the Spanish invasion. Stela 21, for example, depicts a standing figure, one arm rent from his body, who apparently appeals to the Principal Bird Deity perched in a caiman tree, an apparent rendering of the story of the Hero Twins and Vuqub Kaquix from the *Popol Vuh*, as written down in the mid-sixteenth century.

On Izapa Stela 1, Chahk, god of rain and lightning, stands in water and fishes with a net, his already well-stocked creel on his back [62]. A millennium later, on a pair of bones buried in Ruler A's

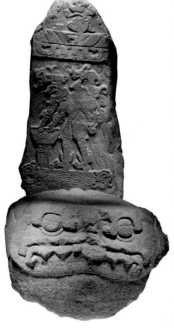

62 Izapa Stela 1 and Altar 1. Fishing creel on his back, Chahk the rain god stands in water to net his catch. Altar 1 suggests the toad-like earth.

tomb at Tikal, three squabbling Chahks catch fish in their bare hands and store their catch in similar creels [173]. In this early representation of one of the most important Maya deities, Chahk has his characteristically reptilian snout, a feature he would bear into colonial times. Not only the god of storms, Chahk was probably the patron of fishermen. Stela 1 took its place on the main plaza of Izapa with a paired altar, which in this case was in the form of a giant toad, symbolizing the earth. The fishing god, then, rose up behind the toad, so that the ordered industry of humankind would be juxtaposed with the untamed natural world. Others feature rulers embodying the Principal Bird Deity, seen elsewhere in the time period.

Stela 5 depicts a mythic origin from a central tree. Representations of natural flora are rare in Olmec and Maya art, but the notion of human origins from a 'world tree' was well known at the time of Spanish invasion and was recorded in the Codex Selden [242]. Dense and difficult to decipher, the scene on Stela 5 may be designed for oral reading, with components recorded as if in simultaneous narrative. Other stelae depict deities and heroes that would play a role in later religious narratives.

Like the rest of the Izapa monuments, these stelae emphasize mythological or supernatural settings. Yet rulers probably are important here, marked by size and scale, and commanding authority in both civil and religious arenas. Borders above and below the Izapa scenes would seem to mark heaven and earth, quite possibly the first use of such conventions, although they emerge simultaneously at Kaminaljuyu (below). The rectilinear 'hill' sign introduced in this era would take its most characteristic form in the Late Postclassic, where it is a standard component of placenames recorded on Early Colonial tribute lists, and suggesting the specificity of location to these Late Preclassic lords.

The greatest florescence of the Late Formative in the highlands took place at Kaminaljuyu, where the richest burials of the era have been recovered, and many monuments have been found in its style over a 50-mile (80-km) radius. Fine carved stelae show both supernatural figures and humans. Stela 11 depicts a standing lord dressed as the Principal Bird Deity [63], like the roughly contemporary ruler at La Mojarra [41]. But he could also be understood in light of the San Bartolo paintings, where an individual like this one is shown splitting open a gourd with an axe. His eye peers out from the mask, and his cape flares out behind him like a pair of wings. An ancestor floats in the sky, and two

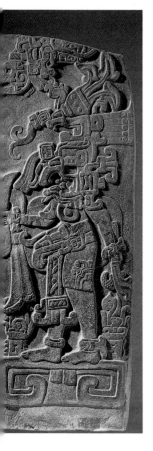

63 Stela 11, Kaminaljuyu. The standing warrior appears in the guise of the Principal Bird Deity. He stands on a place sign, and his feet are framed by blazing censers. Late Formative.

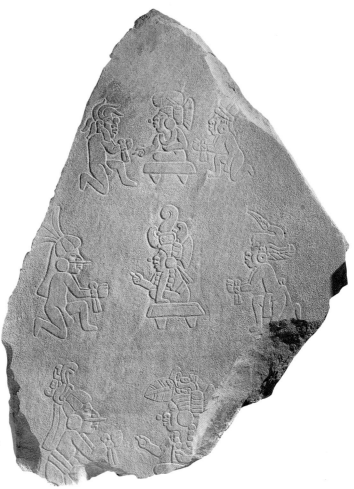

64 Kaminaljuyu Monument 65, a sequence of three enthroned lords, each of whom receives abject captives. This surface of the stone served as a throne itself.

smoking braziers rest at his feet. His deeply-carved feet press into the toponym he stands on, and the knapped surface of the hafted blade at right reveals a skill at carving that the lowland Maya did not achieve until centuries later.

Extremely hard rocks were mastered by Kaminaljuyu artists, who may have sought a durable message to the future. Some human figures and other forms are worked in silhouette with cut-outs, a novel style of very limited distribution. Massive thrones may have recorded systematic genealogies, as on Monument 65 [64]; Stela 10 features a long and as-yet undeciphered text but composed with some recognizable syllables.

At Takalik Abaj, stone monuments were also erected in stela/altar combinations, as they were at Izapa, but the imagery is different. Stela 2 shows two figures flanking a central column of text with a Cycle 7 (that is, before AD 41) date. Like La Venta Stela 3, Kaminaljuyu Stela 11, and the Early Classic portraits of Tikal, the upper margin has a supernatural character. The two humans below were probably historical figures. On Stela 5, two persons also flank a column of text, in this case a legible Long Count date of 8.4.5.17.11, or AD 126. The impossible posture of frontal torso with profile legs and face was a widespread convention which was, within a few generations, to prove typical of Maya representations.

The second century AD brought an end to these achievements in the Guatemalan highlands, and the focus of progress shifted to the Central Peten, where a new iteration of Maya culture began to take shape. From the forms established at Izapa, and already known in the lowlands, the Maya derived mythic imagery; from Takalik Abaj, the conventions of historical portraiture. When the Early Classic emerged in full flower at Tikal and Uaxactun, it clearly drew upon precedents in the highlands for sculpture and from the Caribbean coast and El Mirador for architecture. Indeed, in most of Mesoamerica, Classic achievements in art and architecture were founded upon those of the Late Formative.

Central Mexico

During Early and Middle Formative times an Olmec presence had made a profound impact on sites – and their grave goods, in particular – in the valleys of Central Mexico, but this presence ended in the Late Formative period. These established centers were not cities, and they did not have major ceremonial centers. We might consider them elaborate villages. At Tlatilco, for example, during the Late Formative period, figurines continued to be made; to the west, at Chupicuaro (now under an artificial lake in Guanajuato), charming figurines and vessels with distinctive red geometric slip patterning were produced.

By 100 BC at the latest, two new centers had emerged in the Valley of Mexico, Teotihuacan to the north, and Cuicuilco to the south, now essentially surrounded by the high-end shopping center PeriSur. Positioned like rivals at extreme ends of the Valley, each grew dramatically in size and population. At Cuicuilco, a huge round platform (443 ft or 135 m in diameter at the base) was the focus of construction, rising in four concentric tiers like a giant wedding cake. About 50 BC, the volcano Xitli erupted, burying much of Cuicuilco. Another eruption occurred about 150 years later. Like Pompeii's population, the people of Cuicuilco fled. Teotihuacan no longer had a rival, and it grew rapidly in power and size.

Chapter 4   Teotihuacan

We know the greatest city of all Mesoamerica by the name Teotihuacan, 'the place of the gods,' as the Aztecs would later call it. In recent years the buildings of Teotihuacan have not changed, nor has its signature grid, nor have the tripod vessels that signal the long reach of Teotihuacan traders and the powerful attraction of the goods manufactured there. But much has changed in what is known of Teotihuacan's material world, as revealed by the most recent archaeology. Even at distant Copan, Honduras, Maya lords referred to it as 'Pu,' or the 'Reed' place. This is a translation into Maya of Tollan, as Teotihuacan was known in both its own day and in memory, as a Rome and a Jerusalem but also a Troy to those who never saw the abandoned ruins. To all Mesoamerica and perhaps beyond, the city was legend in its own time.

Centuries after the site's abandonment, the Aztec ruler Motecuhzoma II made regular pilgrimages there, traveling by canoe across Lake Texcoco to follow a well-established route that linked his city, Tenochtitlan, to Teotihuacan and to valuable resources beyond. The conquistador Hernando Cortés and his men would pass near the site on their march to the Aztec capital, although no chronicler noted the ancient city. Teotihuacan's greatest pyramids, and its powerful north–south axis, or 'Way of the Dead,' are all known by the names given them by the great successor civilization, the Aztec; colonial maps marked Teotihuacan's pyramids with a sun and moon.

65 Drawn and colored late in the sixteenth century, the Map of San Francisco Mazapan clearly depicts the Teotihuacan Pyramid of the Moon at lower left, part of a landscape that includes Christian buildings, paths and roads for human movement marked by footprints, and indigenous elite leaders.

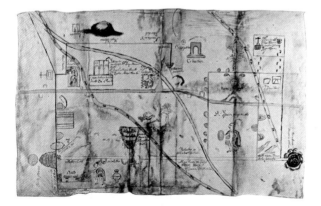

Decades of archaeological research have produced one vision of Teotihuacan after another, starting with the reconstruction of the Pyramid of the Sun for the 1910 Centennial of Mexico's War of Independence; narrow gauge railroad could then bring visitors easily to what quickly became – and remains – Mexico's most important ancient destination, with well over a million visitors

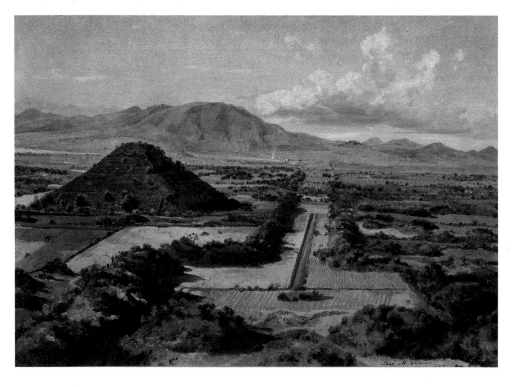

66 Viceroy José Maria Velasco painted Teotihuacan many times in the nineteenth century. Here, in 1878, he captured the Pyramid of the Sun before archaeological explorations began.

annually (at the time of writing). Restoration of the Temple of the Feathered Serpent ensued, to be followed by the investigation, excavation, and reconstruction of residential compounds and the discovery of programmatic paintings limning the walls of spaces for the living. In the 1960s, while the exterior of the Pyramid of the Moon was under reconstruction, René Millon and his team produced the single most detailed map in existence of any Mesoamerican city – and demonstrated unequivocally that Teotihuacan *was* a city, not a shrine. In 1971, workmen installing the Sound and Light wiring on the Pyramid of the Sun fell down a hole, revealing a remarkable cave system under the huge building. In the 1990s Saburo Sugiyama led a project that produced shocking discoveries of great numbers of sacrificed warriors. Ruben Cabrera, Leonardo Lopez Lujan, and Sugiyama subsequently launched the greatest project to date at Teotihuacan: full-scale exploration of the Pyramid of the Moon. These most recent excavations have brought to light major tombs, finally making it possible to ask the question, even if no answers are forthcoming: who ruled Teotihuacan?

Other discoveries make it possible to begin to answer a corollary question: *how* was Teotihuacan ruled? Long after the

79

Maya peoples to the south were acknowledged to have had independent kings who commissioned vast building projects, stone monuments and tiny precious works, the very notion of such rulership has resisted traction at Teotihuacan. Key questions remain about Teotihuacan, including the very ethnicity of its powerful, urban population. The current campaigns of archaeology have much to tell us. Yet with the raw evidence of power marshaled in the control of the life and death of hundreds if not thousands of other humans, alongside the discovery of great tombs, the hand that ruled the site no longer seems invisible. The great first millennium of our era, when dozens of Mesoamerican cities flourished and when cultures across the continent thrived, is shaped by the rise and ultimately by the fall of this great city. Sitting astride the narrow waist where the Valley of Mexico and the Valley of Puebla converge, Teotihuacan's fortunes were never private.

Architecture
Random settlement during the Late Formative period of the city included elaborate cave precincts. By the time of the millennium's dawn, Teotihuacanos had begun to modify every aspect of the cave under the Pyramid of the Sun, widening its entryway and lining the chambers with a mud mortar, although there is also the possibility that the subterranean chambers are entirely manmade. From the entry to the subterranean passages a siting line to the west was drawn that linked the cave, the rising of the Pleiades during the two annual passages of zenith, and the arc of the sun across the sky at that same occurrence, forming a powerful, yet invisible, east-west axis. Perpendicular to this was drawn another great axis, the Way of the Dead, terminating at the mountain today known as Cerro Gordo. By the end of the first century AD, these two axes, one firmly material, the other invisible but ordained by the sky, had determined the grid that informed all positioning at Teotihuacan, with ritual focused at the Pyramid of the Moon (by AD 100, according to the latest radiocarbon dates), the Temple of the Feathered Serpent (by AD 200), and the Pyramid of the Sun (by AD 225). Low-lying apartment complexes of ranging structures filled the interstices in the ensuing centuries, and the great cosmopolitan center flourished, reaching its apogee c. AD 400–550. Archaeology has produced evidence of ethnic neighborhoods and barrios of craft specialists in an urban environment of immense diversity, but all lived along the immutable grid, a tyranny of geometry. Miles away, isolated

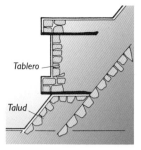

67 The vertical *tablero* sits on the sloping *talud*. This schematic drawing shows the sort of workmanship typical of many Teotihuacan structures. The exterior is finished with fine plaster and polished.

structures still conformed to the city's right-angles, the orientations determined by its grid.

With a population that archaeologists now estimate to have been 200,000 at its apogee – but quickly dropping off to 70,000 by no later than AD 600 – Teotihuacan would have been the sixth largest city in the world in AD 550, in an era when the half-million souls of Constantinople formed the world's biggest urban center and when one-third of the world's population of 300 million individuals lived in China. Cities have long been places of poor sanitation and ill health; not until the invention of modern sanitation and purified water systems would cities cease to depend on immigration for growth. Teotihuacan was no different, even as it spread across 8 square miles (21 sq km). During its rise, the magnet of the great city drew people in, depopulating valleys in surrounding areas. Conversely, when Teotihuacan declined, other Central Mexican cities began to expand.

Within the city, the architecture is of both mass and space – mass in the great temples, open space in plazas, temple enclosures, ritual walkways, and interior space within the palace compounds. Although it is often difficult to distinguish palatial or bureaucratic structures from religious edifices or domestic dwellings in ancient Mesoamerica, the distinctive profile known as 'talud-tablero' delineates much sacred architecture at Teotihuacan, particularly among the smaller structures and within palace compounds [67]. The sloping *talud* (talus) supports the vertical *tablero* (entablature), which is often the surface for architectural ornament or stucco paintings. Perhaps more than any other aspect of its culture, *talud-tablero* architecture marks the presence of Teotihuacan abroad, and the execution of such profiles in adobe at Kaminaljuyu, for example, nearly 700 miles (1,125 km) to the south, is a provincial manifestation of the city's power. The axes themselves took on architectural qualities, not only in orienting the city, but in ordering particular views of the city for participants in ritual. The north-south axis, called 'Miccaotli,' or Way of the Dead, by the Aztecs, may refer to the ancestral shrines that line it, and some may yet hold undiscovered tombs and offerings to the dead. Annabeth Headrick has suggested that the shrines held mummy bundles of revered ancestors, perhaps like the ceramic mummy bundle image from Monte Alban [101]. Brought out for veneration, the mummy bundles would have kept the past present in a tangible way. Often thought of as a 'street,' the Way of the Dead changes elevation several times, forcing pedestrians up and down stairs and commanding attention as a two-dimensional architectural feature. This processional requirement recalls the passage in the cave under the Pyramid of the Sun, where supplicants shifted from kneeling and crawling to walking upright. On a modern map the axis appears easy to access, but in fact today visitors reach it only through the modern gated portals, whose purpose is to control paid admission but which replicate the limited access of the past.

The Way of the Dead leads to the Pyramid of the Moon, and then to Cerro Gordo, a vast clefted mountain, a dead volcano with a sunken cone [70]. Slightly smaller than the Pyramid of the

68, 69 Teotihuacan. An isometric view (above right) of the buildings along the north-south axis, the Way of the Dead; an oblique airview (right) is oriented with the Pyramid of the Moon's back to the viewer. Residential complexes filled the interstices of Teotihuacan's grid, and it became a true city.

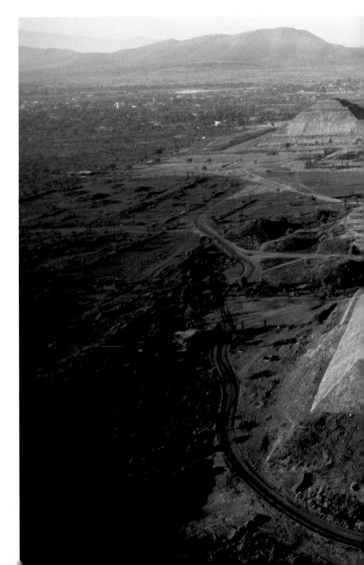

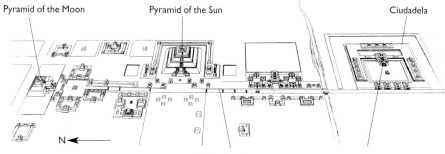

Pyramid of the Moon · Pyramid of the Sun · Ciudadela

N ←

Way of the Dead · Temple of the Feathered Serpent

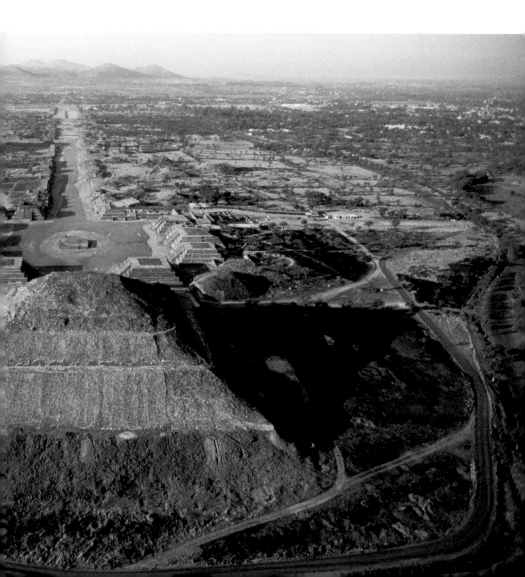

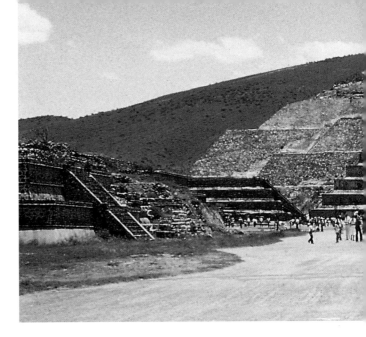

70 The Pyramid of the Moon at Teotihuacan, framed by Cerro Gordo, a dead volcano, in the distance.

Sun, the Pyramid of the Moon also features a huge open courtyard in the rough configuration of the Mesoamerican completion sign that flows from the smaller *talud-tablero* structure that abuts the pyramid. Framed by the mountain, the pyramid appears to possess the mountain and channel its forces to the city, acknowledging and calling upon the greater rainfall and abundance at the still-gurgling volcano once known as Tenan, 'our mother of stone.' The setting of mountain and pyramid is visually compelling at Teotihuacan, as if humans sought to place their works in perfect harmony with the landscape. The concept of *altepetl*, or 'water mountain' to the later Aztecs, referring to a place of civilization, may have had its first manifestation at Teotihuacan.

Recent excavations at the Pyramid of the Moon by Saburo Sugiyama and Ruben Cabrera have upended conventional wisdom about how such massive constructions took form. The pyramid did not grow steadily, one layer expanding another gradually. Rather, the size and scope of the Moon grew exponentially, especially around the year AD 250, when the vast fourth phase multiplied the existing structure by a factor of nine. After this point, the Adosada, the small structure that abuts the Moon itself, did not grow substantially, and further construction did not impinge on the plaza in front of the pyramid. As the Moon expanded, it engaged more specifically with the grid, so that the rectilinearity and orthogonal qualities became more specific

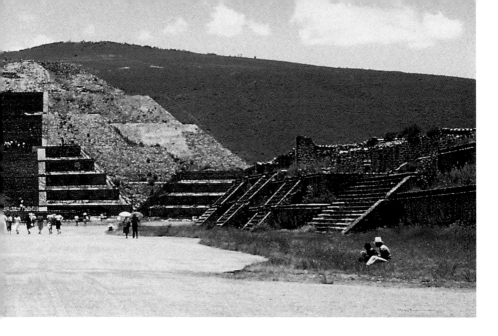

through time, with the huge expansions of the pyramid manifesting extraordinary marshaling of human effort.

Teotihuacan achieved the pinnacle of its political power during the years of vast expansion of the Moon, AD 250–400. Maya epigraphers now know that Teotihuacan invaded both Tikal and Uaxactun in 378: what these new discoveries at the Moon tell us, however, is how little we know of the complexity of relationships between these two quite distant regions. Did the invasion result in the export of luxury goods to Central Mexico, or had the Maya previously established contact with Teotihuacan? And did outright invasion and victory – and perhaps overexpansion – come to undermine Teotihuacan's dominance?

The discoveries at the Pyramid of the Moon lead to tantalizing questions with few answers as of yet. It is now clear, however, that deaths and dramatic interments drove the expansions of the great building. Burial 2 was set atop the third iteration of the pyramid, to be covered by the fourth; Burial 3 lay under the mass of the fifth. Both were sacrificial deposits of highly ritualized characteristics: great raptors – nine eagles, a falcon, an owl, three rattlesnakes, two pumas, and a wolf (and recent DNA studies suggest a wolf/dog mix) were brought to Burial 2 in cages; one can imagine the snarling, caged wolf and pumas, perhaps delivered on a litter, and the horrible carnage that may have ensued or that may even have preceded the interments; a single, bound human –

probably a foreigner, and perhaps a deity impersonator himself – was surrounded by dozens of blades, with attention focused on a single, perhaps female, stone figurine at center. Five Tlaloc vessels with flaring lip marked the four corners and the center of the chamber.

Burial 5, c. 350, probably sealed the fifth construction phase of the structure and launched the sixth. Three seated figures form the focus of the burial, and unlike the other burials of the Moon, they were not bound or tied, nor do they seem to have been within mummy bundles. Rather, once in the tomb chamber, their seated bodies were arranged with respect to two (presumably dead) pumas and an eagle, in a powerful demonstration of the control of wilderness by the most civilized setting in its day north of Peru in the Western hemisphere. An extraordinary seated jade figurine and jewelry accompanied the dead, seemingly a focus of the chamber. There is some sort of narrative to be teased out of

71 The Pyramid of the Sun at Teotihuacan.

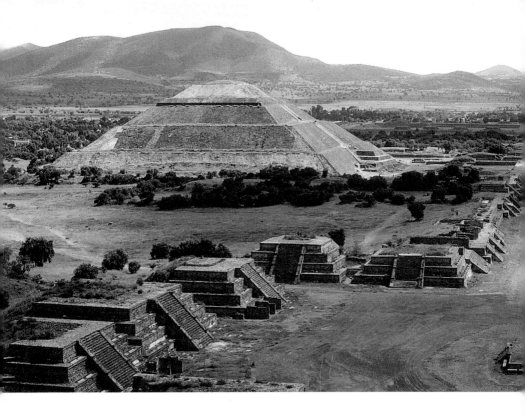

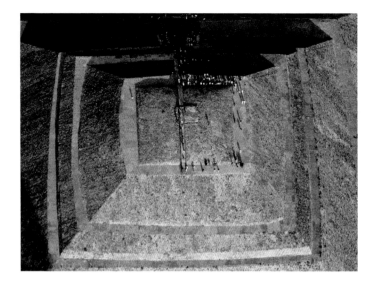

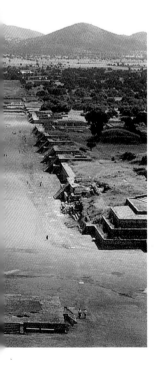

this configuration, as well as a keen sense that the works of the city, from architecture to the tiniest offering, are performative, not static, to be understood by the roles they played.

The Pyramid of the Sun is one of the largest structures of Precolumbian Mesoamerica. In fact, at some 200 ft (61 m) (even without the perishable superstructure that undoubtedly crowned it), it was one of the tallest and largest structures in Mexico until the twentieth century [71, 72]. Built over the multi-chambered cave that may have first galvanized the religious practice and civic order of Teotihuacan, the Pyramid of the Sun perhaps commemorated human creation and emergence from caves. The later Aztecs claimed to have come to Tenochtitlan from a mythic place called 'Chicomoztoc,' or Seven Caves: might not the underground chambers of Teotihuacan have entered into memory as a sacred place of origin?

Like the Pyramid of the Moon, the Pyramid of the Sun was built in various levels, with secrets for archaeology of the future to reveal. Today, the pyramid rises in five distinct and massive levels, as can just barely be discerned in the nineteenth-century paintings made before the advent of reconstruction [66]. The broad staircase is the focus of the building, a fully integrated visual element, in distinction to the fussier Adosada of the Moon. A single flight of steps divides into two and then merges together again: as attendants progressed up the stairs, they would have vanished and reappeared several times to the viewer on the

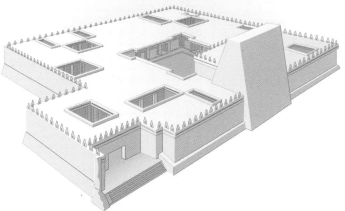

73 The Zacuala compound at Teotihuacan, whose walls were lined with brilliant stucco paintings. Many apparently enhanced devotion, and guided supplicants to chambers for worship.

ground, narrowing to a thin stream toward the summit – and flowing like coursing water down its slope. Like all Mesoamerican architecture, Teotihuacan structures formed specific backgrounds for rituals and public events. Excavations have now been launched at the Sun, and ongoing excavations may yet surprise the twenty-first century.

Although later partly covered by a plain pyramid, the original Temple of the Feathered Serpent always remained at least partly in view, with its elegant display of severe, frontal War Serpent headdresses floating atop the undulations of a Feathered Serpent. At the center of the large residential compound called the Ciudadela, once perhaps the palace of an early charismatic ruler, the Temple of the Feathered Serpent celebrates and commemorates warfare. Recent excavations have revealed what may also be a cave or tunnel on the east-west axis under the Ciudadela, following the pattern known at the Sun. Indeed, the Ciudadela's massive footprint seems to counterbalance that of the Sun. Sugiyama and colleagues have explored the structure and found evidence that a major tomb at the center of the structure was looted in antiquity. It was perhaps a royal tomb, but is perplexing in light of the tombs at the Moon. The discovery of some 200 skeletons, almost all victims of what must have been massive human sacrificial rituals, reveal the chilling presence of war at the heart of society. Dressed as warriors, the bodies were bound with hands behind their backs and dumped in pits lining the sides of the structure, an immolation that may have lived on in memory for generations.

Residential compounds of various size fill out the Teotihuacan quadrants [73] – perhaps hundreds at the city's apogee. Access to these compounds was extremely restricted, often through a single door, providing security and privacy within. Given the inevitable noise and confusion in this city of busy merchants and craftsmen, the inhabitants must have felt relief at escaping from the hubbub of the street to the seclusion of their quiet residences. Walk-in cisterns would have made it possible for some members of the community, whether religious personnel or women, to be secluded from public life for periods of time. Such urban life can be compared to that of Old World, pre-modern cities, but it had no previous counterpart in the New World. Each residential grouping included shrines and a platform for semi-public rituals, as well as many dwellings. Built to conventional standards and using stock materials, the compounds at Teotihuacan appear to have been the result of state construction. Only recently have archaeologists found evidence for slum-like dwellings pressed up against the apartments. The grand compound of Quetzalpapalotl, adjacent to the Pyramid of the Moon, has long been thought to have been a priestly residence, offering both private and discrete access to the city's public architecture that would otherwise have been approached by the Way of the Dead.

Apartment compounds sometimes housed foreigners, as discovery of a 'Oaxaca' barrio has shown. Here, residents lived in typical Teotihuacan housing, but their mortuary rite included traditional Zapotec extended burials with Oaxaca urns. The Zapotecs at Teotihuacan imported utilitarian ceramics from Oaxaca as well. Luxury goods in foreign style for the local inhabitants may also have been prepared in some compounds. Evidence also suggests Maya and Veracruz enclaves, and some quarters may have been embassies or merchants' retreats. At La Ventilla, forty-two individual glyphs have been found painted onto the smooth white plaster floor, perhaps suggestive of taxes or tribute to be deposited and accounted in specific locations, but unlike other Teotihuacan writing, these glyphs would seem to be names of days or of people, rather than of places. In such constant contact with people from across Mesoamerica, Teotihuacanos may have been pushed to enforce their standards and order while notating specifics in ways that only writing can encompass. Notably absent from the architectural record is any formal ballcourt. Teotihuacan was a cosmopolitan city but within a regional framework, both a receiver of and donor to Mesoamerica's cultural landscape. And yet despite all that, Teotihuacan remains profoundly local.

Sculpture

The stone sculpture of Teotihuacan is massive and prismatic, retaining the 'stoniness' that attracted the modern sculptor Henry Moore to Mesoamerican styles. In its sense of materiality, Teotihuacan sculpture aligns with the architecture. Static and serene, both Teotihuacan sculpture and painting long resisted interpretation, the absence of individuality and personality so keen that artistic expression was long considered a reflection of a corporate mentality that idealized the self-consciousness of uniformity, in distinct opposition to the Maya pattern, where individual rulers are the focus.

74 Powerful in her rigid geometry and masked face, the so-called Great Goddess is the largest sculpture found at Teotihuacan. The cavity at her breastbone may have held a jade or obsidian inlay.

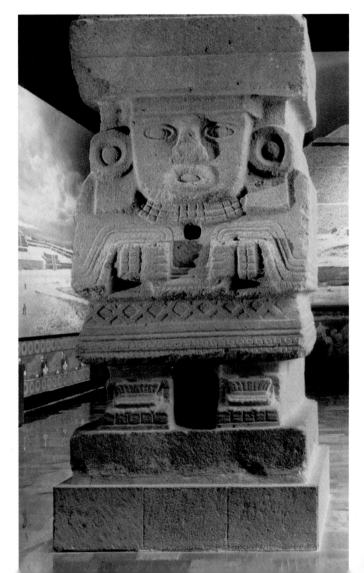

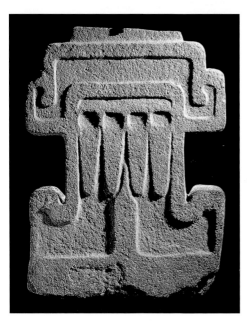

75 Over 3 ft (1 m) high, this large geometric sculpture abstracts essential elements of Tlaloc: his mouth, fangs and tongue stand for the deity. One of several known examples, the work may have adorned a cornice.

In residential compounds throughout the city, archaeologists have recovered blocky, squat, seated sculptures of wrinkled and toothless old men, their backs hunched with osteoporosis. Recently Matthew Robb has shown that these figures, long called Huehueteotl after an Aztec deity known as the 'old old god,' may have served a role in terminating a compound's use. However, no physiognomy or form from the later period can be tied with certainty to this deity's name – and these old gods may be associated most specifically with the hearth, the heat of life extinguished, like the expiration of life itself: the object was turned upside-down or smashed when a building's life also ceased.

The largest freestanding Teotihuacan sculpture is the great female figure discovered in rubble between the Pyramid of the Moon and the Palace of Quetzalpapalotl [74]. The cleft in her head recalls Olmec works, but the 'blockiness' bears little resemblance to the plastic three-dimensional Olmec sculpture. If once set on axis with the Pyramid of the Moon, the cleft in the sculpture's head would have been aligned with the depression in Cerro Gordo, and, as the figure brings her hands to her body, she seems to wring water from her *huipil*, or upper body garment, as if releasing water upon those who venerate her. A cavity would have held an embedded jade or obsidian, indicating divine status. Is this the greatest of all depictions of a powerful female mountain and water deity, sometimes dubbed the Great Goddess?

A badly battered but less orthogonal sculpture remains in the Moon Plaza today, perhaps female, also with a cavity for a stone, and perhaps a successor to the earlier sculpture – and possibly of Aztec facture. The Aztecs turned to earlier sculptural forms time and again, in dialogue with their great predecessors. That these figures and forms of Teotihuacan were widely known, part of a pan-Mesoamerican phenomenon from this point onward, is attested by their presence in contemporary Veracruz and among the later Aztecs.

Teotihuacan sculptors easily worked at all scales, [75] from the colossal to the hand-held, and perhaps according to the value of the material. Carved into human form, precious materials, such as

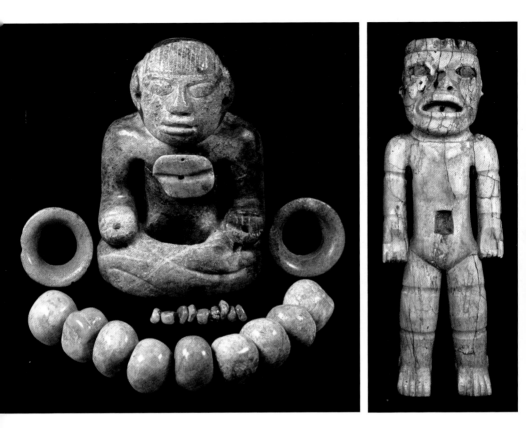

76 Jadeite offerings, Burial 5, Pyramid of the Moon, Teotihuacan. The richest burial to come to light at Teotihuacan, it contained three cross-legged individuals, one of whom may be represented by this seated figurine. The jewelry and adornments in the tomb may have been made by the Maya, although this seated figurine is unlike any previously known work.

77 The Xalla figure may have been bound before being brutally destroyed by dozens of blows. The work has now been carefully restored.

jade, retained prismatic and block-like forms characteristic of Teotihuacan's geometric order. Stunning examples have recently been excavated at the Temple of the Moon, in the most important tombs yet found at the site [76], as well as a brutally and intentionally shattered one within the Xalla residential compound [77]. Leonardo Lopez Luján and his colleagues have looked at the pattern of destruction and burning of religious objects, especially around AD 550, seeing in this pattern an iconoclastic contempt for the ritual object. At the same time, what would seem to be abstracted symbols – the mouthpiece that stands in for a deity, the sections of rattlesnake tail that imply the deadly bite of the serpent – can take colossal size, to be read with ease at distance and to explain and articulate monumental architecture [75].

An unusual sculpture was found at La Ventilla, a residential compound of Teotihuacan. It seems to have been a marker, or perhaps a banner stone, for a ballgame played without a masonry court [78]. The sculpture has four individual components, each worked with an elaborate interlocking scroll design. This type of scroll characterizes Veracruz stone sculpture of the era, particularly at the site of El Tajín, where the ballgame is celebrated with no fewer than eleven courts [103]. One of the sloping *talud* paintings of the Tlalocan shows small, animated figures who play a game around a monument similar to the La Ventilla piece [69]. In the period of Teotihuacan domination of the Peten Maya, Tikal sculptors worked an object of similar form yet in a single piece, and inscribed with Maya texts.

Perhaps best known of all Teotihuacan sculptures are the fine masks [79]. Some may have been attached to perishable supports to form large assemblages that might have been dressed and venerated; others may have been attached to funerary bundles. Made of serpentine, cave onyx (the Aztec *tecali*), or granite, these masks present clear, ageless faces, neither male nor female, neither young nor old. Some seem specifically to shield individual identity, like the mask that covers the face of ill. **74**. When assembled together, however, the stone masks reveal a great range of representation; they may be individuals but executed within a very narrow artistic canon.

Ceramic figurines were made throughout the history of Teotihuacan, and the early ones, tiny, agile, and perhaps once dressed in perishable materials, are the most appealing. Like the stone carvings, these miniature figures seem to wear the anonymous mask of Teotihuacan, yet the face is genuine, gentle and engaging, especially when cocked to one side [80]. They are found in abundance, and by AD 450 or so were moldmade and mass-produced, richer in iconography but limited by their technology to static poses. A general move to mass production characterizes all Teotihuacan production, from ceramics to figurines.

Large-scale ceramic sculptures also survive. Brightly polychromed urns show human and animal faces peering out from almost architectural constructions of mass-produced, stamped elements [82]. The flatness of the surface planes directs attention to the recessed, three-dimensional face. The Teotihuacanos themselves may have taken these assemblages apart and reconfigured different deities from the constituent parts. A compound to the north of the Ciudadela may have been a place of manufacture.

Obsidian and precious shells were worked into fine objects that frequently accompanied burials. Recent excavations at the Temple of the Feathered Serpent have yielded forty similar

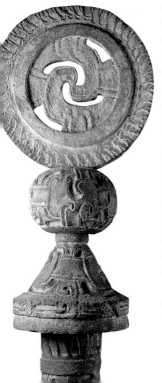

78 Made in four parts, the La Ventilla sculpture served as a ballcourt marker, topped by a shield-like form trimmed with feathers.

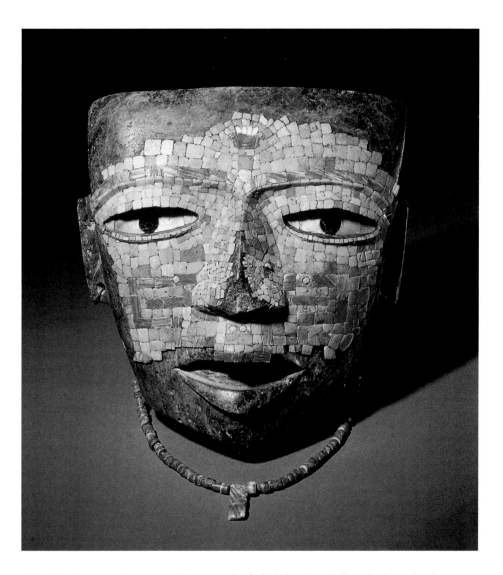

79 Shell, obsidian, and malachite mosaic bring a Teotihuacan greenstone mask to life. The tiny glyph on the forehead may record a name.

necklaces, each of which features shell worked into the shape of human teeth, sometimes accompanied by whole jawbones, forming what must have been potent and eerie symbols of prowess in warfare and sacrifice [81]. These necklaces concentrate death and sacrifice, power that could also be transmitted through ones that merely imitated the human bone. Countless pieces of obsidian have been recovered from all recent excavations in the city's main pyramids, some in dazzling serpentine forms, others as rough references to the human body.

94

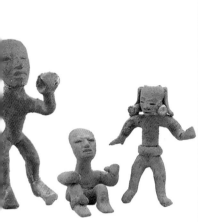

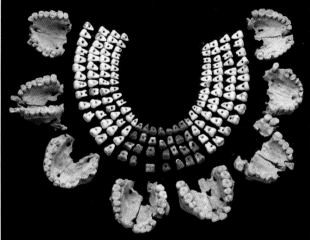

80 Small clay figurines, Teotihuacan, modeled in animated postures. Early Classic.

81 During the second century AD, Teotihuacanos interred an unprecedented human sacrifice of at least 100 victims, many of whom wore necklaces featuring human jaws and teeth, the harvest of previous sacrifices.

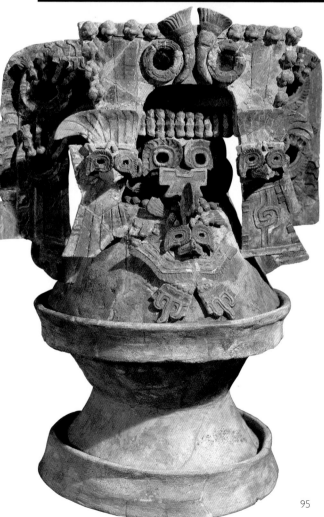

82 Mass-produced of standardized parts large and small, this large urn with its owl imagery served the Teotihuacan war cult. Across Mesoamerica, the Teotihuacan owl entered the inventory of war iconography.

Painting

The histories of painting and architectural sculpture at Teotihuacan cannot easily be separated, for thick polychrome applied to exterior sculptures on early buildings would appear to give rise later to flat wall painting, returning to painted sculpture late in the sequence. Of all architectural ornament at Teotihuacan, the finest is that of the Temple of the Feathered Serpent, set at the western margin of a large enclosure, perhaps the palace of the ruler [83]. On the *talud-tablero* façade uncovered and restored between 1917 and 1920, the huge feathered serpent heads of the balustrade weigh over four tons apiece, and elaborate tenons hold the complete assemblage in place. Because these sculptures were painted, we may consider this the earliest programmatic painting to survive at Teotihuacan, and daubs of blue, red, white, and yellow can still be seen, aided by the recent repainting of the main façade.

The early Temple of the Feathered Shells featured repetitious painted panels with burnished stucco painting of strong greens and blues, some made with ground malachite, before being buried within the very late Quetzalpapalotl structure. But by the third century AD, painting replaced most sculptural ornament, and the palette brightened, with an emphasis on shades of clear reds, most of which depend on hematite as the essential pigment, and resulting in images that bring to mind medieval tapestries or Persian carpets. With little emphasis on line, and what line there is drawn in red, the works can be hard to decipher, particularly when partly eroded. But many paintings are also highly repetitious, and reconstruction of the whole can often be determined from fragments.

Murals covered the *tableros* throughout Teotihuacan, and the apartment complexes in particular were brightly painted. Despite efforts to develop a sequence for paintings, both the range of subjects and nature of paintings from AD 400 until the period of rampant destruction seems to have been fairly consistent, with images of warriors, deities, and sacrifice prevailing. At the Atetelco complex and elsewhere, standard templates must have been used to achieve a repetitious patterning that looks like wallpaper to the casual visitor, especially when executed in only one or two colors, the steady line also suggesting the stencil, rather than the whiplash of the free hand. Burnishing marks underscore the sense of process and erasure that denies the individual gesture. Yet such templates were restricted to individual complexes and did not repeat beyond a single precinct.

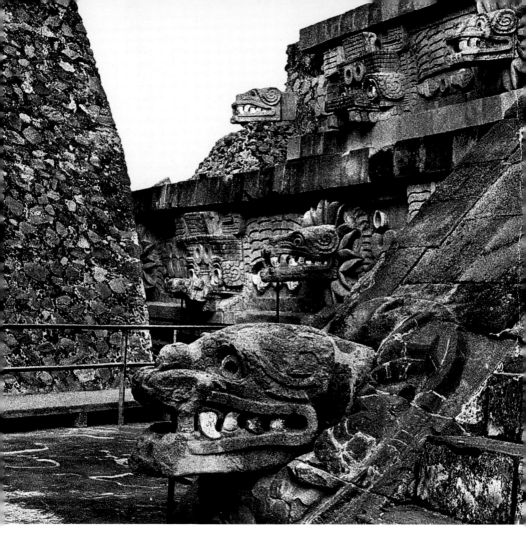

83 The Temple of the Feathered Serpent, Teotihuacan. Early in the twentieth century, archaeologists removed the exterior mantle of the structure and revealed more of the painted, sculptured façade of an earlier construction.

Many paintings are didactic and would seem to instruct observers to conduct themselves appropriately, and particularly to carry out sacrifice, exemplified in the many images of figures in profile, carrying incense bags and standing beside maguey spines and grass balls. Rows of profile figures, including the Netted Jaguar, flank doorways, guiding processional movement [84]. Elaborate backgrounds reveal temples, clouds, and abundant foliage. Processional warriors from Techinantitla follow a footprint-dotted path and speak 'flowery' scrolls; rare name glyphs appear in front of each one. The three-droplet tassel in many headdresses represents an extruded heart; what may seem to be necklaces turn into draped intestines upon closer examination.

Frontality may have been restricted to deities, and representations of goddesses were painted all over the city. Remarkable frontal images dominate the so-called Tlalocan patio paintings of Tepantitla, so named by Alfonso Caso as an image of the Aztec paradise of water long before female deities were identified at Teotihuacan [85]. On the upper *tableros* of each wall, a female cult figure painted with yellow skin gives forth blue-green droplets while a pair of acolytes in profile attend and make offerings. From her head sprout plants along which butterflies flutter and spiders crawl. We might read this repeated mountain imagery as an invocation of the concept of *altepetl* once again. Other *taluds* reveal what may be raised agricultural fields.

On the *talud* below, myriad tiny individuals frolic in water flowing from a mountain; exuberant speech scrolls suggest happy sounds and glyphs articulate speech as 'butterfly,' 'stone,' or 'flower,' among other words. Bodies are red, blue, or yellow but with strongly stylized faces, as if to unify diversity. Some form teams in a ballgame; others play a game resembling *bocce* (a form of bowls). The lively figures are among the few actors in Teotihuacan art, which is more typically nominal rather than verbal; here the figures perform the verbs, while nouns attach themselves to things or dot the background.

Many paintings have eluded identification. One strange clawed goddess features an upside-down head and bosom, perhaps a prototype for the image of a decapitated woman deity, prevalent in Aztec art, who similarly throws her head backward, but with blood usually spewing from the neck. In another, a mountain deity

84 Reconstruction of one of two mirror image paintings that framed a doorway at Tetitla, Teotihuacan. On a path marked with footprints, a priest in netted jaguar suit approaches a temple. Suppliants may have taken on the priest's role in stepping through the doorway.

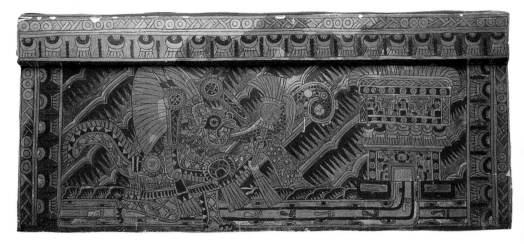

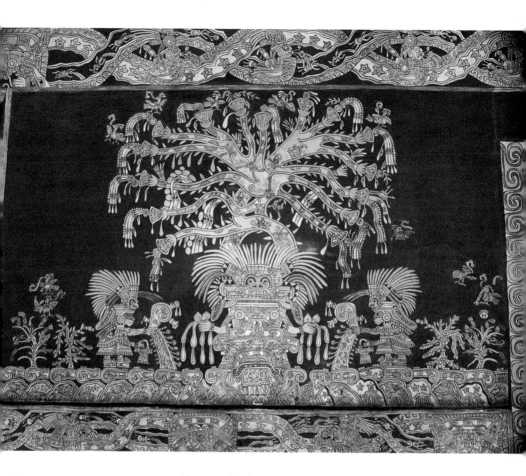

85 One of several nearly identical representations in the Tepantitla patio, this panel features the hands and head of a female figure at center. Under her, an overturned basin spills streams that fertilize the plants in the margins.

presides over the three-mountain image. Supernatural coyotes and pumas may relate to the recent discoveries of these animals in Moon burials.

Most paintings, with the exception of Tepantitla, deploy large areas of uniform pigment, especially the blue-green malachite color used for feathers and then outlined or divided with thin red lines [86, 87]. Shifting background colors at Tetitla, for example, separate a *talud* and *tablero* of eaglets, painted in white and red, and which the viewer reads differently depending on the field behind.

Across Mesoamerica, other cultures imitated and emulated the signature form of Teotihuacan ceramics, the lidded tripod cylinder, especially the Maya. West Mexico peoples, although poorly understood in this period, adopted both the Teotihuacan *olla*, or open-mouthed jar, form and the typical stucco with which many elite ceramics were finished. Stucco on ceramic generally

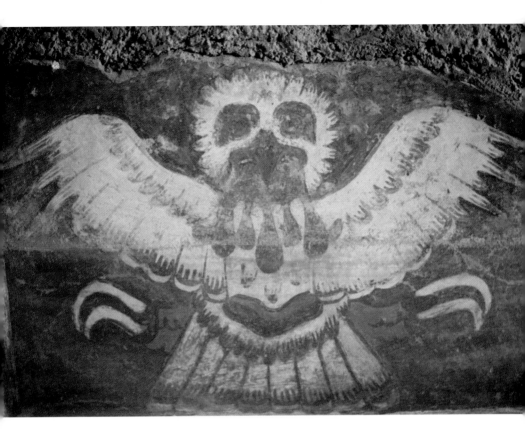

86, 87 Teotihuacan artists used templates to map outlines onto fresh white plaster, creating standardized images that repeat like wallpaper patterns. Burnishing yielded flat, even colors that have endured 1,500 years or more. At left, a frontal – and insatiable – eaglet at Tetitla drips gouts of blood; the image is centered against a built-in bench. At right, in the Palace of the Plumed Shells, a parrot or quetzal spouts precious liquids. Shades of red and pink were based in hematite pigments; the dark green manipulates malachite to create this effect.

shows a chronology and imagery similar to the monumental paintings. Ceramics of a thin orange clay [89] found a wide market across the region. Many stuccoed or carved vessels feature heavy, lipped lids with ornament to match the body; tiny slab cut-outs function as tripod feet.

Although imagery is typically repeated twice or three times on a vessel, with an emphasis on the uniformity characteristic of monumental works, some show continuous imagery that wraps the vessel on the diagonal. Goggled warriors approach mountains or bear weapons [88]. At the time of the Conquest, the Tlalocs were said to pour water onto the earth from their heavenly palace, causing downpours.

Teotihuacan artists also produced hollow 'host' objects that bear tiny solid moldmade figures and adornments inside their bodies [90]. Examples have been found in distant Guatemala and Mexico, with the most extraordinary find coming at Becan, Mexico, 750 miles (1,200 km) from the great city. There, a host

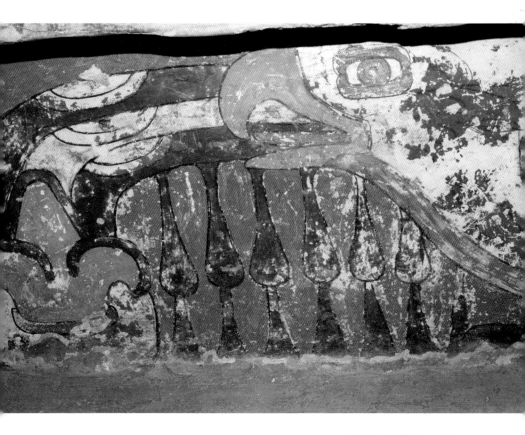

88 Stuccoed tripod vessel in Teotihuacan style. Symbols of Tlaloc adorn both the vessel and its lid. Tripod feet characterize Teotihuacan ceramics. Early Classic.

Below:
89 Teotihuacan potters crafted ceramics that were prized everywhere in Mesoamerica for their extraordinary thinness. This hunchback may have borne maize or gruel on his back.

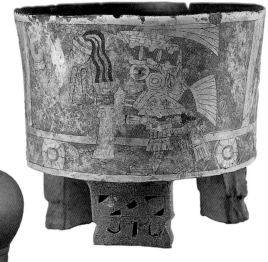

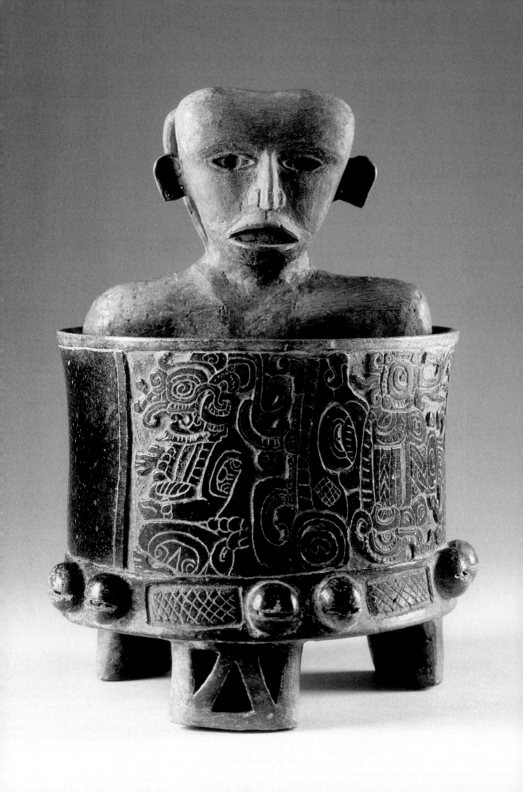

object held ten tiny warror figures and a number of miniature adornments, including shell and jade. Placed into a Maya tripod of local facture, the works collectively dedicated a Maya structure c. AD 550, just at the time of Teotihuacan's destruction, and perhaps making reference to the complex relationships of power and authority between the two cultures.

The end of Teotihuacan

Constant rain and water crises at Teotihuacan probably exacerbated the difficulty of building and maintaining the city. The preparation of lime for mortar and stucco required vast amounts of firewood to burn limestone or seashells, and the more Teotihuacan grew, the more the surrounding forests were depleted. With deforestation came soil erosion, drought, and crop failure. In response, Teotihuacan may have erected ever more temples and finished more paintings, thus perpetuating the cycle. Tlaloc may have turned to war to supplant agriculture; the powerful female deity must have wrung her hands without profit, for the city was doomed. According to radiocarbon dating, Teotihuacan might have been ravaged as early as AD 550. Whether in 550 or as late as 650, Teotihuacan's destroyers burned the central temple precinct and sacked the city. The perpetrators may have been semi-nomadic peoples just to the north, those most disrupted by the expansion of Teotihuacan, and perhaps occasionally in Teotihuacan employ as miners or laborers. The Teotihuacan map itself reveals greater density of construction along the northern perimeter, forming a wall to what was an open city. Although some occupation of Teotihuacan continued, the city never regained its importance, and the production of fine art and architecture rapidly declined, to become instead the model for the subsequent generations of city dwellers in Central Mexico.

Far to the south, in highland Guatemala, Kaminaljuyu was apparently the locus through which Teotihuacan had invaded the Maya region, taking advantage of trade relationships that had previously been established. Although Kaminaljuyu had flourished in Late Formative times, a number of structures were built there in Teotihuacan style before AD 500. Principal among these is a small-scale reproduction of the Pyramid of the Moon, carried out in adobe [91]. Tombs at Kaminaljuyu were filled with luxury goods, indicating the wealth accumulated by those who mediated between Teotihuacan and the Maya, and with patterns shared by both Burial 10 at Tikal and some of the recent discoveries at Teotihuacan itself.

The notion of a 'Classic' era was first conceived to define the span of time during which the Maya used Long Count inscriptions, or about AD 250 to 900 – a period originally thought of as peaceful and theocratic throughout Mesoamerica. Though the idea of peaceful theocracy has since been abandoned, the problematic term Classic remains in use, if only to characterize the richness, variety, and growth of the art and society of the time. What is often called the 'Classic' starts in Central Mexico with the rise of Teotihuacan, and even after the city's demise, its traditions were sustained, if strained, at Cholula and other sites in the Valley of Puebla. Rather than use such a term, we may be better off simply thinking of this 'Classic era' as the first millennium AD.

During the era of Teotihuacan's rise and development, Cholula, in the Valley of Puebla, also thrived. Curiously, about the same time as the burning of Teotihuacan, Cholula likewise underwent depopulation. During the Postclassic, however, the city was rebuilt and expanded. Most ethnohistoric sources link Cholula to Quetzalcoatl, at least during the era of Spanish invasion, but the relationship may well be ancient.

The main pyramid at Cholula was used and rebuilt for nearly 2,000 years, ending with a Catholic church on its summit [92]. Archaeological explorations by the Mexican Instituto Nacional de Antropologia e Historia have revealed many aspects of the pyramid's construction. During the Teotihuacan era, for example, paintings covered the *talud-tablero* temple exterior. These sprawling stucco paintings record drinking rites and may reveal the drunkenness of the painters themselves.

Cholula's identity in the apogee of Teotihuacan is not well known, but sculpture, ceramics, and architecture are all distinct. Stelae survive today with only paneled frames, as if slates for

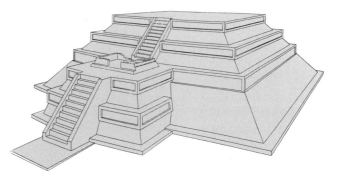

91 Reconstruction of B-4, Kaminaljuyu. At this site, in modern Guatemala, buildings in pure Teotihuacan style were executed on a diminutive scale in simple adobe during the great city's apogee.

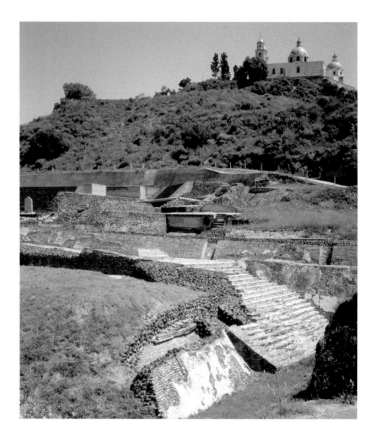

92 The main pyramid at Cholula flourished in many periods, and it probably benefited from Teotihuacan's decline. A Colonial church caps at least 1,500 years of prehispanic construction. Most of the terraces revealed by archaeologists date to the first millennium AD.

painted depiction of rulers – in which case they would have been more analogous to Maya examples of the period. The long sloping talus of the architecture profile may have underscored local identity; years later, Cholula's rulers, like those of nearby Tlaxcala, fought to preserve independence in the face of Aztec imperialism.

A longer sloping *talud* than that known at Teotihuacan characterizes the early pyramids at Cholula, and we may surmise that its population steered clear of Teotihuacan domination, despite the proximity, like the later city of Tlaxcala. At the time of the invasion, Nahua speakers occupied the site and it is possible that distinct members of this large linguistic family dominated the Valleys of Mexico and Puebla in the first millennium, ruling rival kingdoms. In this mix, the ethnicity of Teotihuacan remains the most enigmatic.

Chapter 5   Monte Alban, Veracruz and Cotzumalhuapa

The first millennium AD produced the most widespread flowering of culture in Mesoamerican history. As we have seen, in Central Mexico Teotihuacan was the largest, most powerful and prestigious city to rise in the history of the ancient New World. To the south, in Yucatan, Guatemala, Honduras, and Chiapas, the Maya were equally important, although known for their diversity and variety rather than the monolithic power that characterized Teotihuacan. However, other regions fostered important contemporary developments as well. Independent styles of art and architecture flourished in Oaxaca at Monte Alban, in Veracruz at various sites, among them El Tajin, and on the Pacific coast of Guatemala at Cotzumalhuapa. At no other time in Mesoamerican

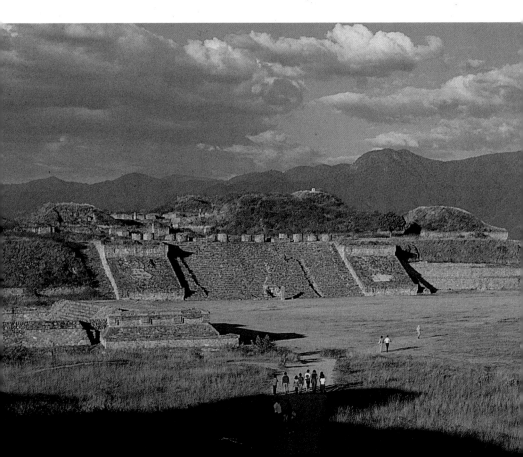

history were so many fine and different kinds of works of art and architecture created. It was also an era of great international contact: just as there was interchange between Teotihuacan and the Maya, so too was there contact between Oaxaca and Teotihuacan and between El Tajin and Cotzumalhuapa, although some of these developments took place quite late in the first millennium. And whereas Teotihuacan – in its forms, iconography, and style – is emulated until AD 500, Maya art, in both its lankier proportions and propensity for narration, plays a great role during the eighth century and until the end of the millennium.

The civilization of Monte Alban

At Monte Alban, the step from the advanced Zapotec architectural and artistic styles of the Late Formative to a Classic stage was easily taken. The traditions of Oaxaca, whether Zapotec or Mixtec, show continuity and shared practices through time, including for generations after the Spanish invasion. At Monte Alban, some sophisticated works of art and architecture survived

93 The view across the plaza of the mountaintop of Monte Alban toward the North Barrier Mound. Buildings echo the topography, channeling nature's power to the site's core.

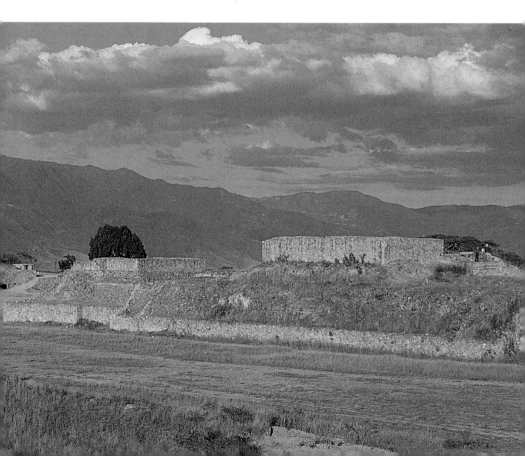

from Late Formative times, and the acropolis had already been artificially flattened. Most of the structures that flank the main plaza, however, date to the Classic era, either Monte Alban IIIa (Early Classic, to AD 400) or Monte Alban IIIb (the Late Classic phase, AD 400–900, according to archaeologists) [93, 94]. Yet despite being home to some of the first profound excavations at a major archaeological site, Monte Alban's architecture remains enigmatic in its function. Javier Urcid and Joyce Marcus have shown that many of the South Barrier Mound sculptures once served as lintels; as re-situated in later times, some sculptural faces became hidden from view, with only a single carved side of the prism left in evidence.

A plan designed to reproduce the rhythm of natural land forms may also help to explain the approximate bilateral symmetry of the acropolis. Structures are not laid out on an axis or grid. Unlike the plan of Teotihuacan [68], they do not radiate from a central point but rather frame the negative space of the plaza. In its general north-south orientation, however, the plan of Monte Alban suggests an axial orientation far more than the organic site plans of Maya cities do.

The general organization of the Monte Alban acropolis also recalls the Teotihuacan Way of the Dead. That great processional way is lined by low-lying temples and modulated by changes in elevation. The North and South Barrier Mounds of Monte Alban not only frame the ceremonial core but also require movement up and down the processional way. Nevertheless, the ceremonial core of Monte Alban is small by comparison with Teotihuacan: the Monte Alban plaza with its surrounding temples could all be placed under the Temple of the Sun.

But there is no need to look at Monte Alban only in light of Mesoamerica's other cities of the first millennium. Constructions of the era made the Monte Alban acropolis a gem, with new buildings that offered additional definition of the ceremonial precinct. A wall enclosed over 1 square mile (2.6 sq km) of the acropolis. Access to the plaza, both actual and visual, from the east, for example, was blocked by the replacement of numerous individual structures almost contiguous with one another. The proportion of balustrade to stair of these buildings is ponderous, and emphasis falls on the alternation between the two forms.

The corners of the plaza were no longer open: at the northeast, for example, the Zapotecs built an I-shaped ballcourt. (Such ballcourts were peculiar to this region in the Classic, but by

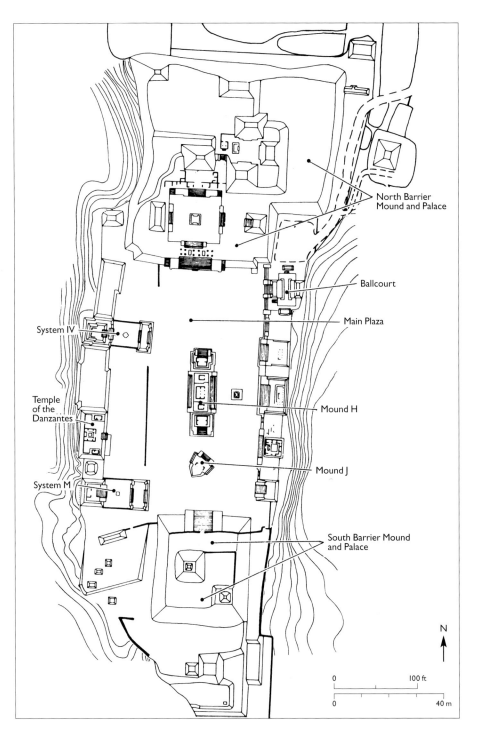

North Barrier
Mound and Palace

Ballcourt

Main Plaza

System IV

Temple
of the
Danzantes

Mound H

Mound J

System M

South Barrier Mound
and Palace

N

0   100 ft

0   40 m

the Postclassic the closed I-form court with sloping walls was known widely in Central Mexico as well.) On the west side of the plaza, similar compounds were erected to flank the earlier Temple of the Danzantes. Known as Systems IV and M, these buildings have been considered amphitheatres, where supplicants would gather in the closed court while attending rites performed on the principal façade. As with all Monte Alban structures, the perishable superstructures are gone. Tomb façades and small stone temple models found in tombs show that the distinctive Monte Alban profile molding was also repeated at the cornice level. Wrapped around exterior corners, this molding consolidated the structure, as did the apron moldings of Maya structures of the same period. In its two separate layers, the molding bears a similarity to the symbol for sky, perhaps indicating the generally sacred quality of architecture so delineated.

By the eighth century, the North Palace compound grew in size, and – particularly during Monte Alban IIIb – it became increasingly inaccessible. By the end of the period of construction, one climbed the North Barrier Mound, passed a colonnade, and descended into a courtyard similar to those of Teotihuacan, but on a smaller scale, and sunken in relation to surrounding structures. One then proceeded along a narrow passageway and up and down stairs before gaining access to palace chambers. Such restricted access has a parallel at Teotihuacan, particularly in the Quetzalpapalotl compound, and in the Maya region, where for instance the core of compound A-V at Uaxactun became virtually inaccessible in Late Classic times.

To the south, an early palace was dismantled, and carved lintels were set upright, like stelae, one side of their imagery now disoriented. Like the South Palace stones, many other monuments were reset through time, and most of them were grouped at the south end, honoring Zapotec lords. Some individuals are Oaxaca warriors [96]; others engage in dialogue with what appear to be visiting Teotihuacanos, whose images were subsequently hidden. In some cases the Zapotecs wear tall headdresses with motifs similar to those of the ceramic urns (see below), but the warrior of Stela 4 features two rings on his headdress: this

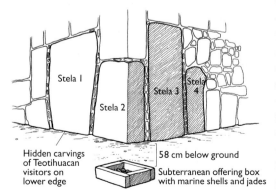

95 South Palace slabs were reset at least once at Monte Alban, reorienting what may have been originally lintels, with carving on adjacent sides of the stone.

Stela 1
Stela 2
Stela 3
Stela 4

Hidden carvings of Teotihuacan visitors on lower edge

58 cm below ground

Subterranean offering box with marine shells and jades

is the same motif of the headdress carried on the back of the Feathered Serpent at Teotihuacan; Maya warriors adopt it as well, along with the turban form. Glyphs record dates in the 260-day calendar or calendrical names. Scrolls indicate speech or song, as they do in Teotihuacan art. Individuals are carved in profile in a flat, linear style.

Alfonso Caso directed excavations on behalf of the Mexican government at Monte Alban throughout the 1930s. He looked for burials in addition to cleaning and restoring structures. Many underground tombs thus came to light, both under structures and as separate chambers, some within the main precinct and others in residential areas. It remains to be established whether the structures that flank the compound were primarily dedicated to ancestor worship, as were many Maya buildings. Caso discovered fine burial chambers containing treasures from the earliest era right up to the invasion. Many tombs of the Classic period were found to be painted, and, of these, Tombs 104 and 105 are the best preserved. Tomb 104 is thought to precede 105, a chronological separation that probably reflects the difference between Monte Alban IIIa and IIIb. The palette of 104 emphasizes blue and yellow, while 105 has many more red tones, like later Teotihuacan paintings. Both had been quickly prepared and show signs of hasty work, such as drips and spills. Yet as Arthur Miller has shown, both tombs were repainted numerous times; we see mainly the final version.

Tomb 104 displays an interesting unified use of architecture, sculpture, and painting. The chamber entry is framed by a doorway with the usual Monte Alban overhanging profile molding, and the door is surmounted by a very fine ceramic figure wearing a

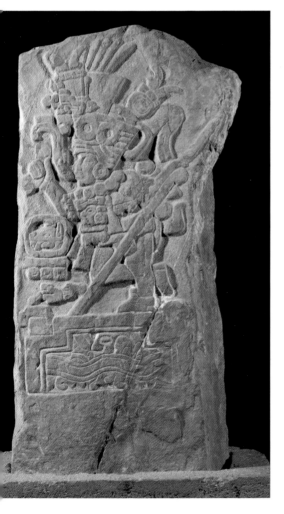

96 Stela 4, showing a standing ruler, Monte Alban IIIa. The ruler stands atop the hill sign, with the upper jaw of a serpent seen within, perhaps indicating the name of a conquered town. The glyph 8 Deer appears at left, indicating either a name or date.

Cocijo, or rain god, headdress [97]. A single skeleton was found extended in the tomb, feet at the chamber door. Sets of small, identical urns had been placed along the body, and other vessels positioned in the three cut-out niches of the wall. Two painted figures flank the side walls, in profile, attending the frontal cult image at the head of the tomb [98]. One of them is an old god with a netted headdress, possibly related to the Maya god Itzamna, an aged creator god known for his wisdom. Iconographically, Cocijo and various maize gods dominate Monte Alban religious art, but Zapotec gods and ritual practice have remained among the most poorly understood in ancient Mesoamerica.

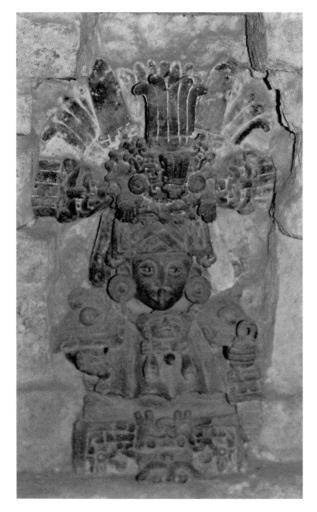

97 The façade of Tomb 104, Monte Alban. A fine ceramic urn remains in place over the entry to the tomb. Monte Alban IIIa.

Compositionally, the painting resembles the central scene of the Tepantitla mural of Teotihuacan [85], the unwrapped composition of Tikal Stela 31 [122], or even the more iconic Río Azul paintings [125]. Given the emphasis on symmetry and frontality, the source for such compositions was probably Teotihuacan. The use of such similar conventions at Monte Alban and Tikal shows both the profound effect of Teotihuacan and the ability of regional artists to interpret its art for their own traditions. Like Teotihuacan painters, Monte Alban painters mapped large areas of color, particularly for feathers, limning individual feathers within great panache, but leaving the general impression of trimmed, clipped feathers. The Tomb 104 paintings and Tikal funerary offerings from Burial 10 both show the widespread use of rich blue pigments, particularly slate blue; Maya blue, a unique color achieved by dying palygorskite clay with indigo, also came into use in this period. Curiously, tomb paintings as fine as this one are not known from Teotihuacan, where we find paintings set in a context for the living rather than the dead. The discovery of a major Teotihuacan tomb, however, could alter this perception.

In Tomb 104, each side figure gestures to the niche in front of him, directing the process of offering, and the central cult image seems to rise out of the central niche, as if sustained by the offerings placed within. Such paintings may have guided the attendants at the funeral rites of the interred, and perpetuated those rites.

The side and rear walls of Tomb 105 show nine male-female couples in procession, accompanied by glyphs that no doubt name them [99]. A single calendrical day sign and coefficient occupies the front wall, probably naming the occupant or the date of his death. Symbols that resemble Monte Alban moldings form the upper register, and what presumably are earth signs lie underfoot. The nine couples represent ancestors who welcome the interred into the afterlife. Some headdresses include what would have been old-fashioned Teotihuacan elements, perhaps a sort of 'period' dress to indicate their antiquity. Tomb 105 includes substantial use of glyphs; symbols in headdresses – such as the trilobe indicating blood – show further development of the regional writing system, as well as connections to Teotihuacan.

The tradition of making large, hollow effigy vases reached its apogee in Late Formative times at Monte Alban. By the Classic era, the urn had supplanted the hollow vase as the dominant form of tomb sculpture. These urns consisted of cylindrical vessels largely hidden by the attached sculptures of human figures, and they usually were made in sets, with four small vessels accompanying the larger urn, often all personified. Evidence of burning in the vessels is rare, and it is more likely that they held foodstuffs or beverages for the interred rather than burnt offerings. They have been recovered both from tomb doorways and from the graves themselves, though many are without provenance. Most have headdresses of deities. Cocijo, the Oaxaca rain god, is worn by the Tomb 104 figure. Lines around the eyes of ill. 100 mark it as the 'God of Glyph L.' The maize of the headdress also indicates a fertility aspect for that figure; the base features the hill sign indicating a place name. As more and more of the imagery of ancient America has been determined to be of historical persons, so the strong individual physiognomies of many Oaxacan urns have begun to suggest portraiture.

Overleaf:
98 Interior painting, Tomb 104, Monte Alban. Hasty workmanship – indicated by spills and drips of paint – would suggest that the final decoration of this elaborate tomb was executed at the last moment. Reconstruction painting. Monte Alban IIIa.

99 Interior painting, Tomb 105, Monte Alban. The painters here chose a darker, redder palette, more like that of many Teotihuacan works. Monte Alban IIIb.

100 One of several fertility gods in ancient Oaxaca, this maize god bears distinctive facial markings. He sits on what is probably a 'hill' glyph, indicating a toponym, perhaps 'hill of maize.'

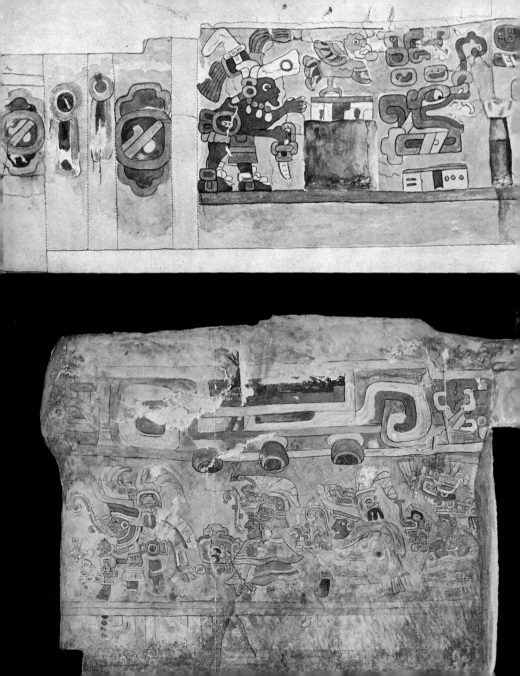

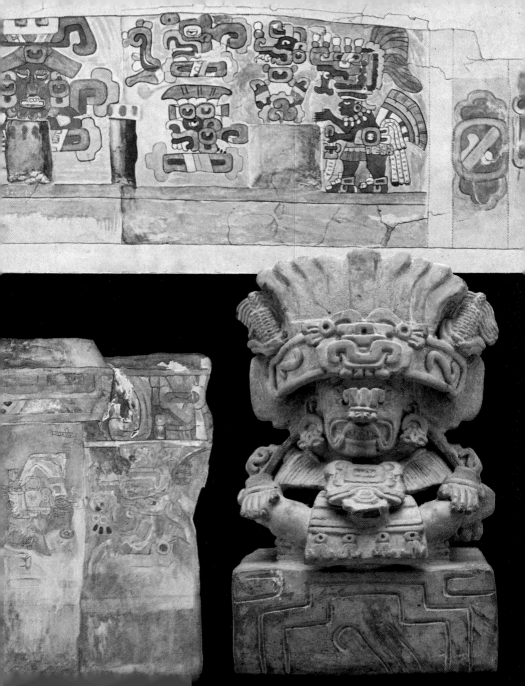

The ornamentation of the urns was built up in layers of pliable clay slabs until a rich three-dimensional texture was achieved over the hollow human form. Eventually, just as at Teotihuacan, individual elements came to be mass-produced. Some human faces are also mask-like and resemble contemporary Teotihuacan stone masks. Many urns have strong rectilinear qualities, despite their three-dimensionality, and can be described geometrically within a rectangle. In this way, they conform to a geometry like that seen in many Teotihuacan paintings.

Tomb 103, in addition to a large urn, yielded an assemblage that may illuminate the funerary process itself. [101] A single, planar figure at the center represents a bundled corpse, adorned with a Teotihuacan-like mask. Five be-feathered attendants hold mirrors; eight members of a musical band perform, and a seated figure may be a miniature Old Fire God, a common form of sculpture at Teotihuacan and associated with termination rituals.

By AD 900 or so, Monte Alban suffered slow and steady depopulation, as the focus of culture in Oaxaca moved to other centers, some of them Mixtec. Finally, Monte Alban became simply a necropolis and a place of pilgrimage, and it remains a place of pilgrimage today.

Veracruz

Distinctive art styles also flowered along the Veracruz coast during the first millennium AD. Today, Totonacs live in the region, but it is not certain that they were the makers of high culture in

101 Excavated in the courtyard in front of Tomb 103, this engaging set of figurines focuses attention on a 'mummy bundle' at center. The standing lords wear bird masks; two feature eagles and three the War Serpent on their removable headdresses. The nine musicians recall the nine attendants in Burial 10, Tikal, some of whom carried instruments.

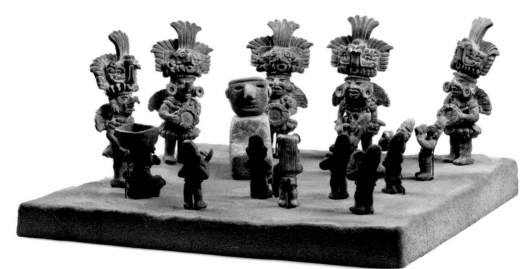

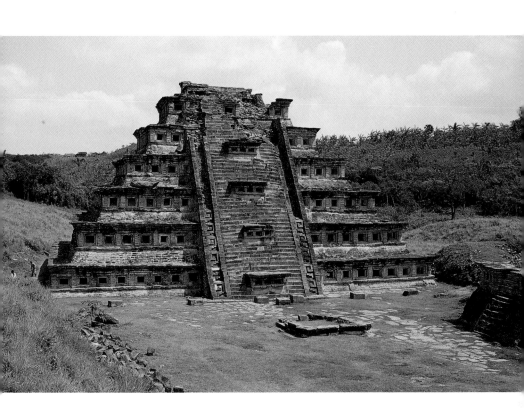

102 Seen early in the twentieth century, before complete reconstruction had taken place, the Pyramid of the Niches, El Tajin, features 365 niches, each setting up a play of light and shadow to make the building shimmer in the sunlight.

Classic times. Fifteen hundred years ago Huastecs and Otomis undoubtedly occupied some of the same territory, while at the time of the Conquest the Olmeca-Xicalanca dominated trade along the coast. We will simply consider the various elements to be 'Classic Veracruz,' as these many quite disparate sites have been called, without ethnic assignation. Connections with Teotihuacan and the Maya area were evident during the period, but the art and architecture of Classic Veracruz also depended upon its Olmec heritage from the Formative era.

Architecturally, the most important city of the region is El Tajin, named after the Totonac rain god. Heavy rainfall yields dense rainforest where mountain meets plain. The Veracruz coast was known for its verdant croplands even in prehispanic times, and the Aztecs coveted the maize, cacao, and cotton grown in the area. El Tajin was discovered toward the end of the eighteenth century, just about the time that Maya sites began to catch Western attention. In 1829, the German explorer Karl Nebel visited the site, and the fine color lithographs he later published evoked the same kind of mystery as Maya ruins. Early travelers believed the

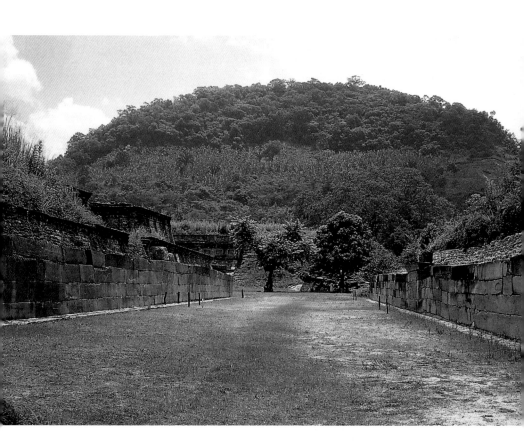

Pyramid of the Niches to be the most important structure at El Tajin, which indeed it is in the sense that it dominates the main ceremonial core, at the center of hundreds of acres of ruins, despite its relatively small size: approximately 85 ft (26 m) on a side and less than 66 ft (20 m) high [102]. Recent INAH (Instituto Nacional de Antropologia e Historia) explorations have demonstrated that little time separates the two layers of construction of the Pyramid of the Niches, completed c. AD 800.

The Pyramid of the Niches rises in six distinct tiers of an unusually busy *talud-tablero* and houses within it a smaller, and therefore earlier, similar pyramid. Each entablature supports a row of niches, making 365 niches in all, which implies that the pyramid refers to the solar year. The niches are each about 2 ft (60 cm) deep, and although it is tempting to think that they held offerings, no evidence is available that they did. Perhaps the niches were for purely visual effect: on a bright day they reflect and shimmer in the sun, giving the illusion of constant motion.

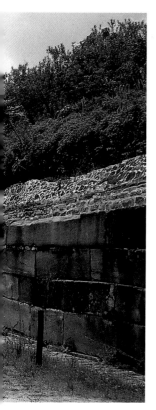

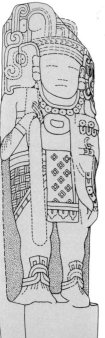

The Pyramid of the Niches has some unusual features that link it to Maya architecture at Copan; El Tajin may well indeed have had some direct contact with that site. Both the Hieroglyphic Stairs at Copan and the Pyramid of the Niches have balustrades with similar running fret designs. In fact, the abutments of the Pyramid of the Niches may have featured seated lords during public festivals, creating a diminutive assemblage closely akin to the Hieroglyphic Stairway at Copan. Moreover, the only true stela from El Tajin was found at the base of the Pyramid of the Niches [104]. In some ways it looks like a rough Maya effort, and in its three-dimensionality, costume, and posture, it bears closest comparison to the stelae of Copan.

The low-lying galleried structures of Tajin Chico, set on a great rise above the Niches and ballcourts, seem to have been largely for noble residential use in the ninth and tenth centuries. Geometric patterning worked on the building façades may correspond to the contemporary designs at Uxmal, in Yucatan, or they may have toponymic value. Dominating the group is the Building of the Columns, now collapsed, but once a very large structure with colossal carved columns. Narrations wrap around the columns on a small scale, many featuring the exploits of a late ruler, 13 Rabbit.

At least eleven ballcourts have been located in the central core of El Tajin [103]. No other site in Mesoamerica has such a preponderance of masonry playing surfaces: indeed, El Tajin was very probably a center for great ceremonial games, in the same way that Olympia served as the recognized meeting point for sportsmen from all over ancient Greece. El Tajin seems also to have been a major center for the collection of natural rubber, and perhaps the solid black rubber balls with which the game was played were made there, using a process of cooking the latex and shaping it in a mold, as is still practiced in parts of Mexico today. Various lineages could have sponsored their own court, or each successive ruler could have been obliged to commission a new one. For whatever purpose, the courts were made in profusion here, and their walls present the most extensive architectural sculpture of Veracruz. As at other Mesoamerican sites, El Tajin lords sited buildings to powerful features of the landscape, and this can be seen most clearly with ballcourts, where rises are typically framed at the ends of playing alleys.

Six narrative panels relate a ballgame myth or story along the vertical surfaces of the South Ballcourt. In the first panel, the

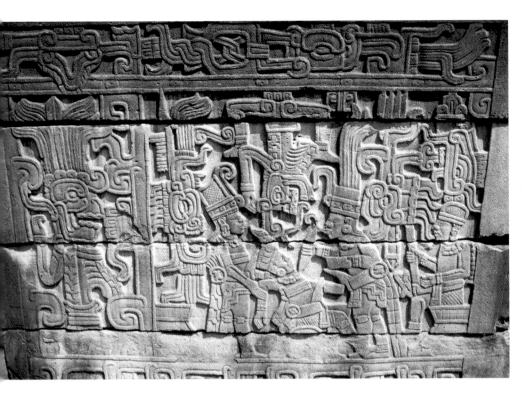

105 Carved panel, South Ballcourt, El Tajin. An unfortunate loser at the ballgame is being sacrificed by two victors while a third looks on. A death god descends from the skyband above to take the offering.

participants dress for the event; in another, one player conceals a knife behind his back. In the illustration shown here, set within a ballcourt (but oddly enough, one with an architectural profile different from that of the South Ballcourt itself), two players hold down a third and prepare to cut out his heart [105]. A descending skeletal monster twists down from the upper margin, presumably to take the sacrifice about to be proferred, while another skeletal monster at left rises from a jar. As the narrative unfolds at El Tajin, the rain god perforates his penis, perhaps yielding *pulque*, the intoxicating beverage of ritual.

At the time of the Conquest, the ballgame was known to be played for various motives. As an athletic event, it was frequently the subject of much gambling. It could also be a gladiatorial contest, where a captive's or slave's strength and desire to avoid death were tried out. The sacrifice of players also informs us that the game was played in order to offer human blood to the gods. The game may have been played for all these purposes, not only at El Tajin, but also in the Maya area and at Cotzumalhuapa, and understood as a cosmic metaphor as well, necessary to the

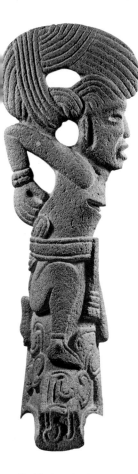

sustenance of the sun. Furthermore, the ballgame often plays a specific role vis à vis warfare. Set in the ceremonial precinct, the ballgame provided the means for controlled re-enactment of warfare. The use of the ballgame as a metaphor for other struggles was known at the time of the Conquest and is perhaps most clear in a K'iche' Maya text, the *Popol Vuh*, where the confrontation of life and death is couched in terms of a ballgame.

The reliefs of the South Ballcourt were probably worked *in situ*, since several flat stones form a single carving surface, like those of Chichen Itza. A distinctive double outline is used to work all the designs, but particularly the scrolls. The reliefs would now appear to have their origins in Middle and Late Formative Olmec styles, as well as in the curvilinear Late Formative style of Izapa. This double-outline workmanship is so characteristic of Classic Veracruz that it indicates the origins and relative date of materials found as far away as Teotihuacan or Kaminaljuyu.

Three kinds of objects – frequently decorated with scroll motifs – have been recovered in great abundance in Mesoamerica: yokes, *palmas*, and *hachas*. Most of them come from Veracruz, but at both Palenque and Copan, Veracruz ballgame paraphernalia were found in a context contemporary with the abandonment of these sites. A similar tradition thrived in Guatemala, along the Pacific coast. The players on the South Ballcourt relief seem to show how at least two of these objects were worn. Yokes were fitted around the waist, attached sideways [107]. Despite the doubt cast on whether these cumbersome stone objects (25–35 lb or 11–16 kg) could ever have been worn (the weight must certainly have altered a player's center of gravity), they were probably manageable for a skilled athlete. *Palmas* were inserted into the

106 The heart has been removed from this unfortunate fellow. In ill. 105 the *palma* springs from the waist, as if directly inserted into the yoke. The thick knotted strands of hair also characterize Maya captives.

107 Ballgame yokes take many forms; this example depicts a great frontal toad, as if to impart terrestrial powers to its wearer. South Ballcourt panels (ill. 105) show ballplayers wearing similar yokes.

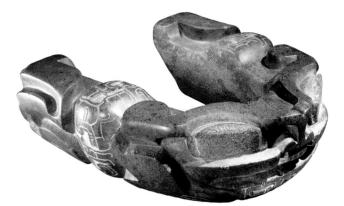

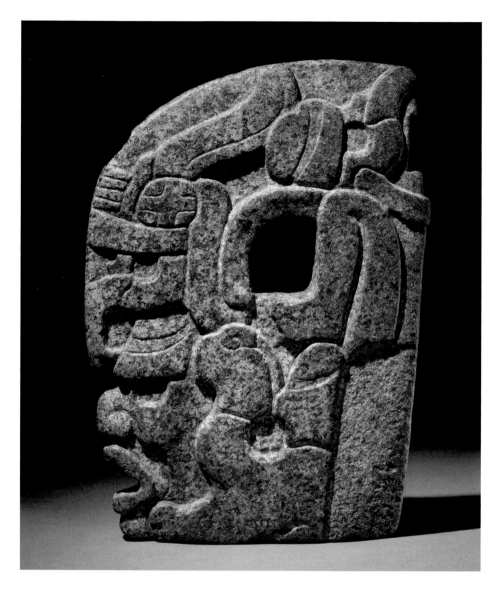

108 Although usually thought to have been trophies, *hachas* in Veracruz style may also have functioned as ballcourt markers. This example features the Principal Bird Deity in the headdress (cf. La Mojarra stela ill. 41).

yokes at waist-level and extended to mid-chest height [106]. *Hachas* may have served as markers for play [108]. The scrollwork of the yokes is sometimes exceptionally fine and complex, and often the design cannot be understood until completely drawn out. Some motifs emphasize themes of the ballgame itself. Despite representations of these objects being worn [105], it is not clear how these objects functioned in the play of the game, or whether they served only as trophies or as replicas of perishable objects.

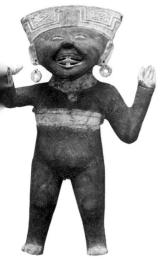

109 A hollow ceramic male figure holds a rattle in one hand and prepares to dance. The frozen smile of his face may be a sign of ecstatic transformation.

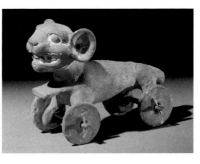

110 Mesoamericans did not use the wheel for practical purposes. Nevertheless, miniature forms, like this jaguar, provide surprising evidence of some knowledge of the wheel.

Overleaf:
111 This large hollow female figure may well have guarded a tomb in ancient Veracruz. Her gesture, as well as the human hands she wears as ear ornaments, relates the figure to later Aztec goddesses associated with the earth. The object may also have functioned as a brazier.

112 At El Zapotal large, hollow ceramic figures stood against painted walls in large funerary chambers, creating powerful scenes in which the deceased played a role. Here, a meditative kneeling figure wears the goggles associated with Tlaloc and also the paper strips at the headdress's side.

Full-scale stone carvings of Classic date have been found elsewhere in Veracruz as well, particularly at the site of Cerro de las Mesas, which may be best known for the huge cache of jade, some of it Olmec, in a fourth or fifth century context. Stone stelae at the site bear Initial Series inscriptions that correspond to Maya dates. Stela 8 records a date in AD 514 and shows an individual who was presumably a ruler of that era [113]. Curiously, he wears a shield emblem in his headdress of the type prominent in the name glyph of Pakal of Palenque, the Maya king who came to power about a hundred years later.

Fine hollow clay sculpture was produced at various centers throughout Veracruz during this era, perhaps continuing a tradition established by earlier Olmec artisans. It was a tradition sustained until the time of the Conquest, with the result that the exact date of some of these pieces is in doubt. Uncertain too is the specific provenance of the majority of the sculptures. Some have been traced to particular sites, but most are isolated finds. Those of Remojadas are particularly lively and are often characterized by 'smiling' faces, which may in fact be the result of ecstatic rituals [109]. Charming couples are found in pairs or on swings, and little animals turn on wheeled feet [110]. Such toys are the only known use of the wheel in ancient Mesoamerica. The potters painted many of these sculptures with shiny black asphalt, locally called *chapapote*, a naturally occurring petroleum product (no other use was known in Precolumbian times for the plentiful oil of Veracruz).

Probably of later date are the large-scale hollow figures, many of which represent gods better known in Aztec times, although the chronology is far from certain [112]. Some are seated, others stand with arms extended, perhaps in greeting but perhaps to warn away a violator of a tomb or cache [111]. Snakes form some of their belts, and some may represent a *cihuacoatl*, or woman snake, a maleficent old female deity.

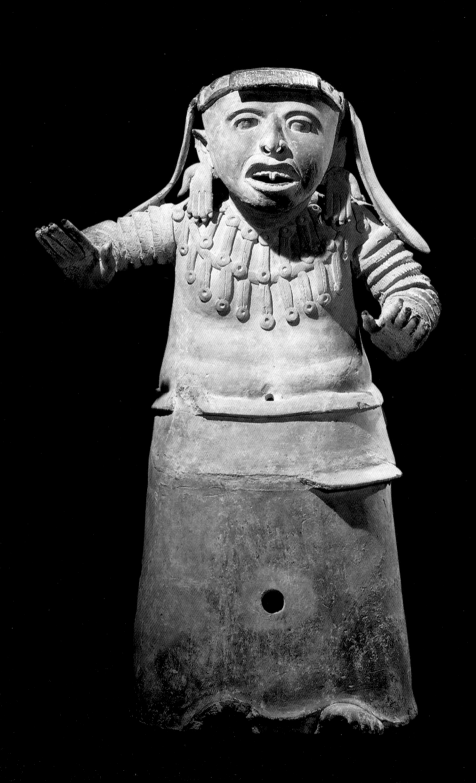

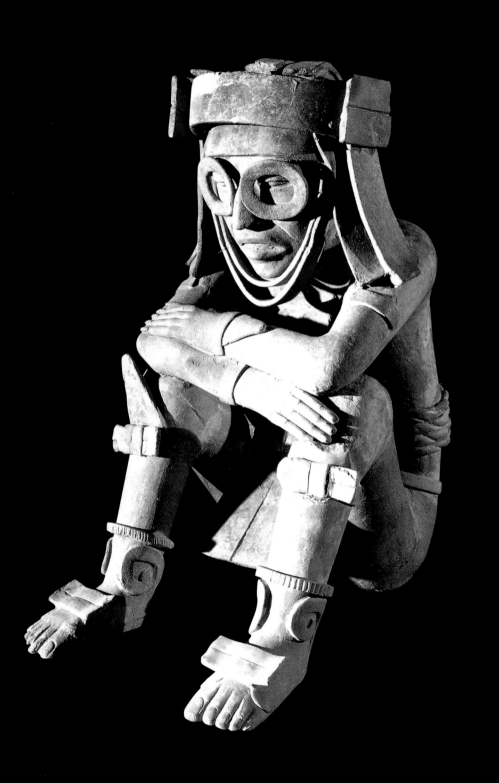

Cotzumalhuapa

A web of artistic and trade connections focused on Teotihuacan during its apogee; later, especially in the eighth century, the network became more complex, particularly as local, regional expressions took root and held on even as Maya cities were abandoned c. 900. Fresh research has brought to light the importance of the regional style of art and architecture known from Santa Lucía Cotzumalhuapa and its environs. Despite its location on the Guatemalan coast and its proximity to the Maya area, Cotzumalhuapa rejected Maya writing and imagery, participating instead in the cultural tradition of the Isthmus of Tehuantepec, where contact flowed from Veracruz to the Pacific Coast.

The makers of Cotzumalhuapa art were probably not Maya, and, although they have often been identified with the Pipil (Nahua speakers in Guatemala at the time of the Conquest), we will probably never know their ethnicity. We do know, however, that they carved stelae and panels rife with images of the ballgame, human sacrifice, and the sun [114]. Glyphs were inscribed in round cartouches – some appear to be part of a Central Mexican calendrical system, although none of the glyphs have been securely read. The figures on the monuments are generally long and attenuated, of proportions similar to those drawn on Maya vases from such highland Guatemalan sites as Nebaj. Right and left hands and feet are often confused in the Cotzumalhuapa depictions. Cacao pods – the source of valuable chocolate – frequently adorn these Cotzumalhuapa figures, suggesting the origins of their wealth.

Ballgame rituals played between humans and supernatural beings appear on several stelae [114]. Whether or not divine, the individuals wear ballgame equipment similar to that of Veracruz, and abundant *hachas*, yokes, and *palmas* have been collected at Cotzumalhuapa sites. Descending solar deities on the upper parts of the monuments may prefigure the Postclassic 'diving gods' of the Caribbean coast. These deity faces are worked frontally in three-dimensional relief, in striking contrast to the low relief of the profile figures below. Some fully three-dimensional monuments were also created, and they may relate to the tradition of sculpture in the round at Copan.

Opposite top left
113 Stela 8, Cerro de las Mesas. Monuments from this site show affinity to Maya works. This one bears an Initial Series date in Maya style equivalent to a day in AD 514.

Opposite right
114 Stela 3, Santa Lucía Cotzumalhuapa. A ballplayer and a death god, both in ballgame yokes, stand in front of a temple. They reach toward a scorpion sun to offer a human heart.

Opposite below left
115 Sylvanus G. Morley kneels beside this fragmentary stela from Pantaleon in Cotzumalhuapa style. Comparable three-dimensional portraits of the Classic period are known from El Tajin and Copan.

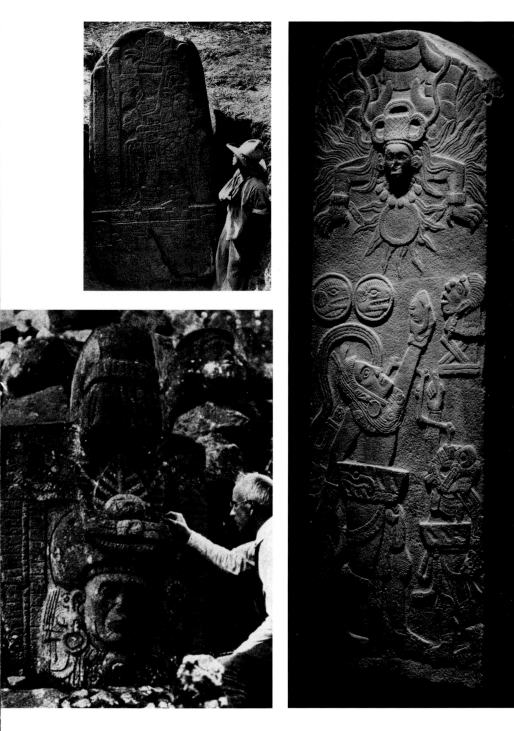

Chapter 6   The Early Classic Maya

Great Maya cities had thrived during the Late Formative period; most seem to have gone into decline around the turn of the millennium. Meanwhile, in Central Mexico, Teotihuacan became an important center and cultural force by AD 150, but it was not until a hundred years later – about AD 250 – that the Maya entered upon their period of greatest prosperity and influence. By this time, Maya temples with corbeled vaults were being constructed, and stone stelae with Long Count dates and ruler portraits erected. All these elements appeared independently long before AD 250, but it was the beginning of their combined, continuous, and widespread use that roughly establishes the Classic era among the lowland Maya. What is also clear now is that the rise of the Maya follows, rather than initiates, developments in Central Mexico. At the same time, the Maya were looking backward, acquiring old Olmec jades and giving them new inscriptions or simply treasuring them, placing them in Maya tombs.

During the first 300 years of the Maya Early Classic (AD 250–550), major growth of cities was limited to the Central Peten, particularly at the sites of Tikal and Uaxactun. Teotihuacan lords and warriors invaded Uaxactun and Tikal in AD 378, marrying into local elites, who then adopted Teotihuacan modes of dress and possibly burial. In the sixth century many other Maya sites started to expand, as Teotihuacan influences waned, possibly because of attacks on the Central Mexican capital. The resulting competition led to warfare, and the largest and most powerful among them, Tikal, suffered terrible devastation at the hands of lesser polities. Simultaneously, the profound influence of Teotihuacan waned. Teotihuacan motifs and costume elements did not vanish, but they became so thoroughly incorporated into the Maya repertoire that they ceased to be foreign. By the seventh century, Tikal was only one of many well-established Maya cities, including Palenque in the west, Uxmal in the north, Altun Ha in the east, and Copan and Quirigua in the south. At its height, Tikal may have had a population of only 50,000, so these Maya cities were smaller than Teotihuacan. They were united by the common use of the hieroglyphic writing system, but their monumental carvings and

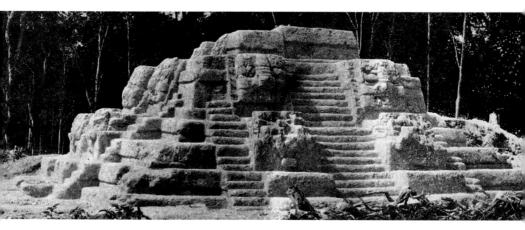

architecture reflect both regionality and innovation, and despite allegiances among them, no unified empire emerged.

Architecture

Using a relatively small inventory of simple architectural forms, the ancient Maya built a vast array of cities, no two of which look alike, with towering temples that crested above the forest canopy and ample palaces that provided the spaces for royal and bureaucratic functions. Archaeological work at Tikal and Uaxactun (literally 'eight stones,' a name given by Sylvanus G. Morley to refer to the early Cycle 8 dates there and also a near homonym for 'Washington,' in honor of the sponsor), has revealed much of what we know today about the Early Classic.

Preliminary architectural and ceramic studies at Uaxactun, initiated in the late 1920s, indicated to the archaeologists that Group E, an isolated cluster of buildings, was the oldest part of the site. In a search for the origins of Maya high civilization, Structure E-VII was dismantled layer by layer, revealing a series of building phases. The earliest one, now known as E-VII-sub, is a small, radial pyramid just over 26 ft (8 m) high, with staircases on all four sides flanked by giant mask façades [116]. The principal orientation of E-VII-sub is to the east, indicated by a stela at the base of the stairs on that side. Postholes on the upper level mark the remains of a perishable superstructure, which suggested to the archaeologists that the pyramid might antedate the general use of permanent superstructures. Indeed, E-VII-sub does seem to date from the first century AD, preceding the widespread erection of dated stone monuments. What we now know is that most Peten sites hold such early structures, and that E-VII-sub is no longer the unique prototype Morley imagined.

Functionally, E-VII-sub works as a simple observatory. From a point on the eastern stairs, the lines of sight that can be drawn to the three small facing pyramids mark the lines of sunrise on the days of the solstices and equinoxes. The Maltese-cross plan of E-VII-sub resembles the Maya completion sign, as do plans of some other radial structures, and most such structures record the completion of some period of time. At E-VII-sub it is the solar year that holds significance, as it is at the Castillo, Chichen Itza, built much later. Twin radial pyramids at Tikal were erected on platforms to commemorate the completion of *katuns*, the twenty year periods, during the seventh and eighth centuries, while the Maltese-cross emblem that functions as a frontispiece to the Aztec-period Mexican manuscript Féjerváry-Mayer is a 260-day calendar. Thus radial configurations, from their earliest appearance at Uaxactun, and as found at Chichen Itza until the Spanish invasion, indicate the passage of time, and structures in such form are generally giant chronographic markers.

Excavations in Group A at Uaxactun revealed a different pattern of construction [117] at the outset, perhaps more like those now also seen for San Bartolo (Chapter 3). A three-temple complex, A-V, was transformed over a period of at least 500 years, its growth inspired by ritual interments of important lords and stone monuments. The term 'temple' generally refers to an elevated platform with a relatively small superstructure where offerings were made. Because new temples were erected over rich tombs of important individuals, or in some cases the inscribed records of those individuals, one can only suppose that the structures were shrines to memorialized ancestors. As we shall see, a focus of Maya religion and architecture was ancestor veneration.

At complex A-V, by the end of the fifth century, small temples obscured the courtyard of the three original temples, which had also been expanded through time. In the seventh century, these single-chambered shrines of A-V gave way to multi-chambered galleried structures, the type of building normally considered a palace (and often called 'range-type' structures by archaeologists). These palace buildings drastically altered access to the old interior platform and shrines, and presumably function changed along with form. Although burials were deposited in the new structures, they were not elaborate and were limited to women and children. At the end of its life, when galleries had replaced all but one of the

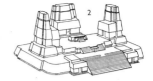

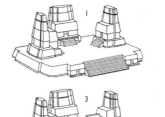

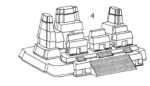

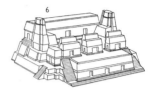

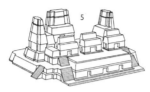

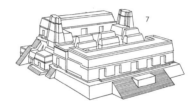

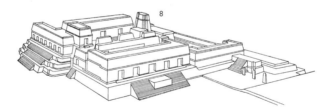

117 Based on the archaeological exploration of Uaxactun, Tatiana Proskouriakoff drew reconstruction drawings (after which these are adapted) of the eight major phases of architectural development at the site. Single shrines of buildings from the third century gave way to a vast complex by the end of the eighth century.

shrines, A-V had become a great administrative or bureaucratic complex, where most events took place away from public view, and where secular or family activities dominated sacred ones. A separate temple raised beside A-V can be interpreted in this light as a new focus for religious activity, and it probably housed a rich tomb at the end of the eighth century.

Many elements of Maya city planning can also be observed at Uaxactun. The gently rolling karst limestone topography of the Peten provides islands of solid foundation separated by swampy *bajos*. Typically, the Maya built their sites so that clusters of monumental architecture on firm ground were connected by *sacbes*, elevated, stuccoed white roads which spanned the

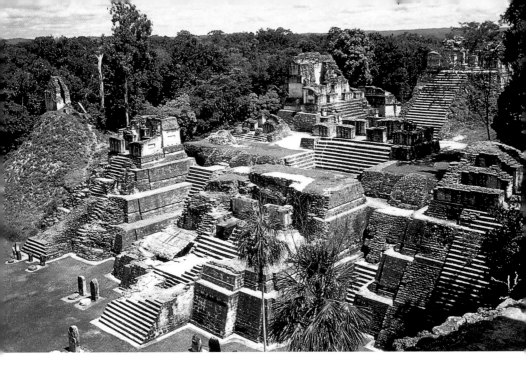

118 Early kings of Tikal were buried in North Acropolis structures (center). In the eighth century, Temple II (at left, out of the picture) and Temple I (from where this picture was taken) framed the ancestors.

swamps. The result is a skyline of towering structures broken by open stretches. We might compare the result with modern Manhattan, where less firm rock long precluded the building of skyscrapers between Midtown and Wall Street. The skyline thus appears as islands of construction, connected by the great north-south avenues. At Uaxactun, Groups A and B are connected by a single causeway, and address one another across the north-south axis of the *sacbe*.

At Tikal, many years of large-scale archaeological exploration in the grandest of all ancient Maya cities has revealed an intricate pattern of architecture and urban planning. Like Uaxactun, Tikal featured a massive radial pyramid with badly damaged stucco masks at the center of what is today called the Mundo Perdido ('Lost World') complex. A row of small temples flanks one side, while addressing the radial construction from the northwest is a large building constructed in something like Teotihuacan-style *talud-tablero*, but in proportions that are unknown at the site of Teotihuacan itself. Was this the focus for worship of foreign gods or a shrine constructed for resident foreigners?

Before AD 250, the North Acropolis and the Great Plaza were laid out to define the strong opposition of mass and space, north-to-south, that prevailed for the rest of the city's history. (The equally strong east-west axis created by Temples I and II was not established until the eighth century.) Massive temples clustered on the North Acropolis functioned primarily as funerary monuments of Early Classic rulers of Tikal [118]. Structure 34, for example, housed the richly furnished tomb of King Yax Nuun Ayiin, nicknamed 'Curl Nose.' Structure 33 held the tomb of his successor, and may have been the last tomb added to the program. Once completed, the North Acropolis must have embodied the spirit of ancient kingship, an invisible yet known gathering of ancestors, dwelling within sealed chambers.

Typical features of these Early Classic funerary pyramids are their squat proportions and the massive apron moldings that wrap around corners. Archaeologists tunneled into the most ancient constructions at Copan, within the Main Acropolis, revealing massive early buildings that retain almost perfectly preserved stucco ornament [119]. On the exterior of what may be the most ancient structure to be discovered yet is the glyph for the founder of the Copan dynasty, Yax K'uk Mo', and his tomb is probably the trove archaeologists have found there.

119 Eighth-century Copan kings interred their Early Classic buildings with care, preserving color, stucco, and detail. Known as Rosalila, the building revealed here contained tombs of early kings – and yet another building smaller but equally elaborate lies hidden within.

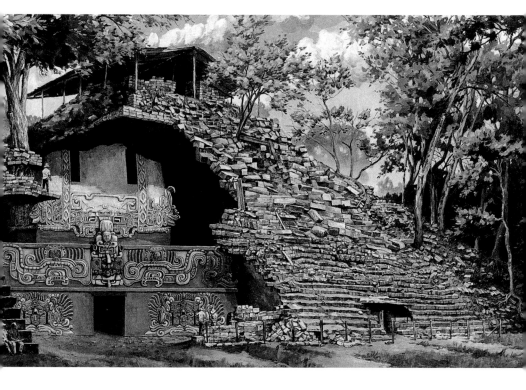

In these early Tikal and Uaxactun structures, we see the most prevalent types of Maya architecture: great chronographic markers, memorials to ancestors (probably religious structures), and bureaucratic structures. Were we to examine buildings of such different function from another part of the world, we would probably find that they were executed using different forms, perhaps separate architectural orders. Among the Maya, there was no architectural style linked exclusively to religious structures that differentiated them from civil buildings. All Maya architecture was composed of elevated platforms and corbel-vaulted chambers, organized in a variety of configurations. This makes the identification of function not always an easy task.

The corbel vault has sometimes been disparaged as a false arch, but the true keystone arch was not a goal of Maya architecture. To form a corbel, masonry walls were built to the desired height. At the spring of the vault, flat stones were placed closer and closer together until they could be spanned by a single capstone. The weight and mass of the walls helped prevent collapse, as did crossties, many of which remain in place today. They were probably useful in raising the vaults and then served for suspended hammocks and other furnishings. Exterior mansard roof profiles often followed the lines of the corbel, resulting in a stone architecture almost perfectly reproduced by the forms of Maya thatched houses today. The stone capstones conform to the hip roof of the thatched house, as if both to sanctify and exploit the domestic space. At Palenque, the conceit of the thatched house was emphasized in the buildings of the Palace, where sheets of shale were sheared off to look like thatch at the overhang of the mansard. On buildings throughout the Puuc region, where sleek vertical lines supplanted the mansard profile, the architectural ornament at vault level featured thatched Maya houses, as if to inform the viewer of the relationship of permanent stone constructions to the humble, perishable dwelling. Almost all Maya interior spaces, then, repeat the forms of the Maya house. It is not a 'false' anything, but a 'true' Maya transformation of simple forms into elevated permanent ones.

Sculpture

A new history of Maya art reveals a developed religious narrative at San Bartolo and historical rulers on stone stelae in the Guatemala highlands. By the third century, at Tikal and elsewhere in the Maya lowlands, at about the same time that the Maya began

120 Stela 29, Tikal, records the earliest contemporary Maya Long Count date, 8.12.14.8.15, corresponding to a day in the year AD 292. This early king wears a deity mask and holds out another god, while his father's portrait faces downward in the upper margin. Drawing by William R. Coe.

to use the corbel vault, they also started to erect stone monuments carved with portraits of rulers and writings of their deeds. Royal individuals now commanded the power to have themselves honored in a permanent medium during their lives, and probably to be commemorated posthumously as divine. The earliest of these new monuments with secure date and provenance is Stela 29 at Tikal, recovered from an ancient garbage dump in 1959 by archaeologists [120]. (Other stelae were found tossed into piles of refuse or cut into building stone, but some had been reverentially buried and still others had evidently never been removed from public view in Maya times.) The roughly hewn shaft of Stela 29 was carved on one surface with a portrait of a seated Tikal ruler; the other face records a Long Count date, 8.12.14.8.15, or AD 292. Such dates denote important events and the names of their protagonists; unfortunately, in this case the butt of the stela was broken off and lost in antiquity, thus depriving us of the complete record.

Typical of the representation of these early Maya lords are the very round and irregular forms. The right hand is drawn curled, as if in a mitten, and it presses a ceremonial bar to the body – many Maya kings throughout the period are shown carrying this object. An ancestor figure looks down from the upper portion of the stela, in a manner similar to the deities in the upper margin of late

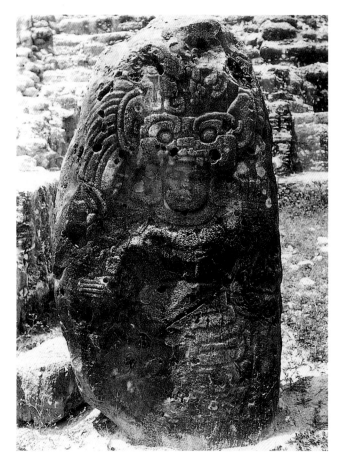

121 In his frontal representation, Curl Nose – the modern nickname of Yax Nuun Ayiin – presents himself as a foreigner from Teotihuacan. Later lords buried the stela upside down, leaving only the feet visible.

Opposite
122 Stela 31, Tikal. Stormy Sky, as this ruler is known, is shown on the front of the monument. He is flanked on the sides (not shown) by warriors in Teotihuacan-style dress, or perhaps just two sides of the same warrior, and the long text at the back recalls the Early Classic Tikal dynasty, up until 9.0.10.0.0, or AD 445.

La Venta stelae. With his left hand, the ruler supports an image of a supernatural figure generally known as the Jaguar God of the Underworld, identified by his tau-shaped tooth, jaguar ear, and 'cruller' over the nose. All early Tikal rulers carry this deity, and he is probably a patron of the city. The king himself wears a mask as well, and his hair is shaved into a 'mohawk' and studded with bones.

Stela 4 of AD 380 records the first Teotihuacan interloper, Yax Nuun Ayiin, to rule Tikal, and the monument was reset upside down in front of his funerary pyramid years later [121]. Technically, the monument is a modestly worked boulder with stone occlusion, with uneven surfaces and low relief, but the image is distinct. The ruler is seated, like his predecessor, and he bears the Jaguar God of the Underworld on his right hand, but he is shown with a fully

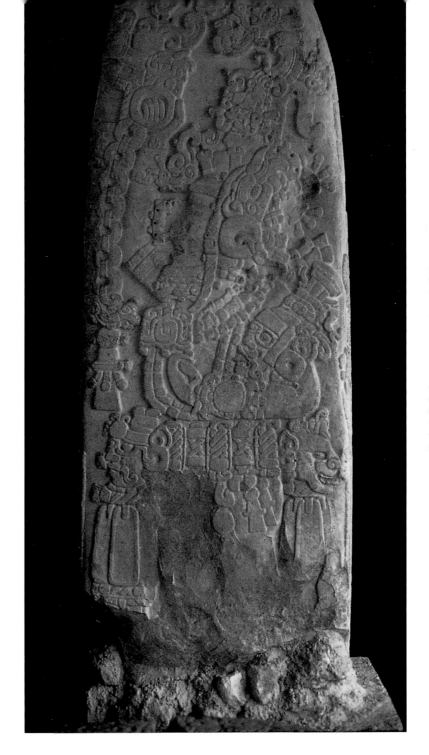

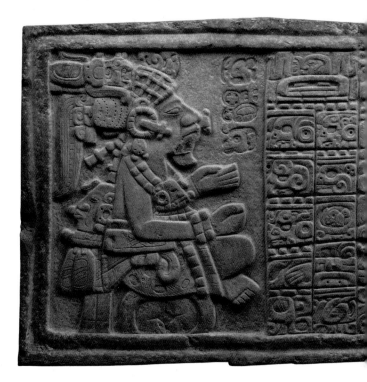

123 The so-called 'Po' panel. Named for the glyph that appears on the thrones on which the two figures sit, this wall panel shows two Bonampak rulers of the Early Classic.

frontal face, like no other king before him: he has been rendered as if he were a Teotihuacan deity. His headdress comes straight from the walls of that distant city, as does the Tlaloc *olla*, or jar, that he cradles in his left arm. In his monuments, including Structure 5D-43, in the East Plaza, Yax Nuun Ayiin demonstrates bilingual skills, with monuments, deities, and architecture that spoke to both Central Mexico and the Maya.

Despite the political intrusion, Yax Nuun Ayiin's son returned to the canon of representation established by early Tikal kings, at least in the representation on the front of his principal monument, Stela 31, erected in AD 445 [122]. Perhaps the child of a local Tikal woman, Siyah Chan K'awiil, nicknamed 'Stormy Sky,' sought to invoke legitimacy on both sides of his family. He had the shaft of stone carved on all four sides, and the two sides flanking his portrait depict a pair of Teotihuacan warriors, and in an uncluttered format that suggests Teotihuacan more than the Maya. Each warrior bears an *atlatl*, or spearthrower, and a shield that reveals Tlaloc on one side. In these representations we see two profile views of the same individual, for shield and weapons are reversed, as if we were looking at a single individual, standing

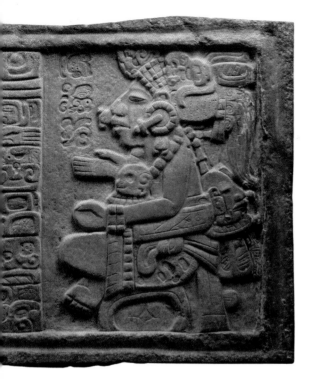

behind Siyah Chan K'awiil himself. Both bear a glyphic text above that identifies a single person, and it is none other than the father, Curl Nose, apparently revealed as a young warrior at the height of his powers.

The stone of Stela 31 is of fine grain, a hard, dense, and superior limestone ideal for recording detail. The sculptor recorded the most complex inventory of ritual paraphernalia of any Maya king: Siyah Chan K'awiil holds the Jaguar God of the Underworld in the crook of his left arm, and with his right, he holds forth the headdress of rulership, crowning himself. His own face bears a small 'X-ray' mask, helping to emphasize that this is a portrait of the trappings of office more than a portrait of an individual. Like Stelae 4 and 29, Stela 31 was removed from public view in antiquity, as Tikal wrestled to revise and codify its past. In the eighth century, Stela 31's broken shaft was hauled to the top of Structure 33 and interred with burnt offerings; it would be found here in the 1960s.

During the era when Teotihuacan warlords seemingly marauded across the rainforest, Uaxactun was particularly oppressed and its monuments badly damaged. But at the end of the Early Classic, as Teotihuacan lost its grip, monuments were erected at many other sites. In a number of cases, even these first hesitant works indicate the regional styles that later flourished at these places. Monument 26 from Quirigua shows a ruler in frontal pose, like all later monuments at that site. In style, it probably drew on both the wraparound conventions of Central Peten stone monuments and early cache vessels: portable goods might have influenced provincial developments. Multifigural designs appeared first on stone sculpture far from the Peten, and the 'Po' panel may be the earliest work in stone where two lords face one another across a panel of glyphs [123]. The establishment of strong regional styles in the Late Classic finds its roots in the earlier period.

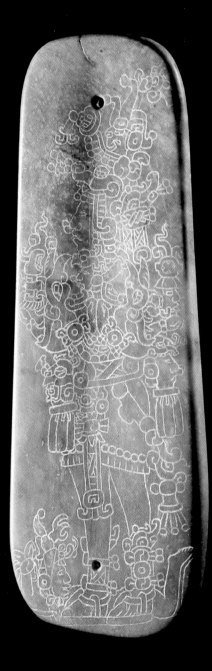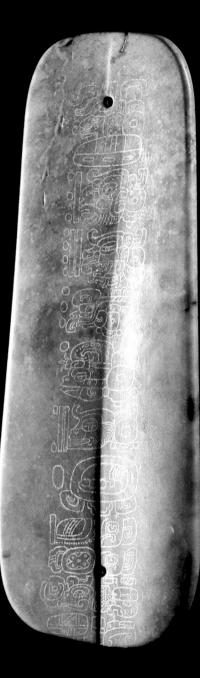

In 1864, workers digging a canal near Puerto Barrios, Guatemala, came across one of the most remarkable of early Maya sculptures, together with a Postclassic cache of copper bells. Now known as the Leiden Plaque, this beautiful piece of translucent jade was once a fancy costume element, one of three jade plaques hanging from a jade bar or head worn at the waist [124]. The imagery suggests that the object may have been a kind of portable stela, for the ruler portrait on the front and the inscription on the back conform to monumental Tikal works of the time. The Maya lord stands over a prone, bound captive, and bears a pliable serpent bar in his arms. Mitten-like hands and the parted profile legs also indicate the early date.

Painting

Several Early Classic wall paintings have survived the ravages of time. Perhaps the most beautiful of these is the tomb painting first encountered by looters at Río Azul, in northeast Peten [125]. An early fifth-century Maya date and text were drawn using guidelines, which artists then scraped away. The writing is framed by deities, including the Maya sun god, at right, with a glyph for *k'in*, or sun, in his cheek. The side walls are marked with wavy, beaded symbols that indicate liquid, probably the watery surface of the underworld. The deceased would have been laid with his head at the text, and

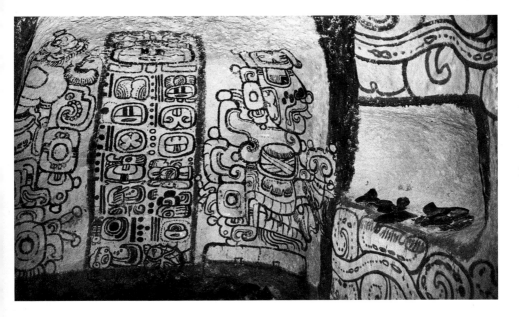

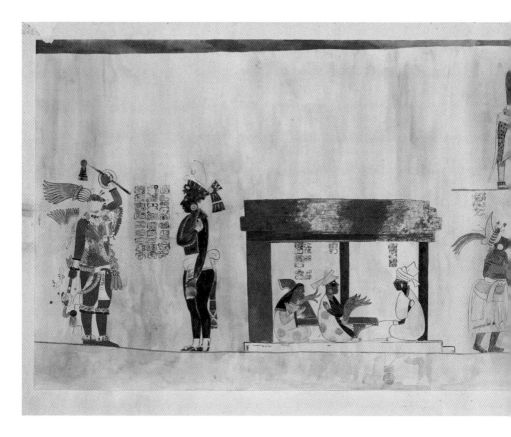

126 Painted across one side of a doorway, this Uaxactun mural depicts the family members of a fifth-century court. Visitors arrive at left; women gather in a palace chamber beside an empty throne; musicians attend at far right.

his body just within the liminal, watery world that the Maya perceived as the entrance to the afterlife. The niches for offerings are similar to those of contemporary Tomb 104, Monte Alban [97].

The Río Azul painting is monochrome, a reddish brown hematite pigment on creamy stucco, and the line is sure, strong, and highly calligraphic, each stroke ending in a whiplash. Contemporary paintings at Tikal (Burial 48) are by comparison less well executed, although the configuration is similar: a Long Count date is surrounded there by symbols of preciousness, asymmetrically painted across the walls of the chamber. A bright polychrome scene at Uaxactun found by archaeologists, copied, and then immediately destroyed by forest workers, showed musicians, families, bloodletting, and a meeting of important lords [126].

At Calakmul, a monumental painted stucco frieze adorned the façade of Group A, North Acropolis; below, archaeologists then came upon a vivid painting 656 ft (200 m) in length, featuring a stylized world of aquatic abundance. Brilliant blue and red

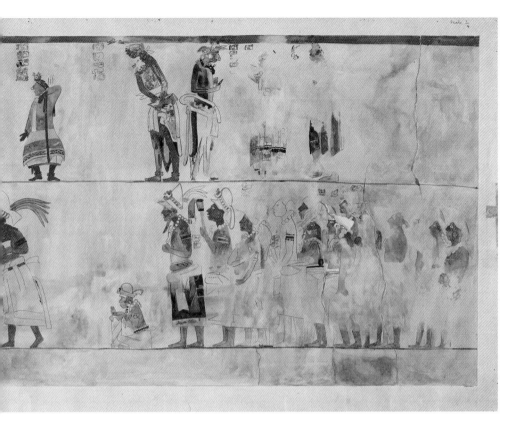

pigments define water signs and glyphs; subtler colors bring waterbirds to life, with shading added to their wings. Both frieze and painted wall closely resemble pots of the fifth century, suggesting the interaction and shared work of painters and modelers of both the small and large scale.

Funerary rites and offerings

The great tombs uncovered at Tikal brought to light the finery and pomp of Maya funerary practices, and in many cases also gave meaning and context to the many objects known without such clear provenance. When Maya kings were prepared for interment, they were splendidly equipped for their journey and transformation in the underworld, and funerary furniture often reflected these concerns in its iconography.

Yax Nuun Ayiin died about AD 425, perhaps leaving the surface of the earth as the Maya calendar turned to 9.0.0.0.0. He was borne on a litter into his tomb – at first a perishable structure at the base of what would become after his death the building we call Structure 34. He was probably accompanied by a great procession of musicians who laid down their instruments, turtleshells and deer antlers, in the tomb. Others in the procession, like those depicted in the later Bonampak murals, may have worn exotic costume: a set of crocodile scales was also recovered from the tomb. Nine individuals, perhaps those very procession members, were then sacrificed and placed alongside the dead king. Many fine ceramics were placed in the tomb, some filled with cool frothy chocolate beverages or maize gruel, as can now be confirmed from the texts on numerous pots. Many of these show strong Teotihuacan influence in terms of imagery, shape, and technique, but most were made locally. Many resemble those also produced at Kaminaljuyu, in the Guatemalan highlands. In fact, burial complexes there contained a similar configuration of exotic materials, and both may reflect a Teotihuacan tradition, although they are also not like the Teotihuacan burials which have come to light in recent years.

Lidded, stuccoed tripod vessels predominated in Maya royal funerary offerings during the late fourth and fifth centuries [127]. Shape and technique derive from contemporary Teotihuacan pots, but the Maya products taper at the 'waist,' and the less weighty Maya lids may have anthropomorphic or zoomorphic knobs. In certain instances the stucco technique is combined with incision of clay at its leather-hard stage, and the two techniques are masterfully worked together. Some of the pots, among them an example from Río Azul, have 'screw-top' lids; others have rattles in the base of the bowl. Many ceramics of this era depict purely Maya imagery in the stucco painting, but Teotihuacan influence is also strong: a ring-stand bowl from Curl Nose's tomb shows Central Mexican deities. Copan archaeologists have excavated examples made in Central Mexico, but specifically, in this case, for a local market: the stucco imagery here shows the founder of the Copan dynasty as the embodiment of an ancestral shrine.

Two-part ceramic effigies have also been recovered from Early Classic tombs. An especially fine one from Yax Nuun Ayiin's tomb depicts a squat old deity on a stool of crossed human femurs holding a human skull in his hands [128]. About twenty-five years after Yax Nuun Ayiin's death, a Tikal lord was interred without head, femurs, or feet. Although he might have been brought back from the battlefield in this state, his mutilated skeleton could also bear witness to the practice of collecting relics from royal

127 Nicknamed the 'Dazzler,' this extraordinary vessel came from the tomb of a woman connected to the founding dynasty at Copan. Tests reveal a Central Mexico origin of the clay, but the vessel would seem to have been made for the Copan founder, whose masked face stares out from a temple shrine.

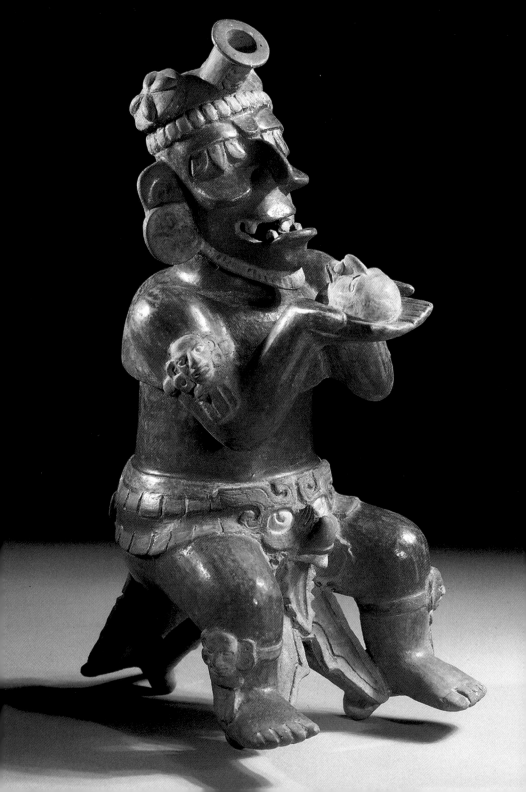

persons. Years later, Hasaw Chan K'awiil of Tikal was buried with a collection of carved bones, some of them cut from human femurs. This old deity, then, may be the patron of a particular form of sacrifice, associated with ancestor veneration and dismemberment.

Other types of fine ceramics were made, including the fourth-century basal-flange bowls that pre-dated the advent of tripod vessels in the Maya area, many with dome-shaped lids. Painted with colored slips before firing, some pots reveal a remarkably wide range of colors, despite the low temperatures at which they were fired. Quadrupod vessels occur with the basal-flange bowls, and many are jaguar or bird zoomorphs. The finest are of dark clay, incised at the leather-hard stage and then burnished after firing [129], including new discoveries at Zotz [132]. The artists enjoyed the interplay between two and three dimensions on these vessels, in a fashion similar to contemporaneous Moche ceramics in the Andes. On one, a three-dimensional cormorant eagerly eats a fish that shifts from a two-dimensional drawn figure to a three-dimensional sculptural one [130]. Like many Asian peoples, the Maya may have used cormorants to help them fish.

Carved and appliquéd cache vessels are also found, many of them formed of two parts – the lower part often with a human face, the upper, one or two supernatural headdresses [131]. Others simply show deities, and one imagines that offerings were placed in these pots. Chahk, god of rain, dominates these representations. He is marked by the curl in his eye, shark tooth, fish fins on cheek, and shell over the ear, and it is in this guise that a Tikal ruler appeared on Stela 2.

Early Classic jade was generally worked in soft, curving lines, rather than with the sharper drill-and-saw technique of the Late Classic. In some cases, the jade was incised; in others, the hard stone was cut into human and animal shapes. A few mosaic masks protected the faces of dead kings, and particularly fine ones were recently excavated at Calakmul, where the dead king was bundled under layers of cloth. Celts like the Leiden Plaque took their place at the king's waist [124].

Internal and external relationships

For some Maya cities, their relationship with Teotihuacan defined the fifth century. They wore Central Mexican dress, added Central Mexican gods to their pantheon, and probably understood distant Teotihuacan to be the hearth of culture. Some other Maya cities

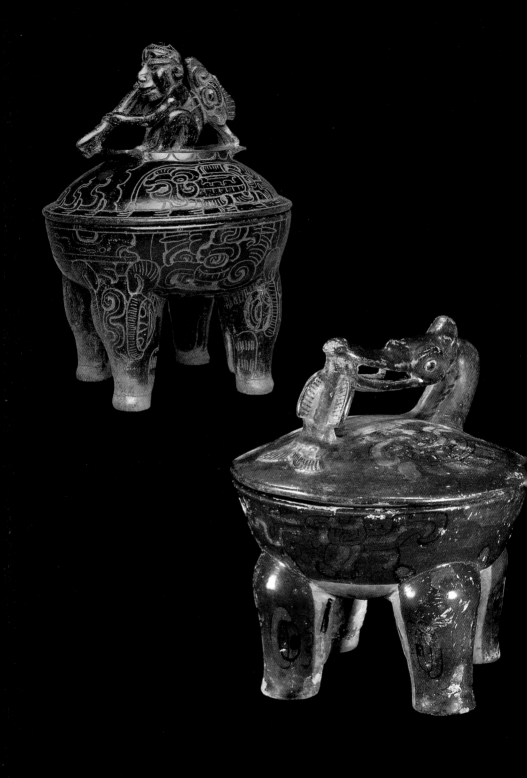

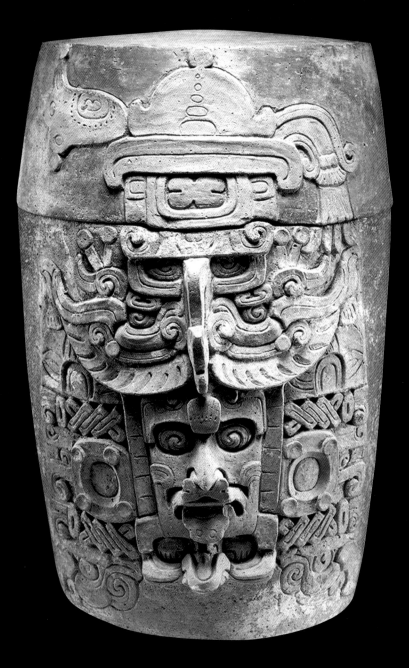

may have defined themselves by their resistance to Teotihuacan. The giant but poorly known city of Calakmul surely resisted all attempts to incorporate it into the Central Mexican orbit. Yet despite clear and indisputable Maya records about the arrival of Teotihuacan overlords, the essentially Maya character of the fourth and fifth centuries, as expressed in writing, architecture, and much of the iconography, remains equally undeniable.

The salient physical characteristic of the city of Teotihuacan is its city plan, with its grid of right angles and its architecture of right-angle geometry [68, 69]. It bears no resemblance to the more random, asymmetrical and clustered plan of Tikal, with its architecture of rounded moldings and variable proportions [142]. Only a single structure has been excavated at Tikal in what appears to be true Teotihuacan *talud-tablero*. Nearby Yaxha, where Teotihuacan influence was strong, developed an urban layout that in part followed 'streets,' perhaps an accommodation of Teotihuacan city planning to Peten geography; but it too is truly a Maya city. Contact with Teotihuacan resulted in an increasingly cosmopolitan and luxurious life for the royalty of Tikal, but it did not necessarily deny the essential Maya character of the period, particularly as expressed in writing, architecture, and much of the iconography. Occasional offerings juxtapose the two cultures' material wealth [90].

Because no inscriptions were known from Tikal or Uaxactun for the period from AD 530 to 580, Sylvanus G. Morley recognized a cessation of cultural production, calling it the 'hiatus,' and used it to divide the Early Classic period from the Late Classic. At Tikal, where Teotihuacan influence had most potently affected religion, ritual, and artistic style, such influence ended abruptly. Although various explanations had been put forward to explain the lapse (Morley had thought Tikal established colonies at Copan and elsewhere in the period) and the absence of any true 'hiatus' outside the Central Peten had become clear in recent years, a recent discovery at Caracol, Belize, seems to provide the clearest explanation of all: according to Caracol Altar 21, in the mid-sixth century Tikal was besieged and defeated by its enemies, led by the lords of Caracol, and, as Simon Martin and Nikolai Grube have argued, with the help of Calakmul, where Teotihuacan's ideological presence had never taken root. If Teotihuacan had already been burned, then Tikal could not turn to its old overlords for help. Whatever the absolute goals of such warfare, Caracol enjoyed an economic boom while a reduced population at Tikal suffered

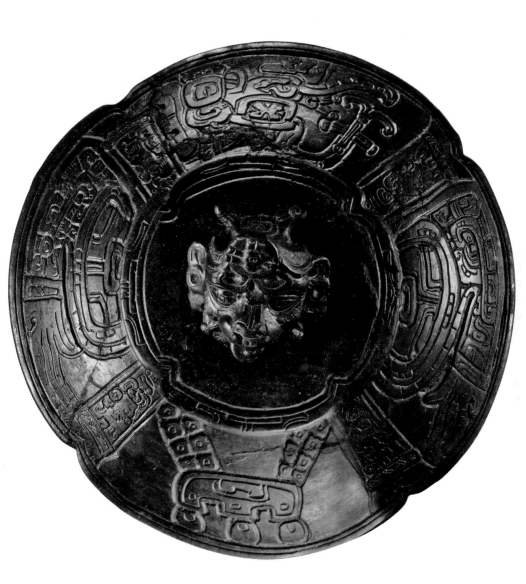

132 Stephen Houston opened an extraordinary tomb at Zotz, Guatemala, in 2010. The lid of this vessel features a Monkey Scribe; his necklace can be seen at the bottom of the picture.

grinding poverty and watched the destruction of monuments and buildings. The Tikal dynasty itself fractured, with a branch of the lineage establishing itself in the Petexbatun region, leading to further seventh-century wars. Cities and lineages far from this interminable conflict seem to have benefited by their distance, capturing trade and talent. When cultural production at Piedras Negras, Palenque, and Copan gained renewed vigor at the beginning of the seventh century, styles in art, architecture, and ceramics all showed dramatic changes.

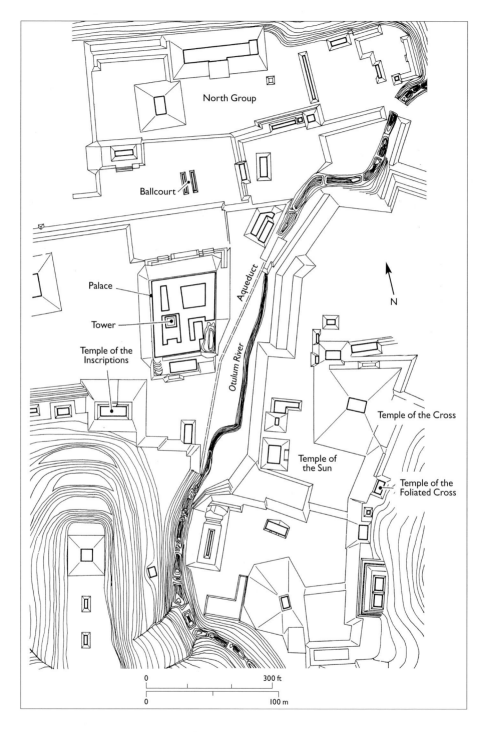

North Group

Ballcourt

Palace

Tower

Temple of the
Inscriptions

Aqueduct

Otulum River

N

Temple of the Cross

Temple of
the Sun

Temple of the
Foliated Cross

0   300 ft

0   100 m

Chapter 7   The Late Classic Maya

Of all Mesoamerican art and architecture, that of the Late Classic Maya has long been the most esteemed. Even before the travels of John Lloyd Stephens and Frederick Catherwood brought the great temple pyramids and stone carvings to public attention in the 1840s, Alexander von Humboldt had remarked upon the naturalism of much of Maya imagery, and students of ancient art had praised the ability of the ancient Maya to draw the human figure. Eighth-century Maya art is undoubtedly very human, and the attention to the individual, whether in the courtly Bonampak paintings or the solemn, three-dimensional stelae of Copan, has always attracted the modern viewer, as has the remarkable preservation of architecture of the period. Moreover, what has always been apparent is the simultaneous flowering of different styles in a profusion of artistic production.

Having already been abandoned to the tropical rainforest for centuries by the time of the Spanish Conquest, most Maya cities were too remote and ruinous to be pillaged in the sixteenth century. Only since World War II have roads opened the realm of the ancient Maya to the modern visitor, and only since 1980 has widespread exploitation of the rainforest run riot, with far-reaching implications for ancient cities, flora and fauna, and the modern Maya. Every year satellite photographs reveal new loss of rainforest. Little forest survives, and marauding drug lords and mobsters have made archaeology perilous.

During the sixth century, the cities of the Peten went into decline, sapped by warfare. Simultaneously, peripheral regions – Chiapas, the Usumacinta drainage, Belize, and the southern lowlands – began to flourish, siphoning economic power and cultural energy away from the center.

Architecture

Just about the year AD 600, in the foothills of the Chiapas *altiplano*, Palenque, the most westerly of major Maya cities, embarked upon a period of expansion [133, 134]. Over about 150 years and under the aegis of just a handful of rulers – in large part, the great king Pakal (whose name can be read phonetically in Maya and which means 'shield'), his two sons, and Pakal's grandson and

133 Plan of the Maya city of Palenque.

Overleaf:
134 The Palenque Palace as seen from the southwest. Behind the tower lies the East Court, famous for its carvings of captives (ill. 136). Subterranean passages honeycomb the section of the Palace in the foreground.

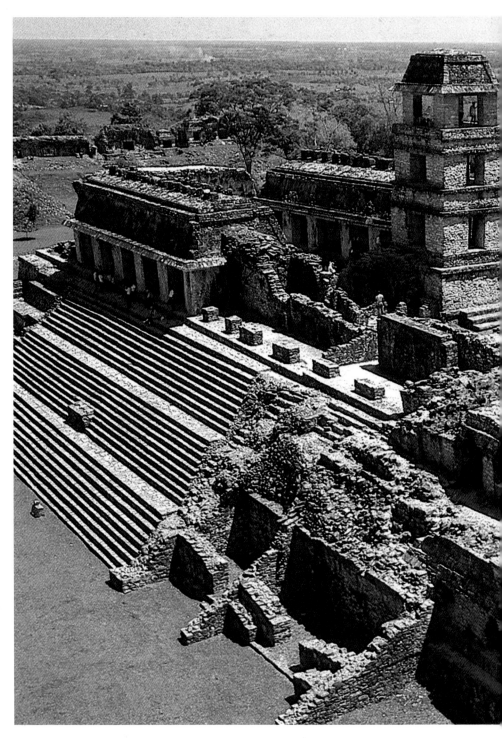

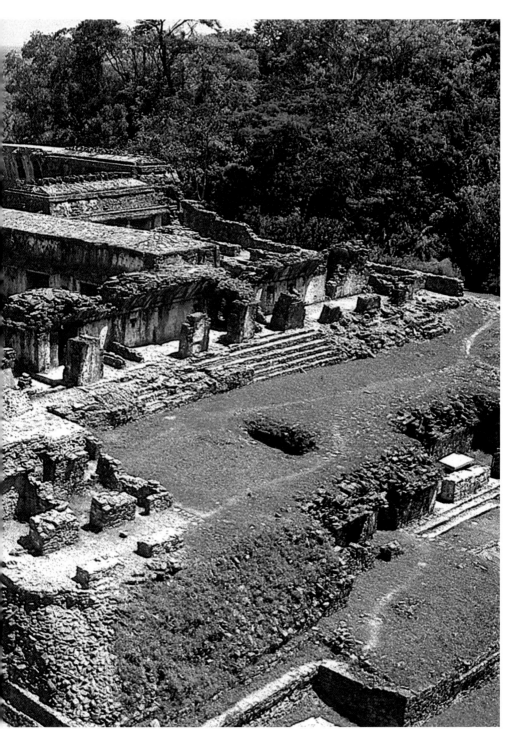

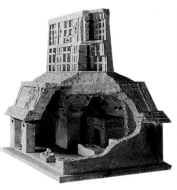

135 Cutaway model of the Temple of the Cross showing the light roofcomb resting on the central wall dividing the two parallel corbeled vaults. The ritual sweatbath can be seen at far right.

great-grandson – the city grew in size, splendor, and importance. Its layout follows the rolling topography of the site, and temple structures crown and emphasize natural rises. Edward Barnhart's map and Kirk French's continuing work reveal the various streams that run out of the mountains above Palenque. Roughly seven streams course like arteries through the body of the site, making Palenque what the Aztec would call an *altepetl*, or 'water mountain,' denoting a place of civilization. The greatest of these waterways, the Otulum, flows from a spring high above the site; its name means 'stone walled water,' and it was canalized to bring running water to the Palace. No *sacbes* characterize the architectural plan, but three distinct levels of construction can be discerned down the hillside.

Early Peten masonry was clumsy and heavy, weighty roofcombs leaving little interior space. At Palenque a different aesthetic prevailed, and its architects set corbeled vaults parallel to one another, with a light, cut-out roofcomb over the central wall [135]. Not only did this allow for greater interior space, but it also stabilized the whole construction, and it is partly because of this innovative technique that Palenque architecture is so well preserved today. Solid mass gave way to a web-like shell for the first time in Mesoamerican architectural history.

What one sees today of the Palenque Palace was probably built over a period of a hundred years, the interior north-south buildings pre-dating the exterior colonnades and the tower. House E, unlike all other Palace buildings, was painted white and adorned with flowers. An inscription names it as the 'white flower house.' Panels celebrating the accession of several rulers were set inside Palace structures, and scenes on such panels undoubtedly reflect the luxury of courtly life at the time. The fine throne of House E was set under the Oval Palace Tablet and the doorway to the East Court was framed by a stucco bicephalic dragon of the sort that provides the border on accession stelae at Piedras Negras. The East Court was ornamented with large slabs of coarse limestone carved with subservient figures of gross and distorted features, including one with a huge scarred penis [136]. The wealth and luxury of the court was quite literally underpinned by tribute and fealty. Sacrificial rituals joined those of accession in the Palace, revealing the rights and responsibilities of kings.

The final phase of construction in the Palace gave rise to the graceful three-story tower, a unique survival in Mesoamerican architecture. Narrow stairways wind around a solid core.

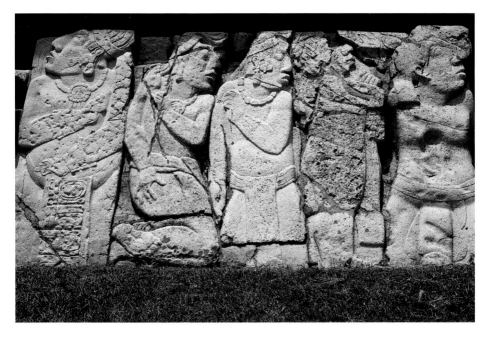

136 Individual carved slabs were placed together to create the great sloping *talud* of carved captives in the East Court of the Palenque Palace. Lords of the region would have stepped down into the court by the staircase that these humbled figures flank. Late Classic.

Although the very idea of a tower has led several scholars to think in terms of an astronomical observatory, the building may also have had a defensive function, for from its upper story one can survey the whole plain to the north.

Supplied with water directly from the ancient aqueduct, the Palace was a comfortable building. It seems to have served as the focus for the various royal ceremonies, rather than exclusively as a residence for the king's family. For dwellings, we look east of the aqueduct, where extensive excavations by Mexican archaeologists have restored the graceful palaces alongside spectacular waterfalls and pools. Here we might well have heard the sounds of children and dogs and smelled the wafting scent of spicy sauces stewing.

The nine-level Temple of the Inscriptions stands just south of the Palace [137, 138]. Set directly into the hill behind, it is highlighted and framed by the landscape. After discovering that floor slabs of a rear chamber could be lifted to reveal interior constructions, the Mexican archaeologist Alberto Ruz cleared the staircase and in 1952 found the extraordinary tomb at the base of the pyramid, set on an axis, north-south, with the stairs. Within, a large corbeled chamber held the uterus-shaped sarcophagus of the great king Pakal, whose remains lay covered with jade and cinnabar. The

137 Reconstruction, Temple of the Inscriptions, Palenque; inset shows the burial chamber and tomb of King Pakal within, accessible only by stairs from the chamber at top.

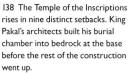

138 The Temple of the Inscriptions rises in nine distinct setbacks. King Pakal's architects built his burial chamber into bedrock at the base before the rest of the construction went up.

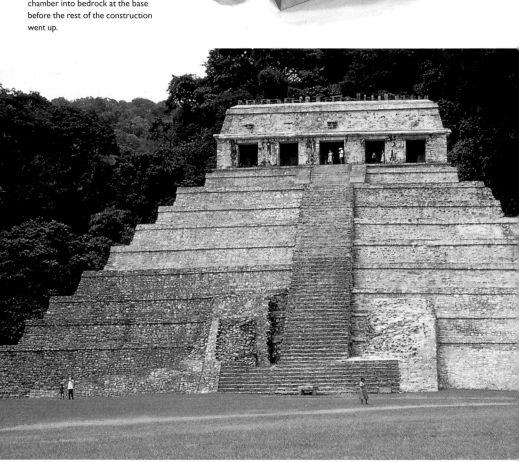

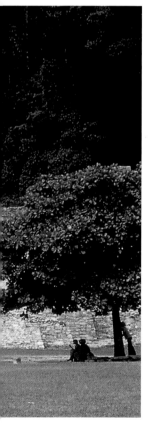

sarcophagus lid shows the king at the moment of death, falling in rapture into the maws of the underworld [143]. The sides of the sarcophagus display Pakal's ancestors, emerging from the ground, while nine stucco attendants flank the walls. The construction was designed for eternity: even the cross-ties were made of stone (the only examples known) and a small stone tube, or 'psychoduct,' as it is called, connects the tomb to the upper level and thence to fresh air. To date, the Temple of the Inscriptions is unique among all Mesoamerican pyramids in having been built before the ruler's death, probably to his specifications.

Three panels of lengthy inscriptions in the upper chamber relate Pakal's life, and the exterior stuccos show his son as an infant deity, perhaps to demonstrate divinity even during the king's lifetime. Immortalized within funerary pyramids, Maya kings were worshipped after death, great ancestors united with deities and visible in the constellations of the night sky.

The Temple of the Inscriptions rises in nine distinct levels. At the time of the Conquest the underworld was perceived by both Aztecs and Maya to have nine layers, and Pakal's funerary monument evidently conforms to the same idea of the afterlife, with the lord's tomb placed at the nadir of the pyramid. Likewise, at the time of European contact, Mesoamericans believed the heavens to have thirteen levels, a vision of the universe reflected in the stratified Maya world of Pakal, for thirteen distinct corbels connect the tomb to the upper galleries. Later lords anchored themselves to Pakal's apotheosis, with burials in smaller funerary pyramids to the west. The Red Queen, whose tomb came to light in 1994 in Temple XIII, may have been Pakal's wife; thick cinnabar – the raw mineral from which yields mercury – coated her bones, and a stunning malachite mosaic mask [2] covered her face.

East of the aqueduct, the three temples of the Group of the Cross (the Temples of the Sun, the Cross and the Foliated Cross) show yet another architectural innovation. In this design – common to each of the temples – the two parallel galleries are intersected at right angles by another corbeled passage, creating a great chamber. Each temple also has an inner shrine at the rear of the building. The post and lintel doorway, as well as the usual mansard roof, conceal the interior space. At Palenque the achievement of private, interior space is as significant as the negative, public space defined by the volumes of the buildings.

Inscribed panels within the Group of the Cross shrines celebrate the birth of three patron deities of Palenque, deep in

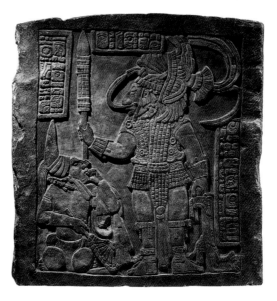

139 Carved stone lintels spanned doorways of royal buildings at Yaxchilan, with the carving visible only from directly underneath. Here, Bird Jaguar dominates a humbled captive.

time, at the dawn of the current era in the fourth millennium BC, under the sponsorship of the late seventh-century king K'an Bahlam, Pakal's oldest son. Stephen Houston has shown that these shrines symbolize sweathouses, places for birth and then the home for the resting image of the deity. K'an Bahlam probably stored cult figures here.

South of the Group of the Cross and creeping up the hillside, Temples 19, 21 and 22 all provide testimony to continuous architectural innovation under Pakal's grandson, Ahk'ul Mo' Naab. New vaulting techniques made it possible to span larger rooms; a new style of royal bench featured multifigural composition and made it possible for several lords to preside at once. The more hidden location and the opportunity for private consultation of large numbers of individuals in interior settings may point to shifting political structures and strategies.

The Usumacinta and Pasión Rivers witnessed a burst of development too, beginning at the end of the sixth century and continuing until about AD 800. River commerce along the Usumacinta was certainly one of the driving forces behind the growth of both Yaxchilan and Piedras Negras. At Yaxchilan, the river rounds an omega-shaped spit of land. Remnants of stone pilings in the silt piers indicate that there was once a bridge or toll gate here. Ranging single galleries are set both at plaza level near the river and on the surrounding hills. Structure 40 and Structure

33 celebrate the inaugurations of the two most important Late Classic rulers at Yaxchilan, nicknamed Shield Jaguar and Bird Jaguar [140]. Rising up from great terraces built into the rugged natural relief, both buildings have commanding views of the river.

The architects of Yaxchilan created a few buildings of the double-galleried sort common at Palenque, but in general they were more conventional in their use of interior space. Moreover, they positioned roofcombs directly over vault capstones, which exacerbated the natural tendency of corbeled constructions to collapse and made it necessary to erect ponderous interior buttresses for added support. Most Yaxchilan structures have multiple doorways, and many have finely carved lintels [139].

At nearby Piedras Negras, only a day or two down-river, different influences are evident. Buildings relate to one another, rather than to the river, and they cluster in groups similar to those of Palenque. The inscriptions suggest a general development of the site from south to north that took almost 200 years. The early

140 Structure 33, Yaxchilan. Narrow doorways pierce this monumental façade dedicated to Bird Jaguar, king in the 750s, whose stucco representation dominated the roofcomb at center. A carved stalactite (foreground) denotes a symbolic cave.

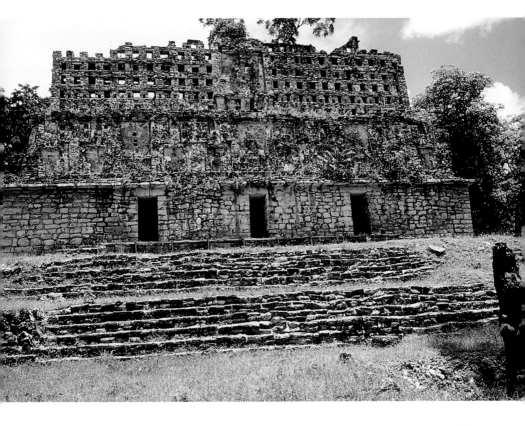

structures to the south are heavy and massive, with great rounded insets similar to those of the Tikal North Acropolis. The West Acropolis at Piedras Negras consists of a central palace compound flanked by two great funerary pyramids, probably the shrines to Rulers 3 and 4 in the dynastic sequence [141]. The palace structures feature double-corbeled galleries like those of Palenque.

At Tikal, the 'hiatus' drifted on into the seventh century, as Tikal sustained further military and political losses [142]. In the eighth century, however, a program of major new building work began that was sustained for about a hundred years. Instrumental in this revitalization of Tikal was Siyah Chan K'awiil (commonly known as Ruler A), who was buried about AD 727 in Temple I, a pyramid located directly across the Great Plaza from Temple II, which had itself been completed just a few years before. Temples I and II dramatically altered the core of Tikal, changing the old north-south axis (conveyed by accretions of buildings with rounded corners and fussy moldings) to an east-west one, defined by just two towering structures with clean lines.

Temple I, like the Temple of the Inscriptions at Palenque, is a nine-level pyramid, and – again like the Palenque building – it was conceived from the first as a complete memorial, from the carved

141 Piedras Negras kings developed a new complex on the West Acropolis during the seventh and eighth centuries. Within galleried palaces, kings reviewed their retinues from elegant thrones, framed by funerary pyramids that rose in great setbacks. Ruler 3's eight stelae stand in a line at right.

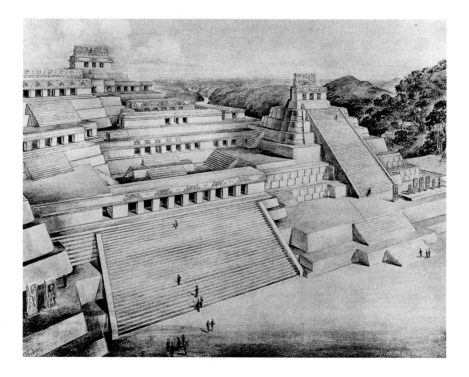

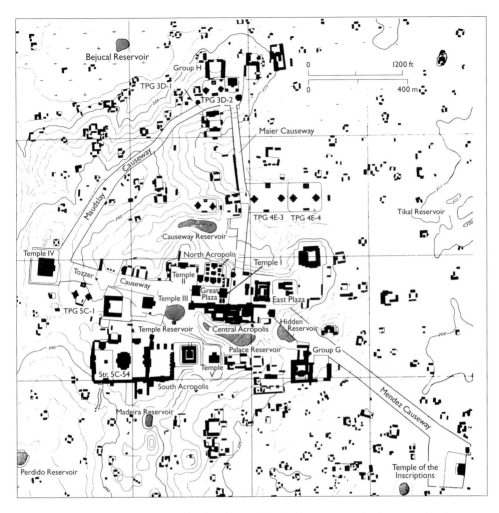

142 Plan of the central part of Tikal. The abbreviation TPG refers to the Twin Pyramid Groups or Complexes erected in the Late Classic. The early so-called Lost World pyramid is marked here as Str. 5C–54.

Overleaf:
143 As if in the moment of death, the seventh-century king Pakal is depicted being swallowed by skeletal jaws on his sarcophagus lid at the base of the Temple of the Inscriptions, Palenque.

wooden lintels spanning the doorways to the funerary chamber below [146]. Such an elaborate building must surely have been planned before Ruler A's death. Unlike the Palenque temple, however, none of the construction work can have started until the body of the ruler was sealed in the tomb at the base of the temple. Temple II was presumably dedicated to Ruler A's wife (though no tomb has been found), in which case husband and wife would have faced each other through eternity, framing their ancestors to the north.

Like great beacons rising above the jungle, other temples surround the original pair of the Late Classic dynasty. These unexcavated pyramids appear to be funerary monuments of later

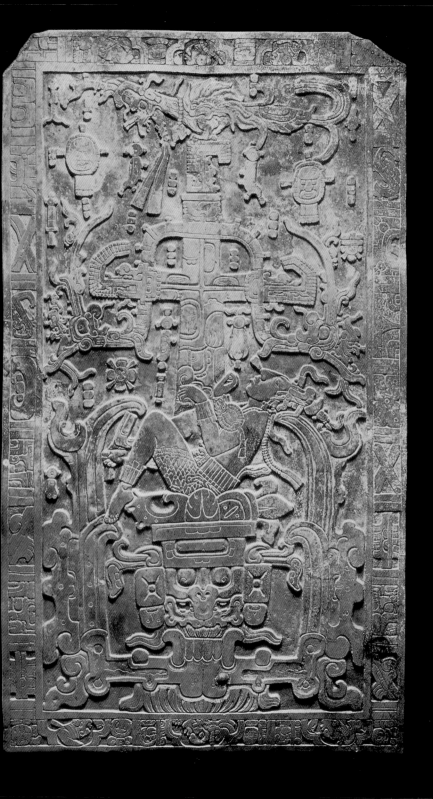

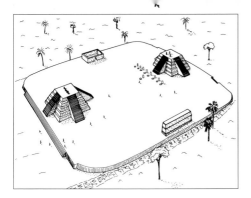

rulers who respectfully address their fore-bears. Temple IV is the greatest in both mass and height, rising to 213 ft (65 m) – or roughly the height of the Temple of the Sun at Teotihuacan. The Tikal pyramids remain visible 12 miles (19 km) to the north, from the last great rise before Uaxactun. Although freestanding and devoid of many of the ornamental moldings typical of earlier Tikal, these pyramids retained characteristics of the North Acropolis that are not limited to their funerary nature. In Temple I, for example, a heavy roofcomb was set over the narrow, dark chambers that are accessible through a single doorway, and its weight runs down the spine of the structure. Inset moldings, more streamlined than those of the North Acropolis, both cover the corners of the structure and create a play of light and shadow across the surface.

144 Reconstruction of a Twin Pyramid Complex, Tikal. Limited to Yaxha and Tikal only, these complexes were erected in the eighth century to celebrate *katun* endings. Although they might have been painted in antiquity, all the altars and stelae in the row at right are plain today.

The strong east-west orientation dominated not only the Great Plaza in the eighth century but also the rest of the site, in outlying groups known as Twin Pyramid Complexes [144]. At least six of these architectural clusters were erected in sequence, presumably to celebrate the twenty-year *katun* cycle which is

145 The Central Acropolis, Tikal's royal palace, invites the observer onto the Great Plaza, although access is carefully restricted.

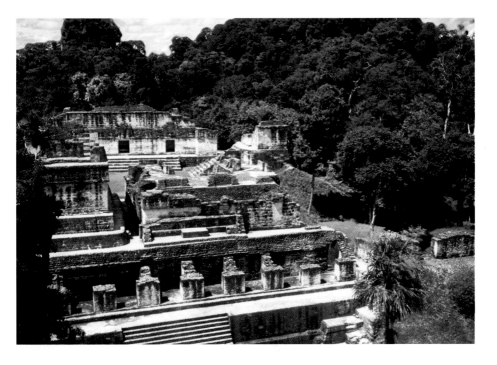

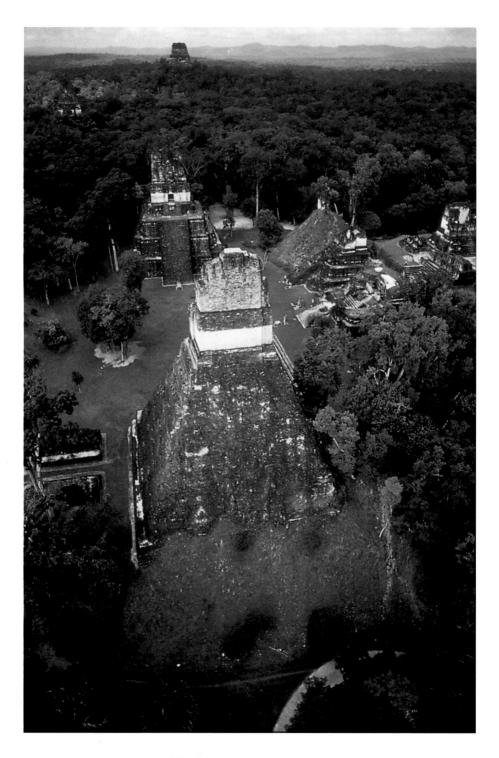

146 Temple I, Tikal and the Temple of the Inscriptions at Palenque (ill. 138) are the two most splendid funerary pyramids of the Late Classic Maya that archaeologists have yet explored. Both structures rise in nine distinct levels, as if a reference to the notion of nine levels of the underworld were incorporated into architectural iconography.

147 By the mid-eighth century, Copan's Main Acropolis and Main Plaza had achieved their full growth, although nearby compounds of wealthy lineages continued to expand. The Copan River, to rear, later ate away structures until the U.S. Army Corps of Engineers constructed a new course for it in the 1930s.

recorded in each group. The elevated platform of each cluster has the shape of the Maya symbol for completion, and the two radial pyramids on the east-west axis recall the chronographic marker at Uaxactun, E-VII-sub. With a range structure to the south and a shrine to a ruler in the open structure on the north, this repeated and well-defined Tikal configuration would seem to reproduce the Great Plaza at its every appearance along the causeways.

No sculpture and little architectural ornament remain *in situ* to help us understand the function and meaning of the Central Acropolis [145]. Its galleried chambers do, however, resemble a palace like that of Palenque, even if organized with less concern for overall plan. Furthermore, the presence of a victor and his captive in eroded stucco – recorded on one of the structures flanking a trapezoidal court at the core of the Acropolis – hints that it may have been a place of sacrifice, like the East Court at Palenque, where humbled captives are depicted [136]. A bank of four large hearths sustained a sort of institutional kitchen for the scribes, traders, priests, scholars, and nobles at work in the Central Acropolis.

Using the same fundamental elements of Maya architecture – platform, stairs, and corbel vault – the architects of Copan [147], Honduras, developed a distinctive aesthetic. The local stone is an easily worked volcanic tuff, ranging from pink to brown to green, so that building stones could be cut and fitted together with a precision rare in the limestone structures of Palenque or Tikal. (The

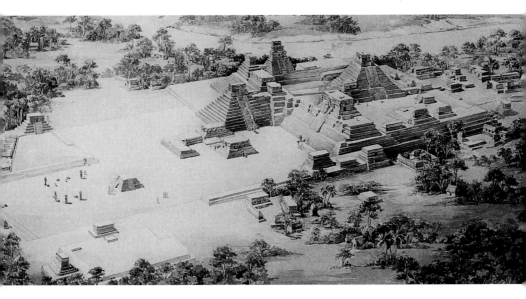

stone, of course, was cut with stone tools.) At Copan, however, as elsewhere, stucco coatings would have hidden any imperfections. Emphasis was placed on tuff architectural ornament, in full three-dimensional relief, and it is the best-preserved iconographic guide to the meaning of Mesoamerican architecture. Surviving façades retain a sheer vertical profile, rather than the usual mansard roof.

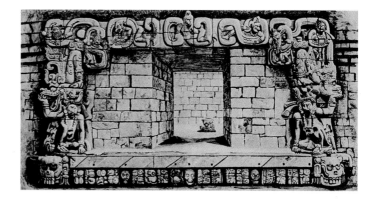

148, 149 The inner doorway, Structure 22, Copan. One first steps through the fragmentary remains of a great monster mouth to gain access to this remarkable carved doorway, reconstructed at right. The king who built this structure was eventually captured and sacrificed by neighboring Quirigua lords.

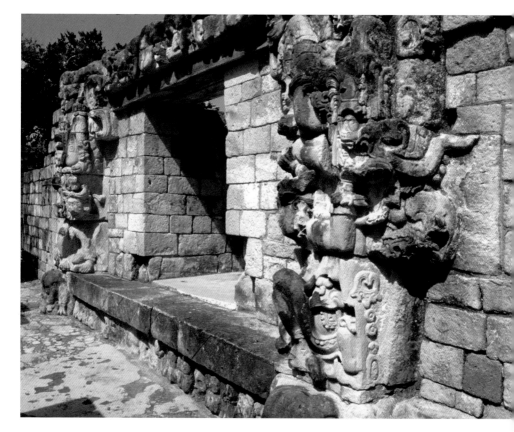

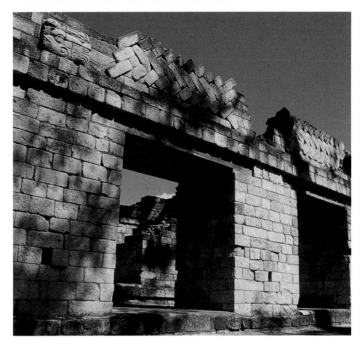

150 Apparently to unite the powerful and wealthy lineages, Copan lords built a *popol na*, or council house, where they might gather to advise and guide the king in his adjacent palace. Now known as Structure 22a, it features a fish on the front façade, probably a reference to the Fish family, whose compound lies south of the Main Acropolis.

These clean lines are echoed in the façades of Central Yucatan and the Puuc region, and may in fact originate at Copan.

The Copan Valley provides superb possibilities for the dramatic siting of architecture. The ancient city planners realized this and located their buildings to take advantage of specific views of the valley and surrounding mountains, especially the saddle through the mountains to the north. The ballcourt, for example, seems to reproduce the valley itself in its layout and orientation.

Eighth-century pyramids and structures dedicated to the rites of kingship crowd the acropolis, the final layer in what was at least a 600-year accretion. Kings were pronounced from Structure 22, where the private, elevated rear chamber framed by a bicephalic dragon is reached through a great open monster mouth, a symbolic cave entry to a sacred mountain [148, 149]. Young maize god sculptures once graced the exterior cornices, and the symbolic mountain may have been where the king brought forth the first corn from the underworld.

An international team of archaeologists has worked to reveal Copan's mysteries, both at its center and along its margins. Just beside Structure 22, a reconstructed Structure 22a apparently served as a *popol na*, or council house, where the king's advisers would have conferred [150]. Local lineages, including the Fish family, promote themselves from its façade, their names juxtaposed with

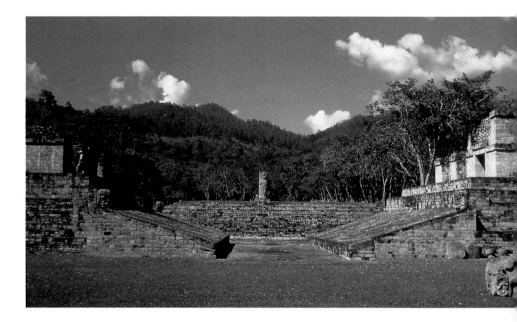

151 One of the most beautifully sited of all Maya buildings, the ballcourt at Copan guides the eye from the Main Plaza to the steep hills beyond.

152 Carved with 2,200 glyphs, the text of the great Hieroglyphic Stairway at Copan is among the longest known. A supplicant would climb back in time as he or she ascended the stairs, reaching a shrine dedicated to the founder of Copan at the top. Eighth century AD.

woven mat, or *pop*, signs. South of the acropolis, archaeologists have now found evidence of the Fish family compound. What might have been thought to be merely idle self-promotions seem, in fact, to have archaeological foundation. And during the eighth century, constituent lineages built luxurious quarters for themselves a few miles from the core that began to compete with the city center. The House of the Scribes in the Sepulturas group reveals the sophistication and wealth of the aristocracy at the end of the eighth century, juxtaposed with nearby tiny and poorly constructed buildings of unknown purpose.

One of the last Copan kings, Yax Pasaw, as he is usually called, rebuilt many acropolis buildings, including Structure 11, his royal palace, and Structure 18, which may have held his tomb, although it was looted in antiquity. Structure 16 is the largest building on the acropolis, housing within it the ancestral structures dubbed Rosalila and Margarita, the earliest funerary pyramids known at Copan, and its nine levels seem to refer to ancestry and the royal lineage in general, rather than to a single dynast.

Below the 82-ft (25-m) drop-off from the acropolis lies the Copan ballcourt, the largest and most beautiful of all Classic courts [151]. Like many smaller ones elsewhere, it unites two different areas of the central city. Unusual superstructures surmount the parallel buildings on its eastern and western sides.

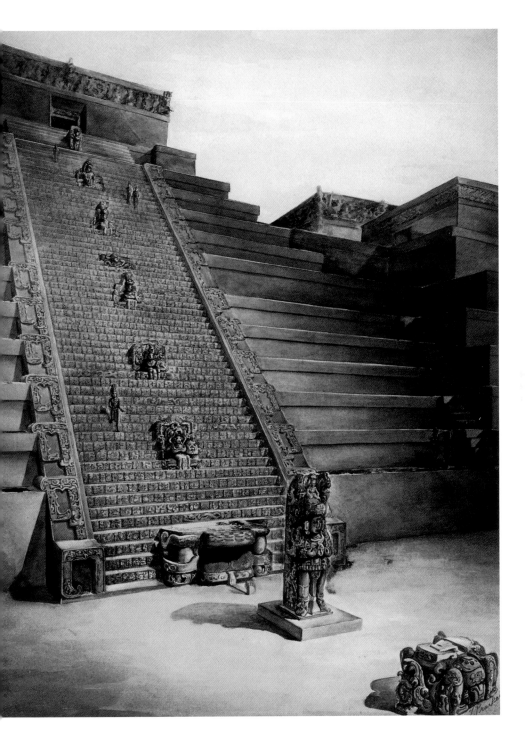

Each of these buildings has a plan cut by a central corridor running east-west, with mirrored configurations to north and south, as if ballcourts themselves. In its final phase, giant sculptural macaws lined the alleys.

Just to the south of the ballcourt stands the great Hieroglyphic Stairway, a large pyramid whose steps are inscribed with 2,200 glyphs that relate the history of the Late Classic dynasty [152]. Five three-dimensional rulers of Copan sit on projections from the staircase, and some are set directly over two-dimensional captive figures. In no other Maya building are sculpture, writing, and architecture more sensitively united. The carved scroll balustrade is an unusual element in Maya architecture, resembling the balustrade of the Pyramid of the Niches at El Tajin. The long Maya text runs from the top of the stairs to the base, from legendary time to the present, so that a supplicant would climb back into time, visiting ancestors in order en route to the summit.

The traditions that may have originated at Copan also thrived in Central Yucatan and the Puuc region. At Chicanna, as at most Chenes and Río Bec centers, the principal structures have great monster-mouth façades – presumably here again associated with

153 Across what is now southern Campeche, Maya lords erected dozens of structures articulated by what seem to be 'monster' mouths. Several buildings at Chicanna feature clearly defined teeth and jaws, surmounted by great eyes with scrolls, so that one stepped into the mouth of the animate being in entering the building.

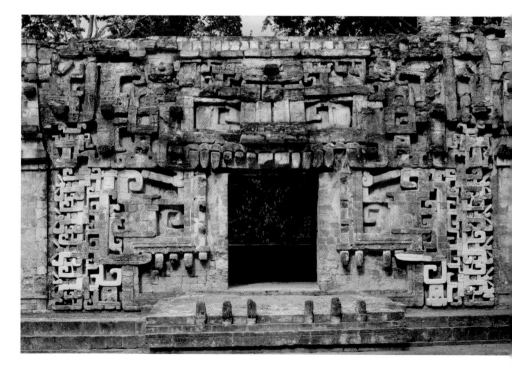

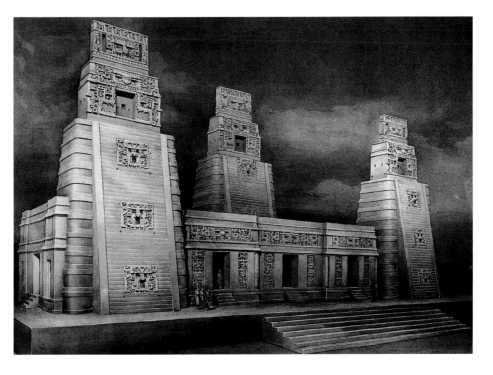

154 What seem to be separate but clustered palaces and temples at Xpuhil are in fact a single building. False openings beckon atop equally illusory stairs, in an architectural style of the seventh and eighth centuries widely known as 'Río Bec' and 'Chenes.'

ceremonies of kingship [153]. Perhaps the proliferation of structures in Central Yucatan with monster-mouth façades reflects the widespread celebration of elite rituals. The mouth of the Chicanna structure is similar to the largely destroyed exterior of Structure 22, Copan, where the interior bicephalic monster framed a removed, interior chamber for private rites. Blocks of ornament fell off in 1994, revealing painting on stucco underneath.

Chenes structures are generally low-lying, galleried buildings. At Río Bec, great false temples frame such galleries – described as 'false,' in the accepted view, because there is no access to temple summits. In fact they may be funerary pyramids, directly combined with palaces, and conflations of the patterns established at Palenque or Tikal. Xpuhil, in southern Campeche, for example, features stucco ornament that looks like stairs, but they cannot be walked on, nor their upper chambers entered [154]. At Ek' Balam, north of Chichen Itza, a vast pyramid with monster-mouth doorways – and adorned with large befeathered stucco figures – encased an important tomb.

Late Classic Puuc architecture first captured the imagination of modern Europeans and Americans through the writings and illustrations of Stephens and Catherwood, who spent months in

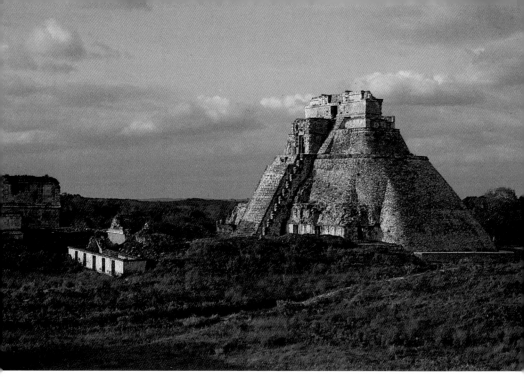

155 The Pyramid of the Magician at Uxmal.

the Puuc region. They visited Uxmal, Kabah, Sayil, and Labna to make drawings and to study the ruins there. There is still no finer introduction to the region and its ancient remains than their report of 1843. What attracted them and what still attracts the traveler today are the elegant quadrangles, fine veneer masonry, and beautiful mosaic façades that reflect shifting patterns of light in the hot clear sun of the Puuc hills.

Most of what is visible at Uxmal today seems to belong to the ninth century, ending with a final hieroglyphic date of 10.3.18.8.12 (AD 907). With two distinct profiles, the Pyramid of the Magician must have been constructed in at least two phases [155]. On its west side, a precipitous stairway leads to a Chenes-style doorway in the form of a monster mouth; a gentler slope on the east leads to a Puuc-style chamber at the top. The eastern profile seems to trail away, like the train of a dress, as the structure appears to gather itself up and address the quadrangles on its western face.

The juxtaposition of quadrangles – say, the Nunnery – with pyramids like the great Magician recalls the Palace and Temple of the Inscriptions at Palenque, although the physical expression of Puuc architecture is new. The Palenque Palace, however, evolves from the inside out, while the Nunnery would seem to have been designed as a quadrangle. Indeed the Nunnery exemplifies the pioneering techniques of Puuc architecture: specialized 'boot' stones in vaults, providing increased stability and making possible some of the greatest vaulted spaces of ancient Mesoamerica; flying façades, the light, airy roofcombs set directly over the front weight-bearing wall, like the false storefronts of the American Old West; and veneer masonry, well-cut stones fitted together without mortar, hiding a rubble core [156].

Many elements from the Nunnery structures are repeated and elaborated in the House of the Governor, the finest of all Puuc buildings [157]. It, too, was probably first conceived as part of a quadrangle, but no other structure was built. The plan of the House itself suggests three semi-detached structures, linked by sharp, corbeled doorways, innovatively used to open cross-corbel vaults within. The greater breadth of the central doorway and the uneven spacing of the flanking doorways (all of post-and-lintel construction), as first attempted in the east and west Nunnery buildings, alleviate the monotony that would result from even

156 The Nunnery Quadrangle at Uxmal.

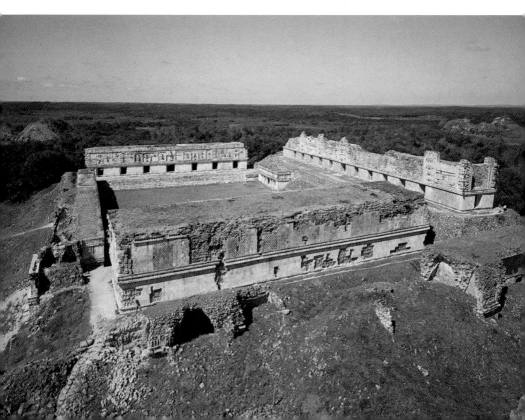

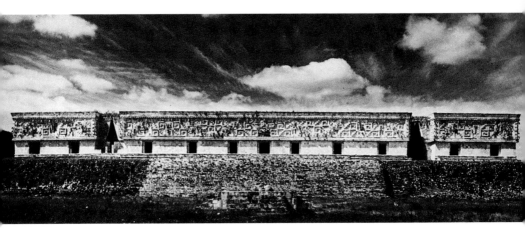

157 The House of the Governor, Uxmal. Built to commemorate the tenth-century reign of the last important ruler of Uxmal, Lord Chahk, this is one of the most elegant and beautifully proportioned structures of ancient Mesoamerica.

breadth and spacing, and the two pointed, recessed corbels vanish from view at sharp angles. The slight outward lean, or negative batter, of the structure gives it the appearance of lifting off its platform. The upper part of the vertical façade is, like most Puuc buildings, covered with a rich stone mosaic. Such mosaic designs may have been emblematic of certain rituals or certain families,

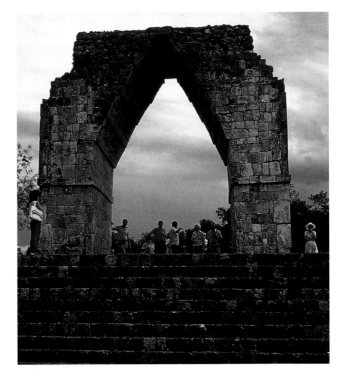

158 The Great Arch, Kabah, is set just at the edge of the city. The massive flight of stairs grants access to the *sacbe* or causeway linking Kabah to Uxmal.

and could be related to textile design. The decoration on the House of the Governor includes many elements: serpents; step frets; netted motifs; Maya thatched houses; and human busts. In the complexity of this ornament, the Uxmal artist seems to have drawn specifically on the east and west buildings of the Nunnery. The ruler of the era, Lord Chahk, presides over the structure, the courtyard, and the range of hills before him from his three-dimensional representation over the central doorway. With its twenty-four rooms, the House of the Governor must have been the greatest administrative structure of its time, overseen by the ruler himself and with ample space to store tribute.

Perhaps the most remarkable feature of nearby Kabah is its monumental, freestanding arch, the only one of its kind [158]. A *sacbe* 7½ miles (12 km) long connects Kabah to Uxmal, and the arch marks the end of the elevated roadway. Unlike European city arches, which either denoted the opening in a wall or commemorated triumph, the arch at Kabah appears simply to proclaim the entrance to the city.

Sculpture

At the beginning of Late Classic times, strong regional styles emerged in monumental Maya sculpture. In the west, particularly at Palenque and Yaxchilan, two or three individuals were represented on a single relief, and the limestone slabs were set as wall panels or lintels, protected from the elements. Conservatism, on the other hand, generally prevailed at Tikal and the Central Peten, where stela imagery continued to conform to canons established in the Early Classic; but some innovative forms were introduced, such as carved wooden lintels and small-scale works like carved bones. In the south, an impulse to three-dimensionality transformed the sculpture of Copan, while at Quirigua, monuments of huge proportion were erected.

The Palenque artists selected a very fine-grained limestone, one that could be quarried in thin sheets, for the interior wall panels that record dynastic history. The Palace Tablet commemorates the accession of the second son of Pakal, who became king of Palenque in 9.13.10.6.8, or AD 702 [159]. On the panel, the young king sits between his dead parents, who offer him attributes of kingship: a jade-plated headdress and a shield. The figures are all simply costumed, and one senses that their individual identity, not simply their ritual paraphernalia, ensures their right to dominion. New, seemingly less formal postures

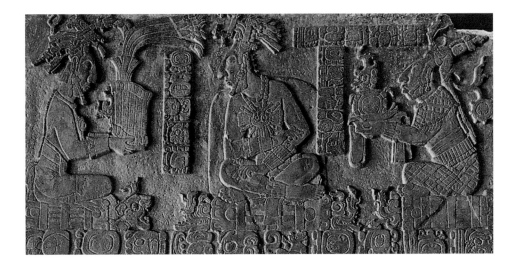

159 The Palace Tablet, Palenque. In commemoration of his accession in the eighth century, Lord K'an Hok' Chitam II was portrayed in the act of receiving the symbols of office from his late parents. Pakal is shown at left, and he holds out a headdress of thin jade squares.

characterize Late Classic Palenque sculpture, and the courtly scenes depicted engage in some fashion with something of the actual life that went on within the Palace chambers where most such sculptures were found.

Technically, the sarcophagus lid of twenty years earlier compares closely to the Palace Tablet, but the imagery of death is couched within the supernatural. The reclining king Pakal, known to have been some eighty years of age at his death, is shown as an idealized youth, and in the guise of two gods, K'awiil, god of royal lineages, indicated by the tube puncturing his forehead, and the Maize God, whose beaded skirt he wears. As the Maize God, Pakal embodies the annual death and renewal of this Mesoamerican staff of life.

A jade mosaic portrait mask was assembled directly onto the dead king's face, without any sort of wooden armature, and two stucco portrait heads were found in the tomb, presumably of Pakal and his wife, whose stern physiognomy may be revealed in the malachite mosaic face of the Red Queen [2]. Many other fine stuccos have been recovered from Palenque. They reveal an interest in recording human physiognomy unparalleled in ancient America.

These fine, sensitive portraits of the ruling family find a foil in the rather gross depictions of subject persons in the East Court. The captives make gestures of submission to the individuals who would have stood above them on the terrace. On these slabs, hands, feet, and faces are crudely worked. Even the stone chosen

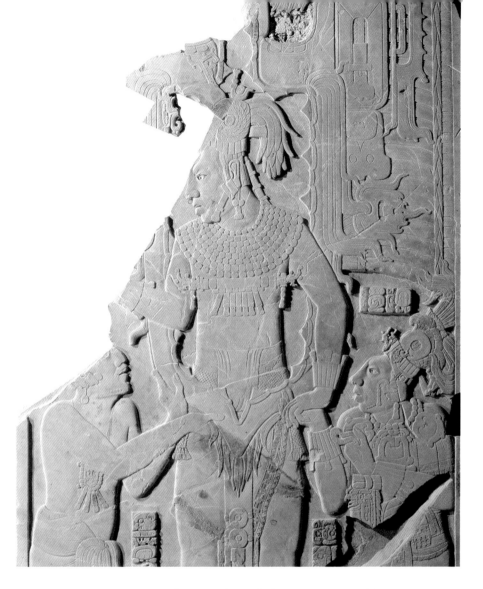

160 The Palenque King Ahk'ul Mo' Naab developed a program just up the slope from his predecessors and featured works where the king acknowledges the fealty of his subjects. Structure 19 has yielded extraordinary sculptures: despite having been smashed in antiquity, this panel retains the eloquence of the sculptor's art.

reflects its subject: the buttery limestone of the accession panels is replaced by porous limestone less suitable for fine carving. Each figure is worked on an independent slab, and the compressed space for each person suggests oppression. The slabs may also have been reused and recut to conform to a new configuration.

For years scholars had puzzled over the seeming gaps in the sculptural record at Palenque, especially following the capture of the Palenque king in 711 by enemies at Tonina, in the highlands to the south. New discoveries by Mexican archaeologists from the

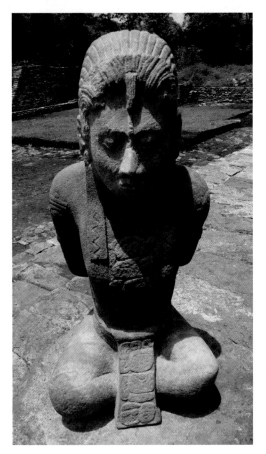

first half of the eighth century, a period until recently thought to be a sculptural drought, have revealed that King Ahk'ul Mo' Naab's programs – Structures 19, 21, and 22 – included some of the most stunning work achieved at the site. A limestone panel from Temple 19 shows the king pressing the hand of an attendant to his right, capturing the sensual charge in the soft sculpting of the stone [160]. The foreshortened torsos and the carved drapery of the two attendants reveal the ability of Maya artists to master the body while confining it to a minimal and fine relief. Additional discoveries at Tonina reveal continued attention to the representation of both two-dimensional and three-dimensional captives, which may have been assembled into a frieze, and which attest to the bellicose practices of the site across generations [161].

Above:
161 One of a pair of captives discovered at Tonina in 2011 in the great ballcourt, this larger-than-life figure exhibits the stoic beauty of Maize God physiognomy. Like many captive figures at Tonina, this pair celebrates the site's victory over Palenque and its environs.

Opposite:
162 Lintel 25, Yaxchilan. Lady Xok', wife of Shield Jaguar, kneels to receive a vision: a warrior, bearing a shield in hand and wearing a Tlaloc mask in 'X-ray,' emerges from a serpent mouth. The rich drapery of the woman's garment is piled at her knees. The bloodletting tools that brought on this vision lie in a basket at her feet.

Often integrated with the architecture of Yaxchilan in the form of lintels or steps, the finest sculptures display a regional style in which relief was executed on two distinct and removed planes. The resulting high relief brings the figures to life, with glyphs as framing devices that suggest architecture. On Stela 11, the figures stand inside a corbeled vault [163]; on Lintel 25, Lady Xok' kneels in the rear chamber of a structure [162]. Rituals associated with royalty were often recorded on Yaxchilan monuments: capture, sacrifice, autosacrifice, and visions of ancestors – all of which may derive from royal manuscripts. Many women are depicted too; the richly garbed Lady Xok' on Lintel 25 receives the vision of a warrior who appears in the mouth of a great serpent amid plumes of smoke. Traces of red, green, and yellow polychrome remain on this and other Yaxchilan lintels, confirming what is supposed of most Maya sculptures – that they were once brilliantly painted.

On Stela 11, in the guise of Chahk, the great king Bird Jaguar stands over three bound captives, prepared to carry out sacrifice [163]. Bird Jaguar's cutaway mask recalls the Oxtotitlan painting of Olmec times, but the conceit particularly characterizes Late

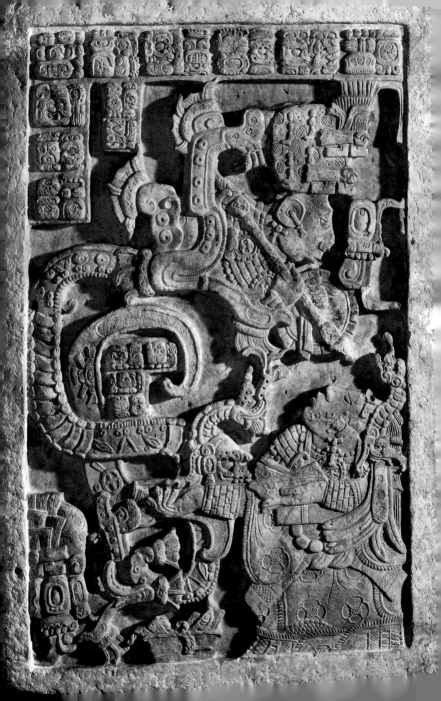

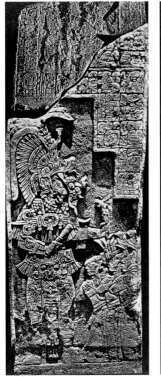
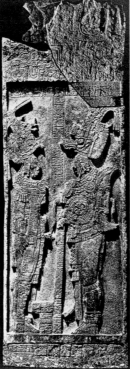

Classic Maya warriors. The dead parents of the ruler sit above, separated from the scene by a skyband, indicating their posthumous place in the heavens. Whether presiding over a scene or flanking it, as at Palenque, venerated parents were frequently recorded, as if to confer legitimacy on a descendant.

The obverse of Stela 11 shows the accession of Bird Jaguar, an event supported by the military success on the other side. Stela 11 and Lintel 25 were probably carved by a small atelier of sculptors whose work spanned two generations of rule. Subsequent sculptors emulated their craft, but none equaled it.

The Yaxchilan artists also pioneered the introduction of new, active postures into normally staid stone sculpture. Lintel 8, for example, shows Bird Jaguar and another lord grasping the hair of some captives, who bear their names emblazoned on their thighs. Such dynamic compositions ultimately culminate in the paintings of Bonampak. As Tatiana Proskouriakoff pointed out over forty years ago, Teotihuacan-inspired Tlaloc motifs adorn the victors here, and throughout Late Classic art the Tlaloc costume appears in scenes of warfare and sacrifice, as can also be seen on Lintel 25. Although Teotihuacan's power had waned generations before, its imagery returned to empower a new generation.

A higher relief distinguishes the sculpture of Piedras Negras. Here special attention was given to human faces. Characteristic of Piedras Negras is the near three-dimensionality granted the ruler's frontal face, especially on the handsome niche stelae. These monuments commemorated the accession to office of the various Piedras Negras rulers. On Stela 14, the young lord's tangible three-dimensionality plays against his mother's flat two-dimensional representation [164]. Footprints mark the cloth

163 Stela 11, Yaxchilan. On the rear of the stela (shown at left), Bird Jaguar, in an 'X-ray' costume of Chahk, prepares to sacrifice three captives who kneel in a doorway. The obverse shows Bird Jaguar (standing on the right) with his father. Mid-eighth century AD.

draping the scaffold or ladder set in front of the niche, and swag curtains are pulled back at the top of it, as if the scene has just been revealed.

At the destruction of the site, enemies of the Piedras Negras dynasty smashed Throne 1 on the steps of the West Acropolis palace, where it remained for archaeologists to retrieve in the 1930s. Made at the end of the eighth century, the carving replaced an earlier throne figured on Lintel 3, another late carving, but whose subject treats détente with Yaxchilan a half century earlier. Along with Stela 12, these late eighth-century sculptures are among the most dazzling of Late Classic efforts and their workmanship runs counter to an identification of artistic decline coupled with societal collapse.

Twelve individuals are grouped on four levels, probably steps, in a pyramidal composition on Stela 12 [165]. Eight captives are tied together in the lower register, and many show signs of torture.

Two captains deliver the well-dressed, uppermost captive seated on draped cloth to the lord above. The text records a war event, and we see its aftermath: victorious Piedras Negras displaying its trophies. Interestingly, the named victims may be from Pomona, a defeated site known for its fine, Palenque-like carvings; the workmanship of this monument resembles that style, not the more three-dimensional style with frontal faces of Piedras Negras. Artistic tribute may have been an aspect of elite warfare, and captives at other sites – including Tonina and probably Bonampak – were worked in the manner of their place of origin.

Static, single-figure compositions prevailed in the Central Peten throughout the eighth century, conforming in

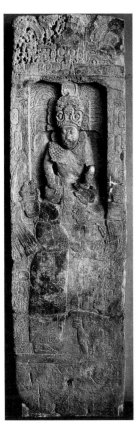
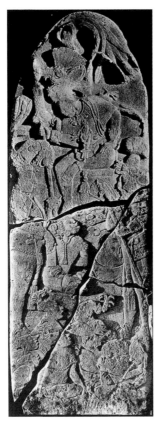

some instances to canons established earlier. At Tikal, the texts on stone monuments were also laconic, unlike most monuments of the western region. Stela 16 presents a formal, frontal view of Hasaw Chan K'awiil (Ruler A), the king later buried in Temple I [166]. Less public sculptures, such as the carved sapodilla-wood lintels of Temples I, II, and IV, display more complicated imagery and texts. The two lintels of Temple IV show Ruler B within a supernatural world. One depicts him being borne on a litter and enthroned under an overarching feathered serpent [167]. On the other, he sits enthroned over a flight of steps marked with symbols of rope and the main sign of the glyph emblematic of the site of Naranjo. A giant, anthropomorphic Jaguar God of the Underworld forms an architectural frame over the ruler. Graffiti at the site depict litters in action, as they parade rulers on plazas.

At Naranjo, many monuments depict female dynasts, and the woman on Stela 24 stands over a humiliated captive. The cramped space of the lower register heightens the abject state of the prisoner. In two-dimensional carvings, frontal faces were generally reserved for captives.

In the eighth century, sculpture at southeastern Maya sites moved from mere frontality to a near three-dimensionality. At Copan, larger-than-life portraits of standing rulers were carved nearly in the round. As at Tikal, many stelae were erected on the Great Plaza. By the reign of Yax Pasaw, the open space was heavily populated by royal ancestors. During his reign, however, there was also a return to two-dimensional works, perhaps reintroduced by his mother, a woman from Palenque. Carved steps, benches, and altars record numerous seated two-dimensional figures in profile. Altar Q, long misread as a gathering of astronomers, actually shows the

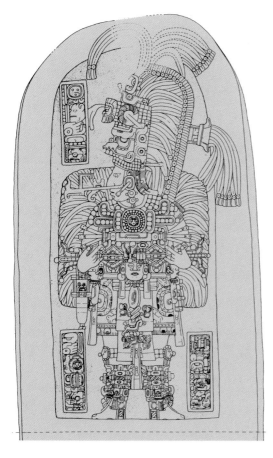

166 Stela 16, Tikal. On this stone monument erected to celebrate the *katun*, or twenty-year period, Ruler A holds a ceremonial bar and wears a great feather backframe. Note the hand gesture of the king and its glyphic analogue in the text.

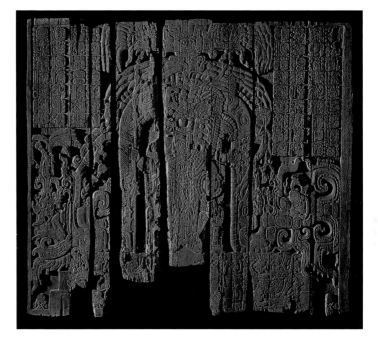

167 Lintel 3, Temple IV, Tikal. Ruler B is borne high on a litter in this depiction – tied beams can be seen at lower right and left. The sapodilla wood of which the lintel is made is about 1,200 years old.

sixteen rulers of the city, all seated on their names, at the end of the eighth century [168]. The ruler, at center right, receives authority to rule from the first, at center left, whose goggle mask indicates his antiquity.

During the reign of K'ak' Tiliw Chan Yopaat (also known as Kawak Sky), nearby Quirigua grew wealthy, and according to the inscriptions this monarch captured the ruler at Copan, often called 18 Rabbit. K'ak' Tiliw Chan Yopaat was celebrated with a series of stelae, among them Stelae E and F, the tallest stone carvings of the ancient Maya [169]. K'ak' Tiliw Chan Yopaat's face is worked in high relief, but the rest of his features are shown in two dimensions. Like their counterparts in tuff at Copan, these great prismatic shafts of sandstone were laid out in the clear expanse of the open plaza.

Later rulers at Quirigua developed one of the most innovative types of Maya sculpture, the zoomorph. Huge river boulders were carved on all exposed surfaces as great composite jaguar, toad, crocodile, or bird forms. On Zoomorph P [170], a ruler emerges from a gaping front maw as if set within supernatural architecture of the sort created in Structure 22, Copan. Elaborate full-figure personifications of hieroglyphs were often inscribed on these

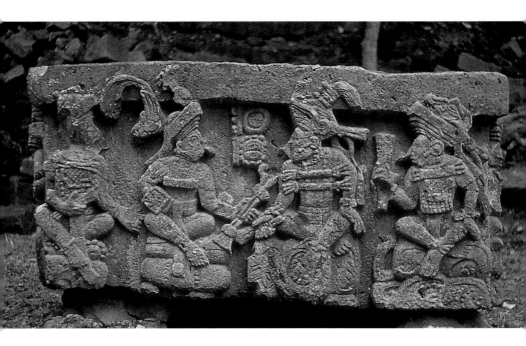

Above:
168 On the front of Copan Altar Q, the first king (wearing goggles at left), Yax K'uk Mo', faces Yax Pasaw, the sixteenth, while the fourteen interposing monarchs line the monument. The nineteenth-century traveler, John Lloyd Stephens, had proposed that these figures are shown sitting on their names, an interpretation finally confirmed in recent years.

Right:
169 Stela F, Quirigua. The tallest Maya monuments were erected at Quirigua, during the reign of Cauac Sky – depicted here – who bested the Copan king in an early eighth-century battle. Most such stelae were double portraits, carved both front and back.

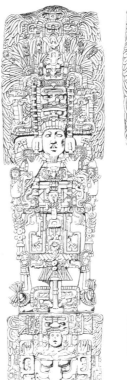
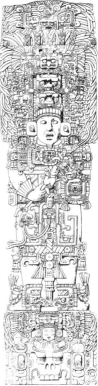

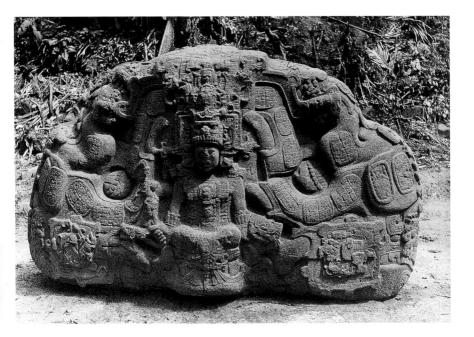

170 Zoomorph P, Quirigua. One of the latest known rulers of Quirigua sits within the open maw of a great monster on this carved river boulder.

great boulders as well, turning script into narrative sculpture. The unprecedented size of Quirigua sculpture commands attention, but it also disturbs, feeling quite out of balance to the modest architectural program.

Hand-held sculpture

Most fine Maya objects of small scale have been recovered from royal burials, and many carry information relating to the life or afterlife of a given individual. The jade-mosaic jar from Ruler A's tomb at Tikal, for example, is probably a portrait of a dead member of the royal family [171]. Jade-plated vessels of this sort are known only from Tikal, and the type is conservative, retaining Early Classic characteristics, such as the knob in the form of a human head. At Altun Ha, a ruler was interred with a 9.7 lb (4.42 kg), three-dimensional carved jade head, an unusual representation of the Principal Bird Deity. Its shape suggests a miniature zoomorph. Fine jade plaques showing rulers accompanied by dwarves have been recovered from Nebaj, in the Guatemalan highlands, perhaps a place of manufacture and not too far from the source of the raw material, but they have also been found far from the Maya region [172].

A number of incised bones (some human) were deposited as a single cache in Ruler A's funerary chamber, the scenes on some of

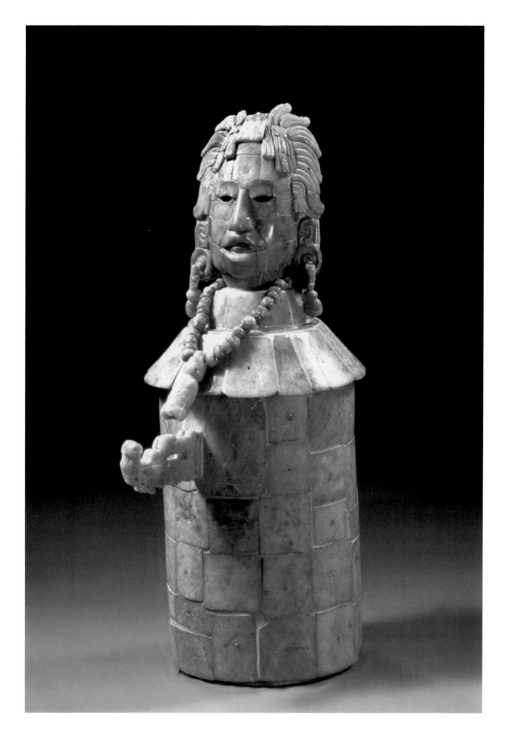

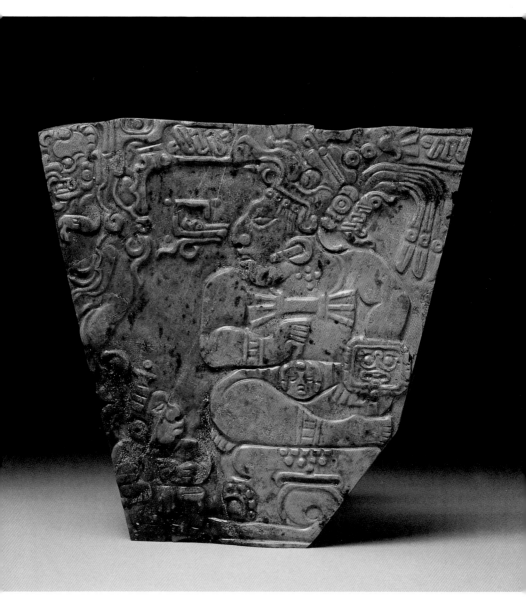

them illustrating what we can presume to be the posthumous journey. On one pair of bones the artist delicately incised and then filled with cinnabar a drawing showing the king as Maize God, the deified ideal of both rulership and renewal, in a canoe, being paddled to the underworld in the company of howling animals. In a gesture of woe, he raises his hand to his brow [173].

Flint and obsidian were worked by Maya craftsmen into many shapes, and these are generally termed 'eccentrics' [174]. Some of the eccentric flints, such as the many examples that reveal the profile of K'awiil, might have been scepters carried by a lord. Others were perhaps designed as funerary offerings. An extraordinary example in the Dallas Museum of Art shows a crocodile with human figures on its back, and it may illustrate a concept of the afterlife.

Figurines

For many years, figurines and shell carvings of high quality have been found on Jaina Island, just off the Campeche coast [175]. The island may have functioned as a necropolis, and people of the Late Classic interred huge numbers of offerings there. Conch was a common material, sometimes ornamented with inlay. Figurines must have been manufactured nearby: hundreds and hundreds are known from the island itself. Most were made in molds, but the finest were modeled by hand, at least in part, and small human fingerprints are often visible (suggesting to some that women made these objects). Tenacious pigments were used on the finished figures, especially blue, white, and yellow. Many Jaina figurines also function as whistles, ocarinas, or rattles. Women are more common subjects among the figurines than in monumental art.

Some known supernatural beings depicted among the figurines, such as the Jaguar God of the Underworld, can be seen on painted ceramics too, but perplexing and possibly humorous scenes such as a young woman embracing an old man are known only from the repertoire of this small island [176]. Even more lifelike ceramic sculptures have been found recently at Río Azul and Palenque. Few figurine cults in the world have produced such animated, compelling human miniatures as has this Maya tradition, now amplified by recent discoveries at Waka': archaeologists there have discovered a grouping of figurines that sat at the feet of a deceased ruler to guide him into the next world, along with an extraordinary Olmec figurine, further testimony of engagement with the past [177].

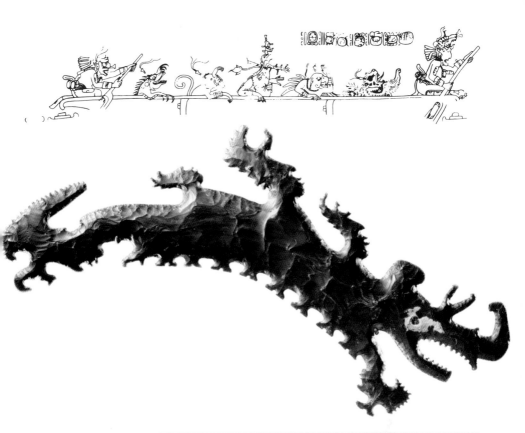

173 Many finely carved bones – some of them human – were recovered from a single deposit in Ruler A's tomb at Tikal. On this one, paddlers guide a canoe and its occupants through underworld waters.

174 To make this eccentric flint, stone was flaked away leaving a design in silhouette. A great crocodile bears Maya lords into the underworld, an image similar to that of ill. 173.

175 Carved shell, Jaina Island. Along the Campeche coast, where the material abounded, conch was cut and carved into fine objects. Here a Maya lord seems to ride a fish monster. The piece may once have been inlaid with precious greenstone.

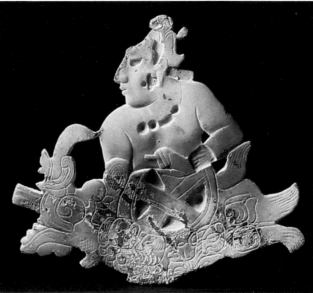

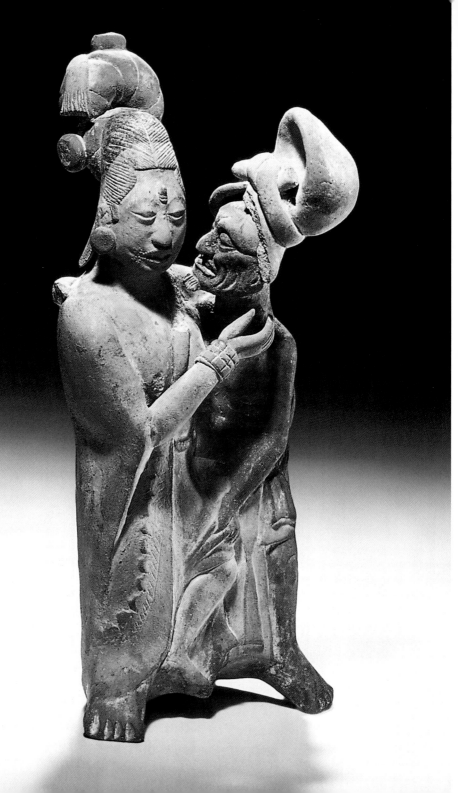

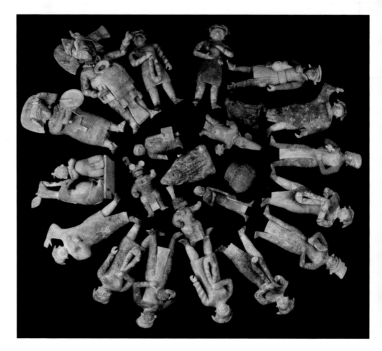

Ceramics

Many of the scenes painted on Maya narrative polychrome pottery elaborate a supernatural world, one the Maya themselves entered through states of altered consciousness. Most once held a chocolate drink [179]. Some scenes occur without regard for geography or chronology, while other nevertheless standard narrations were made only in a single style. Some mythic scenes probably prescribed behavior for success in conquering the underworld, a theme later recounted in the Postconquest manuscript, the *Popol Vuh*. Painted in a fine black or brown line over a cream slip, frequently with a red rim band, such pots may have derived from lost Maya books, which has led Michael Coe to christen the tradition the 'codex' style [178]. The color scheme itself, red and black, was the much later metaphor used by the Aztecs to mean writing itself. Several schools and master painters of this style have been identified, but a common theme celebrates the sacrifice of a baby jaguar by a dancing death god and Chahk, sometimes with a dog and firefly looking on.

On a vase from Altar de Sacrificios, a site at the confluence of the Pasión and Usumacinta Rivers, a red rim and highlights have been added to a codex-style painting [179]. The scene depicts dancers in shamanic transformation. Adjacent texts name these

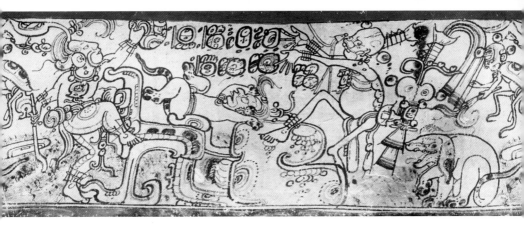

figures as *wayob*, or shamanic other selves, many of whom may be dangerous and even maleficent spirits. One wears snake-patterned trousers, and as he hurls a boa constrictor into the air, he throws back his head, closes his eyes, and presses his hand right through the glyphic border. Particularly in the eighth century, Maya vase painting is self-conscious and theatrical, sophisticated in a way never matched elsewhere in the prehispanic New World.

Other regional vase painting styles can also be identified. In the region of Naranjo, a monochrome red-on-cream style predominated. The western Peten may be the source of the 'pink-glyph' style, in which rose tones were used and figures depicted in cutaway, X-ray fashion. Carved gray slateware was characteristic of northern Yucatan. In highland Guatemala, potters generally included red backgrounds and painted the rim bands with chevron motifs. In Honduras, vases were carved from marble, perhaps by non-Maya of the Ulua Valley, and these were acquired by noble Maya. By the ninth century, a new kind of pottery appeared in many parts of the Maya lowlands, and the iconography of these modeled and carved fine-orange vessels, some of which are mass produced using molds, differs from the earlier painted ones, perhaps to be associated with new people or new trading patterns.

Painting

Fragments of polychrome paintings were uncovered periodically throughout the western Maya region in the late nineteenth and early twentieth centuries, particularly in the vicinity of Yaxchilan. Then, in 1946, Giles Healey stumbled upon a miraculously well-preserved sequence of Late Classic Maya wall paintings at the site now known as Bonampak, not far from the Lacanha River, a tributary of the Usumacinta. The preservation of the paintings was

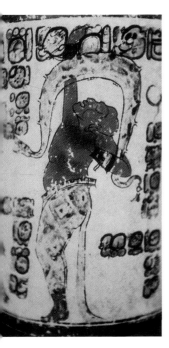

Above:
179 Excavated at Altar de Sacrificios, this ceramic vessel depicts shamanic transformation by the bald dancer, who flings back his head and dances with a boa constrictor. The rim text of most cylinders indicates their use as vessels for a spicy chocolate beverage.

a fluke: shortly after their completion in the late eighth century, water seeped through the poorly made limestone vault, building a layer of calcifications that encased the fragile paint.

In Structure 1, the vaults, walls, benches, and door jambs of the three rooms had all been painted in bright colors on damp stucco. Hundreds of Maya are depicted in a unified work celebrating the festivities and bloodshed of the last major dynastic rituals at Bonampak in AD 790. On three walls of Room 1, nobles in white mantles present tribute to the royal family while three young lords dance at the court's center with musicians and performers contributing to a great celebration. Central to both the program and to Maya kingship is the great battle of Room 2, which might have taken place some time in the past, when King Yahaw Chaan Muwan was at the height of his powers. The battle covers three walls of Room 2. On the north wall, in a scene that encompasses the open doorway, sacrificial victims are displayed on the steps [181].

New paintings have come to light at Calakmul that probably pre-date Bonampak, although their date remains uncertain. Designed as exterior works, simple panels with one or two individuals at very large scale stud a structure at the center of an open plaza, perhaps once the location of a great market. Here we see the Maya artist in easy mastery of the human form, the weight of the heavy *olla* shifting to the woman at left. She has also absorbed the weight of color in the scene: her blue dress and adornments dazzle in the scene, juxtaposing her wealth with the mousy gray dress of the servant or slave in front of her, yet both conform to the convention in which only women wear body paint on the face. Not only color but the absence of transparency may indicate the lower status of the servant woman, indicating the very coarseness of the cloth she wears. The larger woman speaks, her mouth slightly parted to reveal teeth, rarely shown except by captives in Maya art; a distinctive red line outlines her lips.

In the Calakmul painting [183], the artist follows traditions known to both the painter of ceramics and the muralist; the flat, grasping hands so typical of ceramic painters can be juxtaposed with the fleshy hands of the male attendant at right, which are drawn in ways that relate to late Yaxchilan sculptures; the gauzy blue cloth, with its intentional transparency that reveals the voluptuous female body at left shares commonalities with the group of enthroned women in Bonampak Room 3, but here, the artist has paid particular attention to the breast, right down to the nipple, along with the soft curves of her torso. In short, the painter

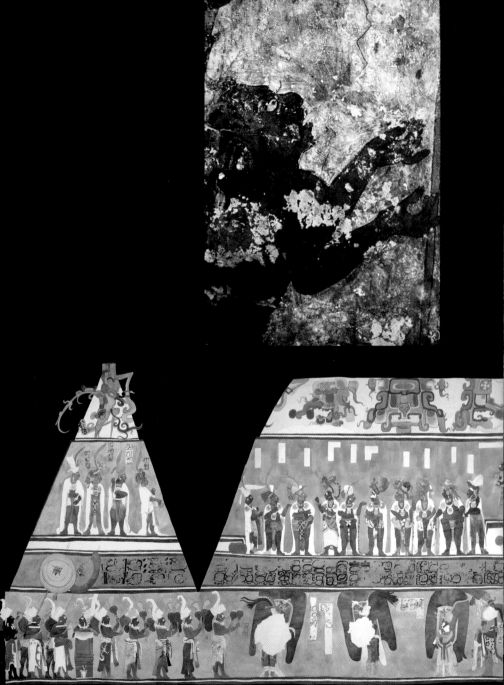

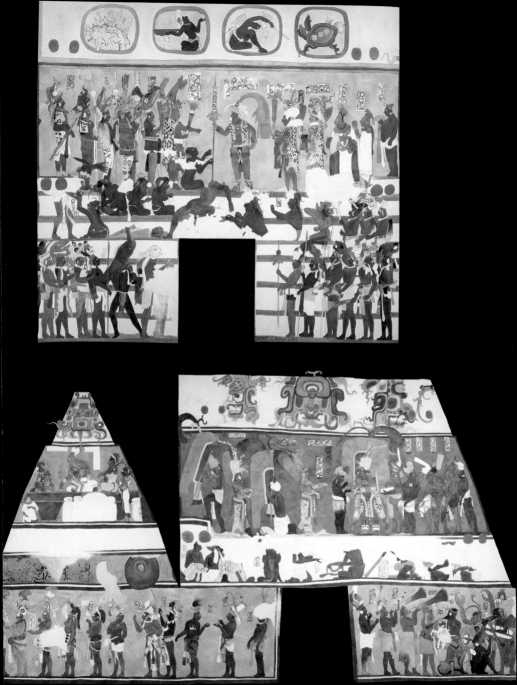

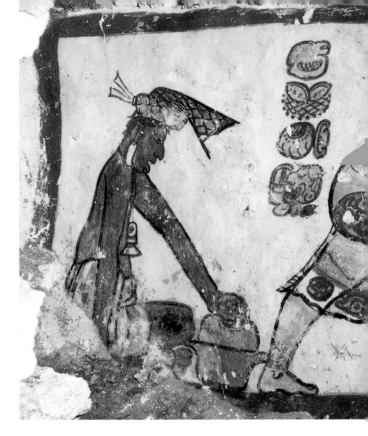

183 Like a Maya pot, this painting at Calakmul is framed by a red border. Rarely does a Maya woman dominate a scene the way this powerful lady in blue does.

reveals himself to be a master of convention, revealed in the familiar representations of hands and feet, but also perhaps a comfortable innovator, especially in the rendering of the woman in blue.

The end of the Classic Maya

The momentum of Maya civilization began to slacken and falter in the late eighth and ninth centuries. Stone monuments ceased to be erected from as early as AD 760 in certain areas, and gradually whole cities were abandoned. At many sites there is evidence of violence: at Piedras Negras, for example, monuments were dragged out of buildings and smashed. At Palenque and Copan, the ritual paraphernalia of the Veracruz ballgame were left by late visitors, or possibly ravaging invaders. Tikal seems to have suffered a slower depopulation. Fine orange ceramics appeared at many sites. By about AD 900, perhaps slightly later in the north, Maya civilization had collapsed.

For the ancient Maya, blood and blood sacrifice were the mortar of dynastic life, and sacrifice accompanied the rituals of

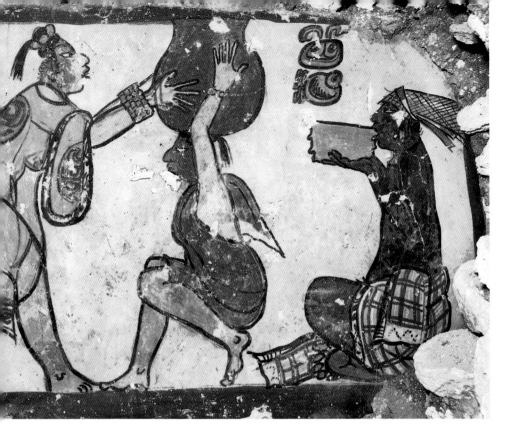

office. At the end of the first millennium AD, however, there is
evidence that the pattern of capture and sacrifice gave way
to warfare and dominion. The latest Yaxchilan monuments
enumerate battle after battle; the final monument at Piedras
Negras is Stela 12, where the booty of battle is laid at the ruler's
feet. The Bonampak murals were never completed, and we can
deduce that the elite perished in a battle like that painted in Room
2. Archaeologists have sought the explanation for the Maya
collapse in buried material remains (did their food supply change?
Was there devastating drought? What happened to the soils?), but
the art and inscriptions relate the Maya's own last record of life
around AD 800, and that record is of warfare. Warfare was the
process, if not the cause, of the Maya collapse that the Maya
themselves chose to record.

Chapter 8   Mesoamerica after the fall of Classic cities

The Maya collapse was a gradual affair, affecting Maya cities at a far from uniform rate. Some well-known centers, such as Palenque, abandoned the time-honored practice of raising stone monuments well before neighbors such as Tonina did so, while a large city such as Tikal continued with limited ceremonial activities for a considerable time. The earlier burning and destruction of Teotihuacan, on the other hand, had marked a dramatic cessation in both the maintenance and the centralized, public use of the Way of the Dead and the major temples there, even if residential quarters remained occupied. Meanwhile, in Oaxaca, when Monte Alban was abandoned other more fragmented centers of population grew up to take its place. By and large, wealthy centers gave way to impoverished ones.

During this period of widespread disruption of cities across Mesoamerica, their characteristic features did not disappear suddenly, nor was all knowledge of the past lost. At the time of the Spanish invasion, for example, the Maya still wrote in a phonetic, hieroglyphic script probably perfected a thousand years earlier, and had a literate Maya of the 1500s seen a monument of 740, he could have read and understood it.

Nevertheless, the turmoil of the late first millennium AD led many Mesoamerican peoples to uproot themselves and form new alliances or move to new territories. 'Foreign' influences can be observed in many places during the Terminal Classic (generally considered to be the ninth century). Maya appeared in Central Mexico and Mexicans among the Maya. It was a time of seemingly unprecedented inter-regional contact, best seen today in the rise and fall of two cities, Tula in Central Mexico and Chichen Itza in Yucatan, both built in a cross-pollinated Maya-Mexican style during the Early Postclassic and probably at their height around AD 1000. Problematically, the current time frames established by archaeologists leave unresolved the twelfth and thirteenth centuries. Yet friezes at Chichen Itza closely resemble those of later Tenochtitlan, executed as if there were no cultural gap, so clearly the unsettled chronology requires additional attention. During the Late Postclassic the Aztecs ruthlessly exploited the weaknesses of their neighbors in order to gain dominion over the whole of Central Mexico, and their civilization will be considered in Chapter Nine. The Maya of the Late Postclassic, however, show neither the innovation nor the craftsmanship of their Aztec contemporaries. Their art drew upon earlier models, and will be discussed at the close of this chapter, in conjunction with Chichen Itza, the strongest influence on the later Maya.

One important marker used by archaeologists to chronicle change is pottery, and among elite wares there was a shift in styles and clays about AD 800 at several Maya sites. Following the precedent established in the pottery of north Yucatan, designs were now modeled and carved, rather than painted – color was no longer an element in fired slip, although colorful stucco painting did continue, especially on perishable materials, including gourd vessels, at Chichen Itza. Some designs appear to have been stamped out, or mass-produced. Even the clay used to make the vessels ceased to be local, and most scholars believe it to be of Gulf Coast origin, suggesting a foreign presence. Likewise, what we find in the art and architecture of the Maya city of Seibal argues for a Central Mexican or Gulf Coast infusion there about this time.

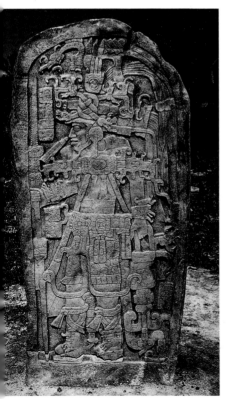

184 Stela 1, Seibal. During the ninth century, new rulers – perhaps the Itza – came to power at Seibal, adopting the traditional stela format but infusing it with new vigor, particularly in respect to portraiture.

Seibal

The later buildings of Seibal exhibit a new architectural style. A great round platform was erected at the site, a rare feature in Mesoamerican, and particularly Maya, architecture. Round structures in use at the time of the Conquest were generally associated with the Central Mexican deity, Quetzalcoatl, and – as we shall see – his cult was beginning to take root. Moreover, a new large radial pyramid at Seibal would seem to recall the unusual forms of Uaxactun E-VII-sub or the radial pyramids of Tikal's Twin Pyramid Complexes.

A stela was set at the base of each staircase of the Seibal radial structure, each commemorating the date 10.1.0.0.0 (AD 849), as if that were a momentous year. One names lords of four separate polities, Tikal, Calakmul, San José de Motul, and Seibal itself, an attempt to draw on ancient lineages to sustain ritual practices. Most striking of all is the distinctive physiognomy depicted on Seibal monuments. Stela 1, AD 869, for example, shows a new kind of portraiture [184]. The ruler's face is not idealized, and the strong, slightly downturned lip suggests both harshness and the hint of a smile. Many Seibal portraits show neither forehead deformation nor the extended bridge of the nose typical of most ancient Maya. Are the men the foreigners who left ballgame equipment at Palenque and Copan? Or have the Maya simply absorbed and articulated foreign fashions once again?

On yet later monuments, both inscriptions and costume change. On Stela 3, for example, a date is recorded in a non-Maya script, and one of the glyphs used is a *cipactli*, or crocodile head, the first day name of the 260-day calendar in most Central Mexican systems. On this same monument, individuals are shown with long, flowing hair and trimmed bangs, rarely revealed by earlier Maya in full dress. On other monuments, traditional Maya imagery appears in odd configurations, as if not understood clearly by the elite artist at Seibal.

Cacaxtla and Xochicalco

It is perhaps too tidy a solution to attribute contemporary developments further north to the same people who dominated Seibal, but powerful cosmopolitan, particularly Maya, influences undoubtedly made themselves felt at Cacaxtla and Xochicalco in Central Mexico at this time.

In 1975, a local schoolteacher led Mexican archaeologists to well-preserved, beautifully executed paintings in what seems to be Maya style at Cacaxtla, Tlaxcala, a hilltop acropolis. One set of paintings had even been packed with fine sand by the ancient inhabitants to help preserve the stucco paint. In Structure A, the doorway is flanked by two stela-like portraits, one showing a standing Maya in bird costume [186]; the other, a Maya in a full jaguar suit. The man in the bird costume and black body paint may be the Terminal Classic prototype of the later Aztec Eagle Knight, but the naturalistic proportions, skilled painting, and attention to both costume details and the human face reveal deep familiarity with Maya style, while the shape of forehead and nose point to the recognition of different ethnicities, perhaps Maya here, of the subject. Other influences are evident as well: borders show Teotihuacan motifs, and the glyphic style is not yet identified. Yet as a whole it is both something coherent and highly local, known only at Cacaxtla.

A second, nearly complete set of paintings framing a staircase features warriors with Central Mexican profiles in jaguar suits and

185 In the battle mural at Cacaxtla, a victorious warrior demonstrates sober concentration.

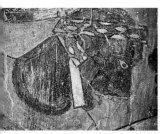

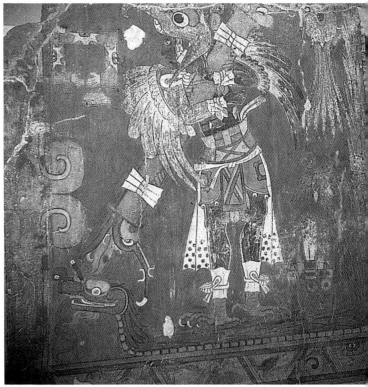

186 Stucco painting of a man in a bird suit, Structure A, Cacaxtla, AD 700–900. Like a Mesoamerican Daedalus, this handsome young warrior in black body paint wears a full bird suit, from headdress to wings to feet.

adorned with the iconography of human sacrifice [185]. They attack, defeat, dismember, and even disembowel warriors with Maya profiles who wear bird suits and lavish textiles, and at least two of the Maya figures may be women wearing upper body garments. The naturalistic representation of spurting blood and spilling entrails derives from a Maya canon of representation, but the subject matter may have troubled those who saw it: within a few short years it was covered over and hidden from sight until the twentieth century. Did Maya forays into Central Mexico result in grinding tribute payments and outright defeat? In the Red Temple, other fragments of paintings have been found that may record an economic reality: God L, the Maya patron of commerce, is depicted with his overstuffed trading pack along a staircase that records both particular victories and emaciated human captives at its foot, juxtaposing luxury with degradation [187]. The rich blue pigments and the quality of line of the paintings correspond to those of Bonampak [180, 181, 182], and they may have been painted around the same time, c. AD 800.

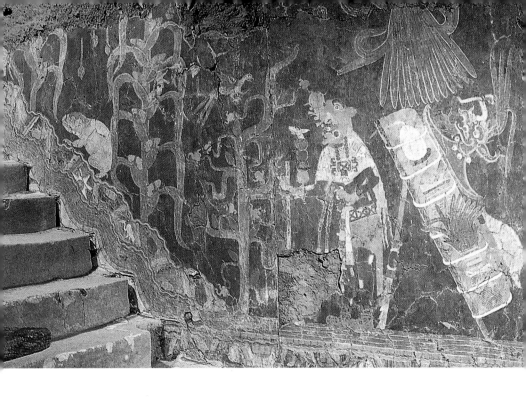

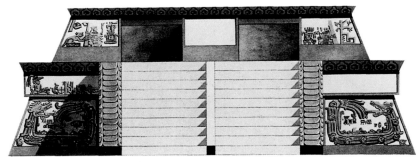

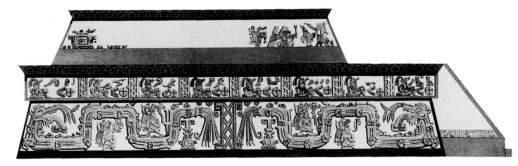

Some 80 miles (130 km) to the southwest of Cacaxtla lies Xochicalco, a contemporary hilltop acropolis high above the Valley of Cuernavaca. Cosmopolitan influences abound here as well, and are particularly evident on the Pyramid of the Feathered Serpent [188]. Seated figures of Maya proportion, in Maya pose and dress, are carved among the undulations of great feathered serpents, or literally, Quetzalcoatl, while shell sections define an aquatic environment like those of Teotihuacan's Temple of Quetzalcoatl. The sculptors executed glyphic notations using an idiosyncratic system that features numerous unidentified placenames, possibly indicating political consolidation or a sort of council house, what to the Maya would be a *popol na*, like the one constructed at Copan [150]. They also gave the images a double outline, a technique characteristic of Veracruz art, particularly at El Tajin.

A large, graceful ballcourt similar to that of Copan was situated at the heart of the site, adjacent to what were probably palace chambers. Other connections with the Maya are seen on the three stelae excavated at Xochicalco. One shows the goggle-eyed and fanged face of Tlaloc, but the two others depict a strikingly three-dimensional human face, set within a helmet, framed by a more two-dimensional calendar sign above and skyband below. These stelae show resemblances to the 'niche' stelae of Piedras Negras, on which enthroned, three-dimensional rulers are portrayed within two-dimensional skyband borders, in scenes commemorating rulership [164]. The works of art at both Cacaxtla and Xochicalco suggest that elites throughout Mesoamerica may have retreated to isolated sites like these, where they left a new, hybridized material culture.

187 God L, a Maya god of trade and tribute, stands atop a stream of bounty. Ahead of him grows first a cacao, or chocolate tree; up the stairs a plant sprouts abundant ears of ripe maize.

188 At Xochicalco, Adela Breton recorded feathered serpents and seated lords. Above the serpents, the *tablero* records a series of glyphs, perhaps the names of places who paid tribute to the hilltop power.

Mitla

The abandonment of cities in Central Mexico and the Maya area was paralleled in Oaxaca by the end of Monte Alban's long reign as the main city of the region, although the mountain continued to serve as a place of ritual activity and pilgrimage even after permanent occupation ceased. Instead, other Zapotec centers grew in the surrounding valleys, particularly to the south. Large, elegant palace complexes were constructed at both Yagul and Mitla, for instance.

The palaces at Mitla have long been admired for their elegant proportion and ornament. Courtyards with both interlocking and open corners are arranged along a general north-south axis.

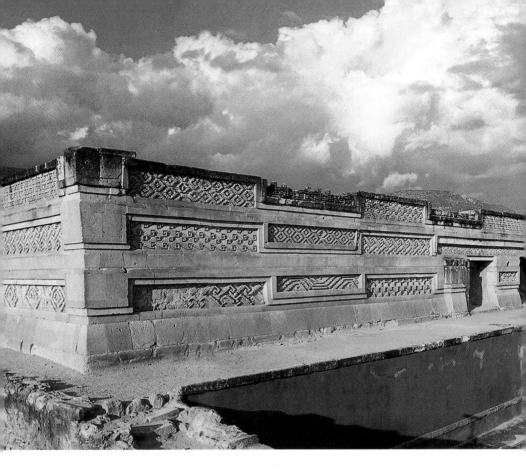

189 Hall of the Columns, Mitla. This graceful building grants entry to private quadrangles within. Columns inside this building once supported a perishable roof.

In Colonial times the townspeople built a church into the northernmost quadrangle and established a chapel on the summit of a large mound southwest of the palaces, thus transforming the ancient ruins into modern holy places.

The Group of the Columns, Quadrangles D–E, is the largest of the palace compounds and the most refined in proportion. Quadrangle E consists of four galleried buildings arranged around the sides of a plaza with open corners, while its northern building, the Hall of the Columns, provides the only access to D, a smaller, fully-enclosed quadrangle, maze-like in its plan. The Hall of the Columns is the most beautiful of Mitla structures [189]. Like the House of the Governor at Uxmal (its contemporary) [157], the building has a subtle outward lean, which visually alleviates the weight of its overhanging moldings, similar to those at Monte Alban.

The façades of Mitla buildings shimmer in the clear sunlight of Oaxaca. Geometric mosaics in a variety of designs and composed

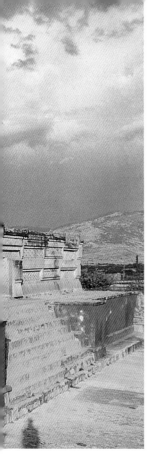

of individual veneer stones are set in rectangles across the exterior walls. In the private chambers of Quadrangle D the interiors are also cast with intricate patterns, quite conceivably replicating in stone fabrics that had once hung within palace rooms. The designs may refer to various family lineages, perhaps derived from woven textile patterns specific to group or place.

The Huastecs

At the very beginning of the Early Postclassic a regional style flourished in north Veracruz, among the Huastecs. This Mesoamerican group is related by language to the Maya, but generations of separate evolution led to a distinct artistic expression. Particular emphasis in the Huasteca (as the region is known) was given to the cult of Quetzalcoatl, and as we shall see this was also true at Tula and Chichen Itza. Circular buildings dedicated to Quetzalcoatl are found at small sites throughout the region.

Characteristic of Huastec sculptures are prismatic yet slab-like three-dimensional works. These have been called 'apotheosis' sculptures because of their dual imagery [190]. A life-sized human figure is worked on the front of the monument, while a smaller image appears on the back – sometimes an infant, borne as if in a

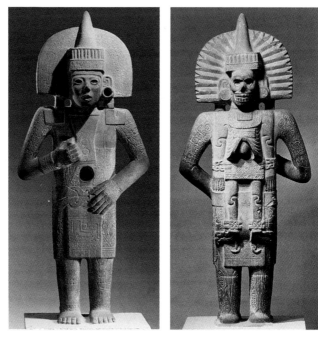

190 A so-called 'apotheosis' sculpture, Huastec culture (Early Postclassic). The strong three-dimensional quality of Huastec stone sculpture may be related to works at El Tajin and Veracruz ceramic sculptures (ill. 111). The death deity on the back of this monument (right) is carried like a burden by the human on the front (left).

backpack, or in the case of the example shown here, a skeletal death image. The oversized hands and the rich, incised pattern that covers the stone can be compared with later Aztec workmanship, particularly as seen in ill. 223. In fact, the carpeted body may represent the custom of body paint; the pleated adornments represent folded *amate* (fig) paper. The Aztecs conquered the Huastecs in the mid-fifteenth century and may have used Huastec art as a model for their own imperial style. It is also possible that these Huastec sculptures have a prototype in the Maya sculptures of Copan. There, a ruler and his predecessor are often recorded in three-dimensional relief on the front and back of a stone shaft. The adult males of Huastec sculpture may be rulers, paired with their infant successors or dead predecessors.

The Toltecs

The rise of the Toltecs at Tula, in the state of Hidalgo, and at Chichen Itza is generally attributed to the tenth century, although both sites were occupied long before. Ironically enough it was the later Aztecs who ensured the Toltecs a prominent place in history. No other people played such an important role in Aztec and Maya chronicles at the time of the Conquest. These historical annals – some of which were transcribed into the roman alphabet – provide information for events going back as far as the tenth century, even if for the period AD 1000 to 1300 the record is not at all complete. For earlier historical records in Mesoamerica, one must turn to Maya inscriptions (scarce as these are from AD 800 to 1000) and use them to compare contemporary archaeological data from other places.

The sixteenth-century documents weave a story of cyclical occurrences, where myth and history are one, and – unfortunately for us – geographical locations are often vague. We learn, for instance, of great events at the ancient city of Tula, but Tula, or Tollan (literally, 'place of reeds,' but generally understood to mean an urban settlement) is the name ascribed to many important centers from early Postclassic times on. To the Aztecs, both Teotihuacan and Tula, Hidalgo, were the Tula of the past, but their own city, Tenochtitlan, was also a Tula, as was Cholula, perhaps Chichen Itza, and even Copan, as well. The sixteenth century reveals a particular view of the Toltecs:

The Tolteca were wise. Their works were all good, all perfect, all wonderful, all marvelous; their houses beautiful, tiled in mosaics, smoothed, stuccoed, very marvelous....The Tolteca were very wise; they were thinkers, for they originated the year count, the day count; they established the way in which the night, the day, would work; which day sign was good, favorable.... (Sahagún, Book 10)

The later commentaries seem to have telescoped all past glories into the Toltec era, but they retained the term 'Toltec' to refer to their contemporary skilled craftsmen. As we shall see, the skill of the builders of Tula, Hidalgo, was not exceptional, and in fact, much of the workmanship there can be considered shoddy.

The historical annals recorded after the Spanish invasion came to emphasize the story of the Toltecs and their cultural hero, Topiltzin Quetzalcoatl, the latter name meaning 'Feathered Serpent,' who ruled at Tula in the tenth century. Postconquest Maya sources relate the arrival of a great cultural hero, Kukulcan, in what may have been the same period. Kukulcan is a translation of Feathered Serpent into Maya, and representations of feathered snakes flourished at both Tula and Chichen Itza, mostly in contexts of war and sacrifice. Archaeology demonstrates that a series of structures that were constructed at Chichen Itza and Tula bear close resemblance. Chichen Itza clearly benefited from the Toltec relationship: precious trade goods, including turquoise from what is today New Mexico and gold disks from lower Central America, flowed into the city.

Meanwhile, at Tula, Hidalgo, the Toltecs developed military and mercantile prowess, maintaining commerce and perhaps some social control far to the north and south. In the mid-twelfth century, however, the last king of Tula, Huemac, was forced to flee before growing factionalism and encroaching barbarians, repeating the pattern established by Topiltzin. Huemac settled in Chapultepec, on the western banks of Lake Texcoco in the Valley of Mexico, sources tell us. Tula was ravaged. Toltec power waned, but no later dynasty in Mesoamerica, whether Mixtec, Aztec, or Maya, would fail to invoke their glorious past.

Tula

Tula, Hidalgo, lies farther north than any other ancient Mesoamerican city. Located on the Tula River, the site is arid and windy, and although the stark surviving art and architecture suggests a military outpost, it was once a thriving urban center.

Tula was not only ravaged at its abandonment, but it was also looted systematically by the Aztecs. It has taken years of patient archaeological work to reveal the nature of the ancient city. What is now clear is that dense urban housing, laid out along a rough grid, surrounded the ceremonial core. Pyramid C is the largest of the central structures, but it was trenched for treasure and stripped of its sculpture in prehispanic times. Pyramid B is just slightly smaller, and stands today as the best-preserved major building at Tula [191]. Its contiguous colonnades, which we can imagine to have had a perishable roof, may once have served as a royal residence. This relationship of massive pyramid to large, interior space formed by piers and courtyards recalls the arrangement at Teotihuacan, where the late Quetzalpapalotl Palace adjoins the Pyramid of the Moon, but on a reduced, even spartan, scale at Tula.

The colonnade protects the single staircase of Pyramid B, restricting access to the summit of the pyramid. Against the four distinct levels of the structure, tenons once supported a façade of carved stone, which in turn was brightly polychromed – but only a small portion of the façade survives. Where still in situ, friezes of prowling jaguars, coyotes, and seated eagles with hearts in their beaks are punctuated by frontal single images of feathered, jaguar-like creatures from whose mouths emerge the faces of supernaturals with large eyes and bifurcated tongues, sometimes

191 Pyramid B, Tula. The French explorer Désiré Charnay first posited a direct connection between Tula and Chichen Itza, and he recognized the similarity between this pyramid and the Temple of the Warriors at Chichen (ill. 202).

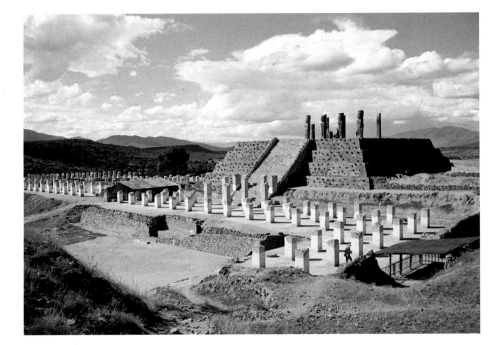

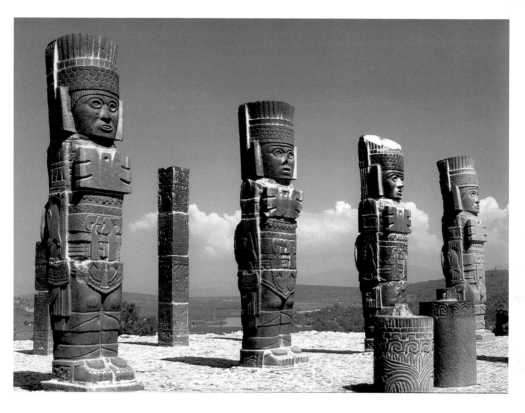

192 Atlantean columns, Pyramid B, Tula. These giant Toltec sculptures are warriors ready for battle; an *atlatl* is held at the side, and the butterfly pectoral and drum headdress are costume elements of those in combat.

thought to represent the Morning Star, or Quetzalcoatl, but who in fact represent the War Serpent, whose headdress figured at Teotihuacan and in the Maya region.

Great atlantean columns depicting Toltec warriors and feathered columns surmount the pyramid [192]. The atlanteans functioned like caryatids and held up the roof; the feathered columns framed the doorway. Square pillars with warriors in low relief supported a rear chamber. Within the chamber, the atlantean Toltec warriors must have been an intimidating group. Their huge, blank faces convey the anonymity of the Toltec war machine, and the *atlatls* – or Central Mexican spearthrowers – borne in their hands threaten the viewer. Scant traces now remain of the bright polychrome that once colored these sculptures: the warriors' legs, for example, were painted in red-and-white candy stripes, usually indicative of sacrificial victims in Aztec art. Each atlantean consists of four drums held together by dowels, and both their uniformity and method of construction suggest mass production. That uniformity speaks to the control of a deep chain of production, from concept to quarry to final execution.

193 A *chacmool* from the Palace, Tula. These reclining sculptures of fallen warriors were set in front of thrones. The receptacle on the chest is for sacrificial offerings.

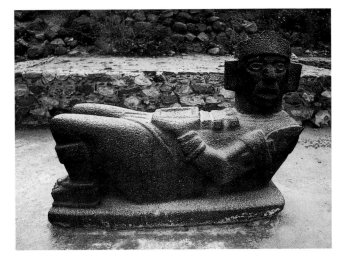

An innovation at Tula is the *coatepantli*, or freestanding serpent wall, which forms an L on the north side of the pyramid. With a border of geometric meanders, a single broad entablature supports a repeating relief of great rattlesnakes belching skeletal humans. Cut-out shell motifs of the sort associated in later art with Quetzalcoatl run across the top of the *coatepantli*. Off to the north, the Toltecs built the Corral, a round building designed to align with a sacred mountain. Along the Tula River, the Toltecs built dense housing complexes, probably some for extended family living and craft production.

Elevated benches within the palace adjoining Pyramid B may have served as thrones for the elite. Three-dimensional *chacmool* sculptures stood in front of these thrones [193]. The discovery in the nineteenth century of similar *chacmool* figures in both Central Mexico and Yucatan helped spark the notion of Toltec hegemony, but, as we shall see below, the *chacmool* may be a Maya invention. The illustration here shows a fallen warrior, knife still held in place by an armband, and he holds out a flat paten, probably a receptacle for offerings brought to a ruler or deity on the throne behind. Ill. 195, a cuirass made of Pacific shells, was buried under the palace floor, a testimony to craftsmen worthy of the term *tolteca*.

194 Plumbate wares mark the Toltec era of the ninth and tenth centuries, from Yucatan to Tula, although manufacture seems to have taken place in Chiapas. These ceramics carried new iconography across Mesoamerica, including the Maya god Pauahtun, featured on this vessel.

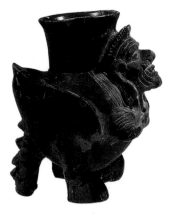

Although carved stelae are not unknown in Central Mexico, they are not common, and the full-figure, frontal portraits roughly worked on Stelae 1 and 2 at Tula strongly suggest a Maya influence. Like earlier warrior stelae at Piedras Negras, the Tula stelae show the face worked in deep relief and the costume in shallow carving.

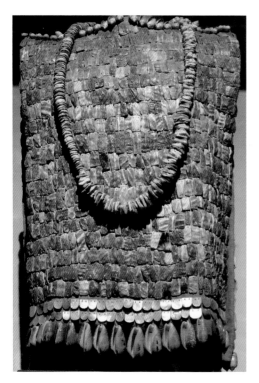

195 Skilled craftsmen cut spiny oyster (*spondylus*) shells into tiny plaques, assembling over 1,200 into a cuirass or warrior shirt, and trimming the garment with oliva and mother-of-pearl.

In the illustration on the following page the figure is probably a ruler in warrior garb [196]. The headdress of these warriors comprises three 'bowties' surmounted by Tlaloc year-sign insignia and feathers. Among the Classic Maya and at Cacaxtla, Central Mexican motifs are worn both by warriors and by those engaged in sacrifice. These Tula stelae may reflect a strong Maya contact at the end of the Classic, and they may date to the early ninth century, when the tradition was still alive in the southern Maya lowlands. At Xochicalco, contemporary stelae called upon Maya forms and motifs in celebrating rulership; at Tula, the precedent is the Maya warrior.

During the Toltec era a distinctive type of pottery known as plumbate ware was widely distributed throughout Mesoamerica [194]. Traditionally thought of as a chronological and geographical marker of the Toltec Early Postclassic horizon, plumbate is nevertheless now generally considered to be of southwest Guatemalan origin, whence it dispersed to the rest of Mesoamerica. The name plumbate suggests a true, lead glaze of the sort used in the Old World, but in fact the glossy, metallic appearance derives from the high iron content of the clay and the reduced oxygen at the completion of firing. Indeed, plumbate perhaps deliberately imitates the sheen of metal, in much the same way as do wares made by the Chimu in the northern Andes. Even though metal objects have not been recovered from Tula itself, the Toltec era ushers in metalworking in Mesoamerica as a whole.

The plumbate potters often made human or effigy jars. Some of the human faces suggest portraits, while others seem to be those of deities. One unusual portrait is worked with mother-of-pearl over the terracotta, and the bearded face recalls accounts promulgated at the time of the Spanish invasion of the Toltec king, Topiltzin Quetzalcoatl, reputedly fair and bearded.

Tula was sacked in the late twelfth century. Its ravagers hurled the atlantean columns from the summit, interred them, and then dug a huge trench through Pyramid B, presumably looting any treasure there. The Aztecs later established a nearby hill as the

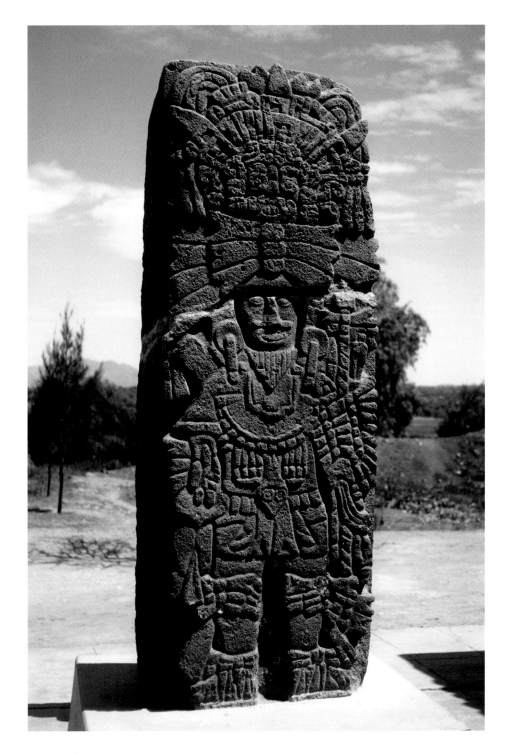

Opposite:
196 Although crudely carved, this Early Postclassic stela from Tula is nevertheless dressed like a Maya warrior. The Tlaloc-and-year sign headdress is similar to that worn by the warrior in ill. 162.

locus of an important cosmic myth, so perhaps it was their ancestors, nomadic barbarians, who were among the despoilers of Tula. Whatever the truth of this, the Aztecs actively drew on the conventions and iconography of Tula when they designed their own capital.

Tula was in many ways an experiment: a seeming union of the Maya and Central Mexico, with a center farther to the north than any other in Mesoamerican history. In the end the experiment failed.

Chichen Itza

The Toltec florescence at Chichen Itza is far more exuberant and expansive than at Tula. Similar architectural features and motifs appear at both sites, among them serpent columns, *chacmools*, and Toltec warrior pillars, but the innovation and skill at Chichen suggests Maya stimulus and craftsmanship. To understand the transformation of Toltec Chichen, however, we must turn first to its earlier history as reflected in its architecture.

Chichen was undoubtedly occupied during the Classic, but despite many excavations and much speculation no precise chronology has so far been established for the site. What is most clear is that many buildings relate closely to the Puuc developments at Uxmal, during the era when Teotihuacan had fallen into decline, perhaps unleashing new migrations across Mesoamerica. This early phase was then probably followed by a period of contact with a Mexicanized Maya group, the Itza, according to chronicles that are contradictory but nevertheless suggestive. Subsequently, Chichen began an era of construction when Toltec influences were pronounced. The relationship between the Itza and the Toltecs remains obscure.

Yet for all the differences that are in sharp relief, Chichen Itza shares much with its predecessors in plan and its architectural vocabulary. The juxtaposition of likely funerary pyramid and palace recalls the practice at Palenque, and the colonnaded Temple of the Warriors features finely wrought corbel vaults.

An examination of the site plan itself hints at the different phases of construction [197]. The south half of the mapped portion, perhaps focused on the use of water from the Xtoloc Cenote, follows the more dispersed plan characteristic of Classic centers, with a rambling emphasis on a north-south axis. The north half of the site, on the other hand, has ordered colonnaded structures, mostly built during the Toltec era and perhaps all within a very short timespan, which spread from east to west,

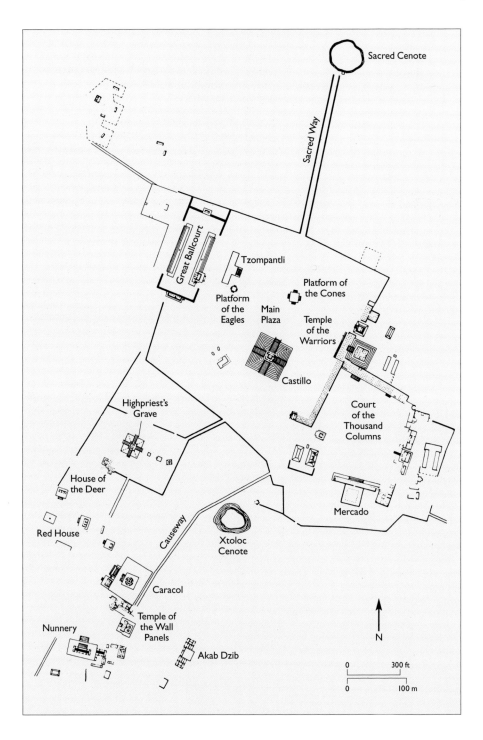

Sacred Cenote

Sacred Way

Great Ballcourt

Tzompantli

Platform of the Eagles

Platform of the Cones

Main Plaza

Temple of the Warriors

Castillo

Highpriest's Grave

Court of the Thousand Columns

House of the Deer

Red House

Causeway

Xtoloc Cenote

Mercado

Caracol

Temple of the Wall Panels

Nunnery

Akab Dzib

N

0   300 ft

0   100 m

Opposite:
197 Plan of Chichen Itza.

defining their own axis. Presumably multi-ethnic, Chichen Itza unified its peoples through a program of public architecture. A causeway or *sacbe* runs north to south, offering organization to the plan. The *sacbe* terminates at the Sacred Cenote, a great natural sinkhole, and probably the source of the name of the site, literally, 'the mouth of the well of the Itza' [198].

In 'Old' Chichen, buildings such as the Temple of the Three Lintels (a low-lying range-type structure with Chahk masks at the corners) recall the galleries of the Puuc. The Red House and the House of the Deer are small temples set on raised platforms; their private rear chambers and orientation to one another suggest the plan and arrangement of the Cross Group temples at Palenque. Stonework, however, is limited to heavy blocks, and the finely cut façade masonry of the Puuc is missing, in favor of the traditional block masonry of the Peten, and perhaps indicating an origin of some Chichen lords near Lake Peten Itza. Nor are the specialized boot-shaped stones used for vaulting, and the arched doorway – so important visually at Uxmal – present at Chichen. In fact the

Below:
198 Maya pilgrims made offerings to the Sacred Cenote at Chichen for generations and continued to do so from time to time after the Spanish invasion. The murky green water has yielded human bones, jade, and gold.

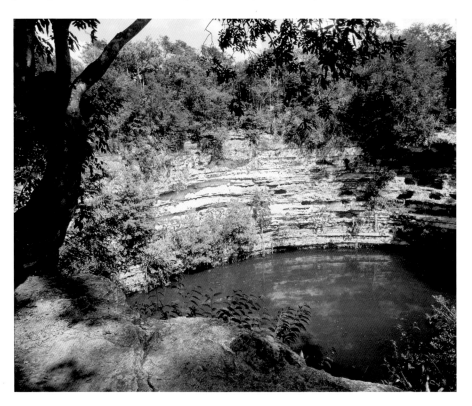

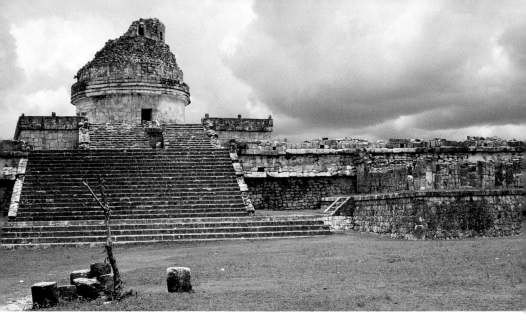

199 The Caracol, Chichen Itza. Tiny windows in the uppermost story were oriented for astronomical observations. The principal entrance does not align with the staircase, creating the sense visually that the building is turning.

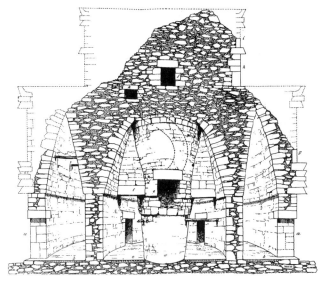

200 A cutaway drawing of the Caracol.

visual refinements of negative batter and uneven spacing of doorways are entirely lacking in Chichen architecture, which in general cannot match the lyrical quality of Uxmal.

The first building that shows a dramatic shift away from more traditional Maya architectural practices is the Caracol, so-called for its plan, the core of which may deliberately resemble the section of a conch shell [199, 200]. Concentric vaults lead to an upper chamber via a spiral staircase. Stonework and vaulting remain of high quality. The great Mayanist Sir Eric Thompson decried its architectural style, claiming that it resembled 'a two-decker wedding cake on the square carton in which it came.' But one can equally well argue that the circles described within a trapezoid within a rectangle express an interest in geometry similar to that of Vitruvius in the Old World. The Caracol's unusual plan and placement of openings allow observation of the movements of Venus, whose synodic cycle of 236 days (Morning Star), 90 days (superior conjunction), 250 days (Evening Star), and 8 days (inferior conjunction) was of great importance to all Mesoamerican peoples. For the later Aztecs, round buildings were always dedicated to Quetzalcoatl (astronomically to be identified as Venus), who was seen with a conch shell in his manifestation as Ehecatl, the wind god.

Quetzalcoatl may have been known in earlier times – perhaps even then associated with feathered serpents, which can be seen on many monuments – but it is clear that this god grew greatly in significance during the Early Postclassic, very possibly coincident with the life of the historical individual of the same name (Topiltzin Quetzalcoatl, or Kukulcan to the Maya, literally 'Feathered Serpent'). His analogue among the Mixtec people, known by his calendrical name 9 Wind (also the birthdate of Quetzalcoatl in Central Mexico), was a great bringer of culture: he introduced kingship, designed a sacred landscape, and initiated the ceremonies that would keep it all in order. But, as we have seen in earlier constructions at Teotihuacan, feathered serpents bear an integral relation to the cult of warfare. Just what this meant at Chichen Itza remains unclear, but the era was one when some of the tenets of Classic religion changed, with some new prominence for different deities. What provoked the changes in sacred imagery remains unclear, but ideological shifts often accompany geographic movement and chronological development.

The first Christian bishop of Yucatan, Diego de Landa, visited Chichen in the mid-sixteenth century, and made the earliest surviving European sketch of a Maya building before 1566, when he wrote his *Relación*. He drew a plan of what he called the Pyramid of Kukulcan, or Quetzalcoatl, which is now generally known as the Castillo [201]. His plan shows a building of several levels with staircases flowing down all four sides of the building: even more remarkable is his written description of the ninety-one steps on a side of the structure, with the north staircase heading off to the

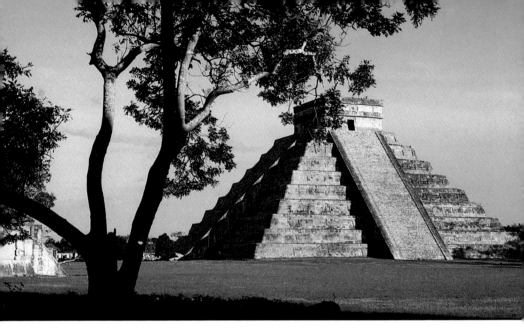

201 The Castillo, Chichen Itza. Like the funerary pyramids of Palenque or Tikal (ills. 138 and 146), the Castillo rises in nine distinct levels. The vertical profile and upper molding of the superstructure are characteristic of Toltec-era buildings at Chichen. This photograph was taken on the autumnal equinox, when seven serpent segments are illuminated along the main stairs.

Sacred Cenote. Landa also noted the two 'dance platforms' in the plaza between the Castillo and the *sacbe* to the Cenote.

Landa's description includes many interesting observations for the modern viewer, not only in what he said but also in what he did not say. He noted the practice of making live human sacrifices into the sacred well (the theory of virgin sacrifice does not depend on Landa: for that we must turn to Tomás Lopez, who had already visited the site in 1552) and speculated that 'if this country possessed gold, it would be this well that would have the greater part of it.' Once Brasseur de Bourbourg rediscovered Landa's manuscript in 1864, feverish imagination focused on the Cenote, with dreams of great treasure: divers at the turn of the twentieth century would eventually haul gold disks with Maya imagery from the well.

But given the state of both ruin and overgrowth that we might expect at Chichen Itza by the sixteenth century (evidenced by Landa's own failure to see much of anything else at Chichen: he mentions only four buildings altogether and does not include, for example, the Caracol, which surely he would have been interested in and would have mentioned had he seen it), Landa's ability to see this one particular cleared portion of the site, from the Castillo to the Cenote, suggests that this quadrant had remained in perpetual use. Landa's attention was also drawn to the particular number of steps on each side of the pyramid and to the massive serpent

220

heads on the northern face, perhaps indicating that the observation of astronomical phenomena at this building had continued unabated from the time of its construction.

Like the Caracol, the Castillo was oriented to acknowledge movements of the heavens, and on the equinoxes the nine levels of the pyramid cast a shadow that reveals a segmented serpent along the northern balustrade. The flight of stairs on that side has ninety-two steps, if one counts the serpent heads at the base; each of the other three staircases has ninety-one, for a total of 365. Thus, both in numerology and orientation, the building recognizes the solar year. As we see the Castillo today, it is a radial pyramid of the sort first observed at Uaxactun in Protoclassic times and whose primary role would seem to have been to commemorate the completion of time.

Today, twice annually tens of thousands of visitors swarm onto the plaza in a modern ritual of equinox observation at the Castillo. The phenomenon was not rediscovered through careful archaeological observation and measurement, but rather seems to have grown up organically at Chichen, probably by means of local Yucatec Maya, who had kept the plaza cleared in Landa's day and who had sustained memory continuously through the Colonial era.

In 1937, Mexican archaeologists exploring the Castillo found within it a complete pyramid-temple, also of nine levels, but with a single stairway to the north. Preserved in the temple chambers were a *chacmool* and jaguar throne, which remain *in situ* today. Given the pattern known at Tikal and Palenque, where earlier pyramids of nine levels held tombs of great kings, it seems likely that this one may also house a royal burial. Although the identity of that individual may never be known, the fact that this structure has always been associated with Kukulcan suggests that the great Toltec king himself may lie within the mass of the pyramid. The High Priest's Grave, a similar building that yielded a tomb in the nineteenth century, was recently restored to its ancient grandeur; a text from that building bears the site's last certain date at the end of the tenth century.

A typical feature of the final phase of construction at Chichen during the Early Postclassic is the colonnade, punctuated by serpent columns, particularly framing a raised shrine, The greatest of these is the Temple of the Warriors [202]. Connecting colonnades extend to define a large, semi-enclosed court, the south side of which is flanked by the so-called Mercado and a small

Overleaf:
202 Temple of the Warriors, Chichen Itza. This structure shares the proportions and the use of a colonnade with Pyramid B of Tula, but the Chichen Itza building is larger and far more beautiful. The colonnade in front of the structure supported a perishable roof. Early Postclassic.

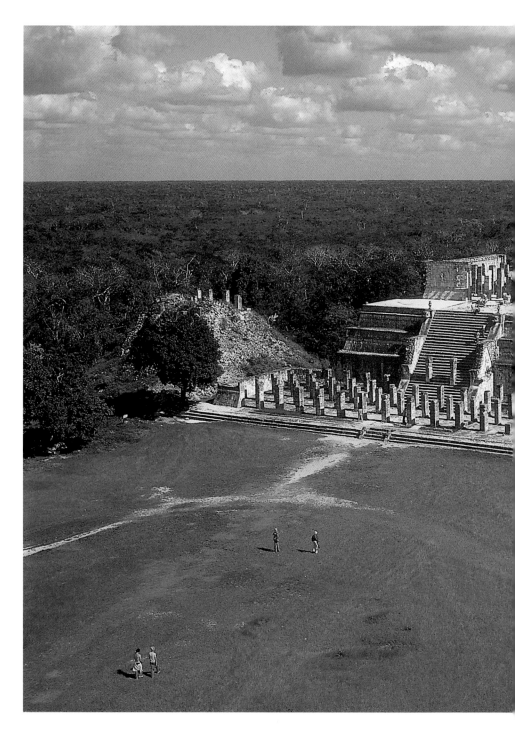

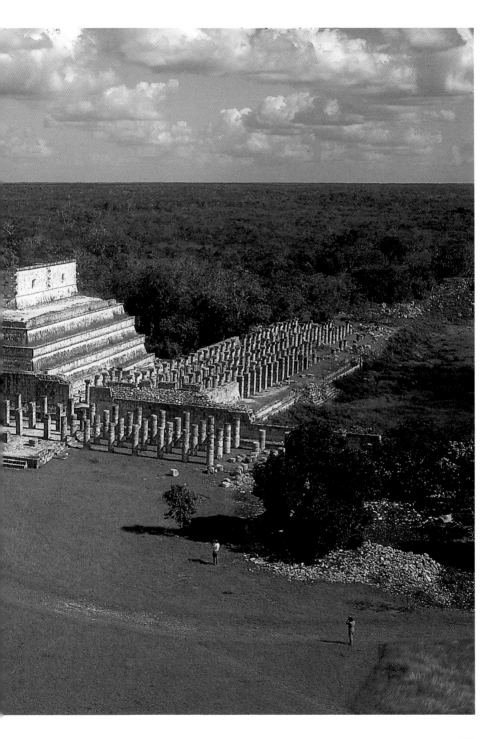

ballcourt, probably a palace compound. Like the Castillo, the outer building of the Warriors was discovered to enclose a smaller but similar structure, now known as the Temple of the Chacmool. Although lost from view, these buried structures would have been known through memory and oral tradition.

One gains entry to the Temple of the Warriors itself through the field of square pillars that would once have supported a perishable roof. Each pillar is carved on four sides. Some reliefs feature standing warriors with Toltec 'pillbox' headdress and weaponry; others show skirted figures, probably women, bearing offerings. Similar reliefs are worked on pillars of the rear chamber of Pyramid B at Tula, but the imagery there is limited to warriors. Anyone entering the Temple of the Warriors must have felt both the guidance of the offering bearers and the threat of the warriors.

The doorway at the summit of the temple is flanked by great feathered-serpent columns, whose plumed rattles once supported the door lintel. In the first chamber, a *chacmool* was set to receive offerings; in the rear chamber a great platform raised up by miniature atlanteans once served as the ruler's throne. A building such as the Temple of the Warriors may have been a seat of government, its function largely bureaucratic. The platform supports suggest the literal pillars of government, the warriors and offering bearers the means of its sustenance. The abundance of administrative buildings at Chichen Itza is perhaps accounted for within a short construction era if we imagine that every regional governor – possibly an individual similar to the *bacab*, or governor, of the Conquest period – built a new establishment.

The Temple of the Warriors undoubtedly bears a striking resemblance to Pyramid B at Tula, but it also provides contrasts, and the scale and quality are Maya. Chambers within the Temple of the Warriors, for example, supported corbeled vaulting; stonework was elaborate and finely crafted – and the Temple is only one of several such buildings at Chichen. At Tula, the stonework seems mean and sparse by comparison, poorly worked and dependent on stucco covering, and Pyramid B stands alone as an impressive edifice. It is almost as if Toltec ideals were first given architectural expression at Chichen, and were then returned to Tula around the year 1000 in a provincial form. With the recent restoration of the adjacent and similar Temple of the Tables, the extent and repetition of the warrior template has become more obvious.

The most unusual structure at Chichen is the Great Ballcourt, the largest of all ballcourts in ancient Mesoamerica [203]. Its playing area extends over a length of 479 ft (146 m) and a width of 118 ft (36 m), defining a surface almost identical in size to a modern American football field, and several times the size of the average ballcourt. Unlike most Maya courts, the Great Ballcourt has vertical sides, a feature it shares with the Uxmal design. Vertical walls rise above a sloping *tablero* that by itself is higher than most other ballcourts. Rings, carved with entwined rattlesnakes, set into these side walls – presumably hoops through which the solid rubber ball passed or against which it was hit – are placed 26 ft (8 m) above the playing surface, almost out of range.

Centered under the rings are carved reliefs, comprised of individual slabs and probably carved *in situ*. They reveal grisly scenes, with references to ritual events on the court [204]. On the east side, two opposing teams of seven members face one another. In the middle of the scene, the first player of the left team has decapitated the first player of the right, who, headless, kneels in front of a large ball marked by a great laughing skull. Six serpents of blood and a tree issue from the severed neck. The apparent victors on the left are more uniformly dressed than those on the right, who wear a variety of headdresses. All these ballplayers sport equipment of the sort generally associated with Classic Veracruz: *palmas*, yokes, and handstones; and the padding on arms and knees was designed to take the bruising blows of the heavy

203 Almost too large to be played in by mere mortals, the Great Ballcourt of Chichen Itza is the largest in Mesoamerica. Entwined serpents are carved on the rings set high in the side walls; carved reliefs adorn the sloping talus.

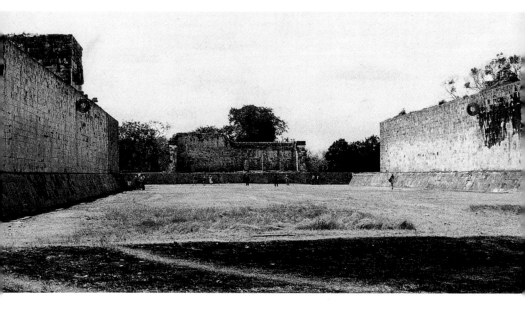

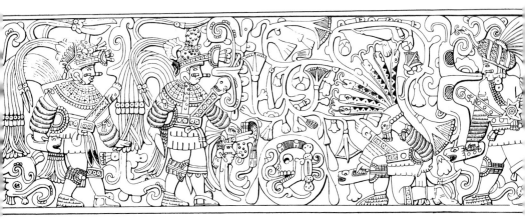

204 Part of the Great Ballcourt relief, Chichen Itza. Members of the victorious team have begun to sacrifice their opponents. At the time of the Conquest, the Maya claimed that Mexicans – often specifically the Toltecs – had introduced human sacrifice to their land.

ball. Beaded scrolls with embedded crossed bands of the kind usually intended to represent precious liquid, particularly blood, form the background and take on vegetal shape, underscoring the renewal from death and sacrifice.

Three large platforms without superstructures guide supplicants toward the Sacred Cenote to the north. One of these platforms, the so-called *tzompantli*, or skull rack, is carved with rows of human skulls. A precedent for depicting human skulls on platforms exists at Uxmal, but the scale and number here indicate an increasing preoccupation with death at the end of Chichen's development, to which this platform and the two associated with it are generally attributed. Alternating jaguars and eagles devour human hearts on the Platform of the Eagles. These motifs also appear at Tula, and at both sites they linked the rituals of the ballgame to those of human sacrifice.

Three-dimensional sculpture regained prominence at Chichen during the Early Postclassic. Particular attention was given to thrones, *chacmools*, and mini-atlanteans, but even the design of plumbate pottery reflects the new concern for images in the round.

Thrones and *chacmools* are generally found together – for instance in the inner Castillo structure, Temple of the Chacmool, Mercado, and Temple of the Warriors – and they seem to replace the stela and altar of times. In this we see the office itself commemorated rather than its occupant, whereas in Classic times the individual – and even the personality – who held such an office was the focus of the record. Thrones include large platforms supported by mini-atlanteans and built-in benches, but the most splendid one is the red jaguar found in the rear chamber of the inner Castillo structure. Bright red cinnabar covers the jaguar body and jade disks form feline spots in a color scheme characteristic of Classic thrones. On the seat of the red jaguar throne was a mosaic disk, or *tezcacuitlapilli*, a Toltec ornament worn at the back of the waist, assembled of precious shell and the rare turquoise traded from distant New Mexico or Arizona.

In front of the majority of thrones are *chacmools*, the most famous of which was excavated from the Platform of the Eagles in 1875 by Augustus LePlongeon, who gave them the name by which they are known today [205]. The variety and number of Chichen *chacmools* exceeds that of Tula. Perhaps the inspiration for them came from the recumbent captives often carved beneath the feet of figures on Maya stelae, an image which the Toltecs transformed into the three-dimensional idiom of their day. In recent years it has become apparent that Maya materials, forms, and iconography, often with roots in the Classic period, made a more profound impact on Central Mexico than has been previously acknowledged.

Stucco paintings and low-relief narratives have miraculously survived throughout Chichen Itza. Scenes of Maya and Toltecs

205 The *chacmool* excavated from the Platform of the Eagles, Chichen Itza, in 1875 by Augustus LePlongeon, who unsuccessfully tried to take the stone sculpture to Philadelphia for the 1876 Centennial celebration.

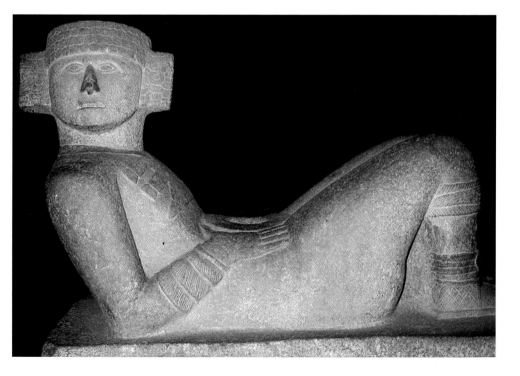

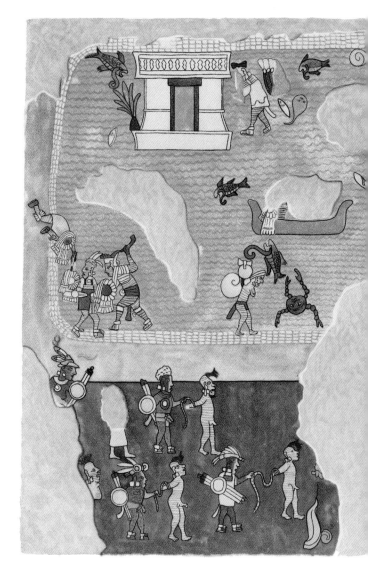

206 A wall painting from the Temple of the Warriors, Chichen Itza. Copy and reconstruction by Ann Axtell Morris. Such scenes would seem to show a foreign conquest. The lake may be a distant one in Central Mexico or in northern Guatemala. A single female can be seen at the upper center, atop what seems to be a mountain.

once covered the interior of the Temple of the Warriors. In the illustration shown here, dark warriors lead away their bound, naked captives with red and white candy cane stripes, yet other striped figures reign victorious above [206]. The thatched houses depicted appear to be Maya, though the stone architecture resembles Central Mexican models. One temple stands within a body of water: is it Lake Peten Itza, where the Itza Maya may have lived before coming to Chichen? The naturalistic human renderings of earlier paintings, as at Cacaxtla or Bonampak, give

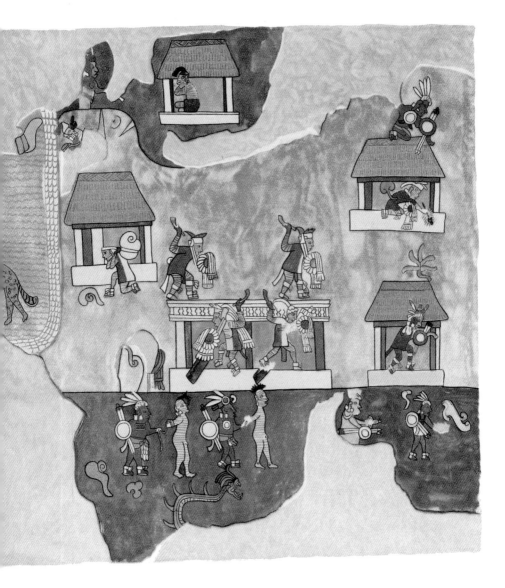

way here to some shorter proportions, but non-naturalistic conventions reveal an intricate and lively landscape. Stylistically, the paintings have more in common with early Teotihuacan painting than with the tradition of Maya murals.

Pilgrimages to the Sacred Cenote continued to be made long after the Conquest, and objects dredged from the silt at the turn of this century spanned a millennium. The discovery of human skeletons confirmed the long-held suspicion that human sacrifice had taken place at the well. Among the finds rescued from the

Cenote mire were offerings of copal, jade, and finely crafted repoussé gold disks. With their lively scenes of war and sacrifice, the gold disks are not only important narratives but also among the earliest Mesoamerican works where art is created from metal. The drawing of the human form and the layout of the scene, with basal panel reserved for an earth monster, reflects a development from the Maya tradition. On most of the disks warriors in Toltec dress dominate defeated Maya.

Toltec, or Toltec-Maya, preeminence in the Early Postclassic may recall patterns of highland political dominance established earlier in Mesoamerica, and it certainly presages the tremendous success of the Aztecs. Such political success, however, does not guarantee priority in the aesthetic arena. Archaeologists may indeed prove one day that Tula truly reigned over the Maya, but the beauty, craft, and abundance of Maya works of the era will not be undermined.

The decline of Postclassic Maya art and architecture

Late Postclassic Maya art and architecture is mostly unimpressive, whether judged against Maya precedents or the splendors of Postclassic Central Mexico. Following the decline and abandonment of Chichen Itza, Yucatan was loosely governed in the fourteenth and fifteenth centuries by a confederacy based at Mayapan by Hunac Ceel, following a rebellion against Chichen. Mayapan in turn eventually fell prey to treachery and was abandoned in the mid-fifteenth century. Although remembered as a great city at the time of the Conquest, Mayapan was poorly built and highly derivative of Chichen Itza in terms of its art and architecture.

What did set Mayapan apart, however, was its plan, which was unusual for a Mesoamerican city. It was apparently designed as a walled city, with a population that dwelt mainly within its bounds. Set at its heart is the Castillo, a small and ill-executed structure built along the lines of the Chichen Itza Castillo. The Mayapan builders constructed the Castillo in roughly cut stone held together only by mud and stucco. Mayapan lords also hauled old Chahk masks from a site in the Puuc; they may have been delivered up as tribute to the lords of Mayapan.

At least ten stone stelae have been discovered at Mayapan. The local limestone from which they are cut is of poor quality, but the stelae nevertheless show interesting imagery. Stela 1, for example, depicts a pair of figures inside a thatched shrine, underneath a long but eroded glyphic text [207]. Chahk sits on a throne and gestures

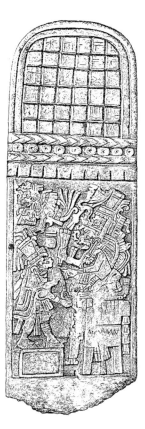

207 Despite the absence of stelae at Chichen Itza, the lords of Mayapan revived the practice of erecting such monuments, although with a change from the historical iconography of the Classic period. Texts do not survive, but glyph blocks construct a shrine, topped by thatch, in which the god Chahk receives adoration.

at a smaller figure, who may be a stone or clay image, placed on a box, possibly once a *tun* glyph. This stela, and the others like it, may in fact bear scenes connected with the *acantun*, a part of the New Year's ceremonies shown in the Dresden Codex and discussed by Bishop Landa.

Large ceramic figures of the Late Postclassic have come to light throughout northern Yucatan. Most prevalent among these are images of Chahk, who was thought to exist both as a single deity and as a group of four. Typically, these figures hold human hearts in the hand: they must have looked gruesome anointed with blood, as Spanish chroniclers tell us they were. The Postclassic potters used a coarse clay, with various substances, or tempers, worked into the clay to lower the firing temperature. Most of the figures were once brightly polychromed, some with a stucco paint that obscured imperfections. Only the most tenacious pigments, particularly blue, survive.

Christopher Columbus's son Ferdinand accompanied his father on the Fourth Voyage to the New World, and he described the great seagoing canoes of Maya traders that they saw among the Bay Islands off Honduras in 1502. Some canoes were piled high with fine cotton mantles, a standard unit of exchange at the time of the Conquest, along with other embroidered garments. Women may have specifically journeyed to the coast to sell their cottons to the traders; we know that women were among the forty-odd persons described by Columbus as passengers on the canoe. Other canoes carried foodstuffs – grains, roots, and fermented corn beverage – and copper bells and hatchets, as well as cacao beans, another unit of exchange. What is clear is that the Caribbean coast sustained considerable commerce, and that commerce in turn provided the basis for the growth of Caribbean Yucatan centers. Tulum and Tancah were probably the largest of these. On his voyage to Yucatan in 1518, Juan de Grijalva sighted what may have been Tulum, and reported that the city was bustling with activity. The small shrines on the island of Cozumel and at other places along the coast may have been no more than way-stations for travelers – a function they later served for famous Caribbean pirates who worked the same coast. Additionally, women came to the Caribbean coastal shrines when unable to conceive a child, and the movement of traders and travelers may have improved one's true odds of conception.

Tulum is beautifully situated overlooking the Caribbean [208]. The sea forms the fourth side of a rectangle with the three walls that surround the main ceremonial structures. Unlike Mayapan,

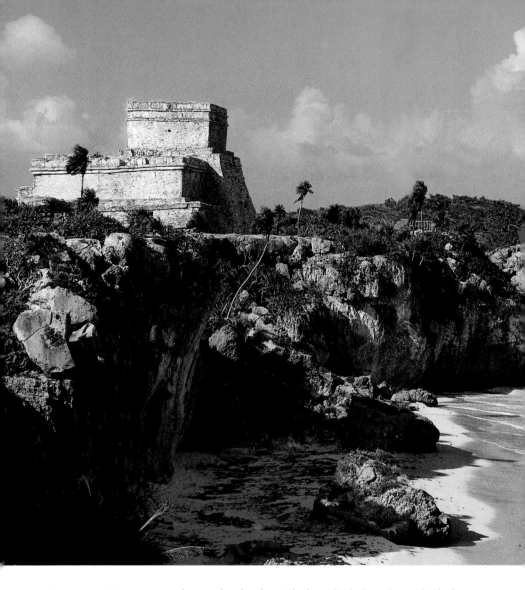

208 The Castillo of Tulum turns its back to the Caribbean Sea; the watchtower at right is one of the few buildings that addresses the turquoise expanse.

the populace lived outside the walls; high-ranking individuals probably lived in the low-ranging palace structures. The temples of Tulum are small, even diminutive, with some doors too small for easy entry. Most buildings were shabbily constructed and heavily stuccoed. The negative batter, used to subtle effect at Uxmal, was here carried to such an extreme that some buildings look as if ready to pitch over. The cornices of Structure 16 reveal great faces of aged deities, and the sharp outward slant of the structure makes the eyes bulge and the chin recede.

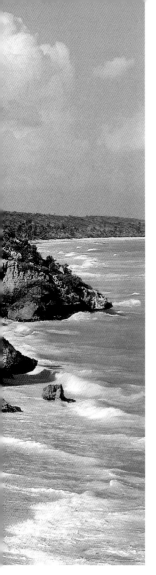

Elaborate paintings cover the walls – both interior and exterior – of many Tulum buildings. The palette of these works is limited to red, blue, and yellow, all outlined in black. Stiff conventional gestures as well as the proportional system suggest influences from Late Postclassic Mixtec painting. Some of the imagery also hints at contact with Central Mexico: the example here shows a deity covered with turquoise mosaic; his eyes are banded with what appears to be black obsidian [209]. This masking is typical of the Central Mexican deity, Tezcatlipoca. The most famous turquoise mosaic masks to have survived the Conquest were those given to Hernando Cortés by Motecuhzoma, but Grijalva's record shows that he also collected some in Yucatan, and perhaps such costume elements provided the means by which religious iconography was shared. Although the Aztecs were not well informed about their Maya neighbors in Yucatan, the Maya nevertheless knew a great deal about this Central Mexican power by the eve of the Conquest. Foreign elements and even a foreign

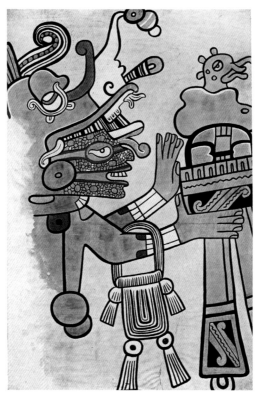

209 Many interior wall paintings have been preserved at Tulum. Here a figure wears the turquoise mask and black eye band of the Aztec deity Tezcatlipoca (cf. ill. 239).

Opposite:
210 Pages 47 (right) and 60 (left)
of the Dresden Codex. Perhaps
dating to as early as the thirteenth
century, this folding-screen book
written on bark paper includes
elements that may have been
copied from an older, perhaps
ninth century, manuscript. At right
the malevolent Venus gods prepare
to unleash devastation onto earth.

stylistic impact, however, should not be taken as evidence that Tulum was occupied by foreigners: the glyphs that accompany the paintings of Tulum are purely Maya, indicating that they were written for a literate Maya audience. Outside influences do nevertheless show the complicated iconographic interaction at the time of the Conquest. At Santa Rita, in what is now northern Belize, Thomas Gann had copies made of Late Postclassic paintings that were destroyed shortly after he found them in 1896. Their style also bears a resemblance to Mixtec painting, but the unusual iconography is largely Maya, as is the writing.

Probably contemporary with the paintings of Tulum are the four surviving Maya manuscripts. Of these, the finest, most complete, and oldest is the Dresden Codex, preserved today in the Dresden Sachsische Landesbibliothek [210]. Cortés was given several Mesoamerican manuscripts in 1519. He sent these to his king, Charles V of Spain, also the Holy Roman Emperor, with his seat in Vienna, where the Dresden Codex was purchased in the eighteenth century, so it may have come as part of the Cortés collection. The survival of the Dresden is fortuitous, since the first bishop of Yucatan, Diego de Landa, gathered up and burned every 'idolatrous' manuscript that he could find. Technically a screenfold rather than a bound codex, the Dresden was painted primarily in black and red, but with bright polychrome on some pages, on a stucco surface over native fig-bark paper. This red-and-black color scheme may have been an ancient one for Mesoamerican writing. The Aztecs used the metaphor *tlilli tlapalli*, 'the black, the red' to refer to writing, although their own books did not conform to such a color scheme. Pages are divided into registers, and the glyphs and figural illustrations create a unified text. Most of the book is filled with auguries and predictions most useful in an agricultural context. The rituals of the New Year's ceremonies are described. Calculations deep into the past and future are also related, as are the movements of the Venus gods and Chahk, the rain god. The Venus calculations also provide confirmation of the standard correlation constant used to derive equivalents for Maya and Christian calendars.

Only a few pages survive of the Paris Codex, and the third of the remaining Maya texts, the Madrid manuscript, is less interesting artistically: it appears to have been made with great haste. Its style is very close to the paintings at Tancah. In 1973 a few pages of a fourth text, an ancient Maya Venus table, came to light, known as the Grolier Codex after the club in New York

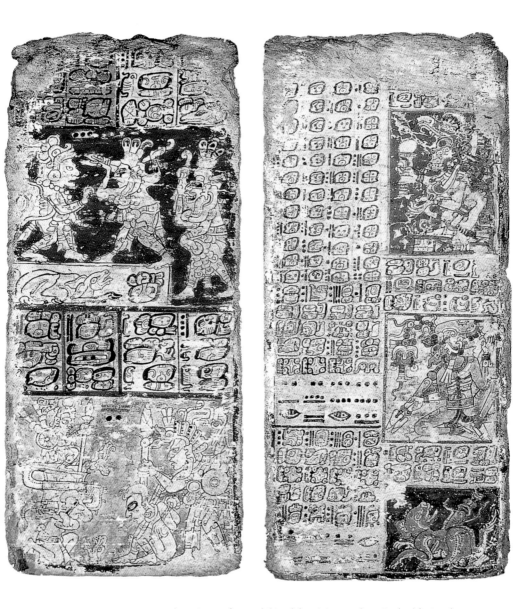

where it was first exhibited, but it is now kept in the National Museum in Mexico City.

At the time of the Conquest various highland Guatemala Maya ethnic groups – Kaqchikel, K'iche', Poqomam, and Tz'utujil – warred over territory and, perhaps more importantly, access to resources. Hilltop acropolises provided strongholds during this era, at Iximche, Utatlan, Mixco Viejo, and Cahyup, among other places. Following the Conquest of Central Mexico, the victorious Spaniards swept down into Guatemala. From Iximche the Kaqchikels took the foreigners' side against their old enemies, the K'iche', and the Spanish joined them there. By 1527, all groups of Maya had been subjugated, and the Spanish were able to establish a new capital at Ciudad Real, the first in a series of modern capitals that would be racked by severe earthquakes. Iximche, like the other fortified cities, was abandoned. Its plan reveals the nature of political organization there. Iximche was laid out to accommodate, architecturally, two important Kaqchikel lineages. Buildings were largely executed in duplicate: two ballcourts, two palaces, and so forth. The steep profiles of the structures, with emphasis on the *tablero*, recall the profiles of Monte Alban [211].

Sculptural efforts continued in what is now Guatemala after the Conquest. Cortés left his sick horse with the Itza lords in Tayasal, in the Peten, and after his departure, the horse died. Many years later, when Spaniards passed that way again, they found a stone or wooden image of the horse, enshrined in a temple! Stone cult objects have been made in Guatemala even more recently: on a hill near Chichicastenango, a stone image is still venerated by local K'iche' Maya.

Both in highland Guatemala and in Yucatan the Maya quickly adopted the Latin alphabet, and various systems of romanization of Maya languages have developed. In some cases, ancient books were transcribed. The *Popol Vuh*, for example, the single most important sixteenth-century document in terms of Maya religious narrative, was written down by a noble K'iche'. Others, such as the many books of Chilam Balam, emphasizing cyclical historical events and prophecies, were written by noblemen in Yucatan. In the margins of the Chumayel manuscript of Chilam Balam, the eighteenth-century scribe added glyphic cartouches, perhaps from the source he was copying [212]. The glyphs he drew had lost most of their meaning: the meaning was now carried by the alphabetic script. Here we see one step in the end of an ancient tradition and its transformation into the form that would help sustain memory in the modern world. Interestingly enough, in both Guatemala and Yucatan, through seminars led originally by Linda Schele and Nikolai Grube, many Maya have seized on the opportunity to write in glyphs once again. The ancient writing may yet live on.

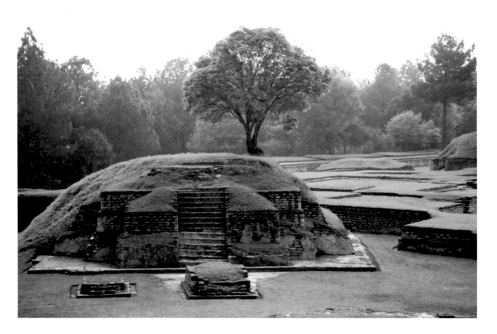

211 Pyramidal platforms, Iximche. Kaqchikel lords reigned from Iximche at the time of Pedro Alvarado's brutal sweep into Guatemala. They helped the Spanish defeat the K'iche'.

212 Page 23 from the book of Chilam Balam of Chumayel. By the time this manuscript was written during the Colonial period, the glyphs – here showing the Maya months – were little more than vestigial ornaments. The text is in Maya, written in the Roman alphabet.

Chapter 9   The Aztecs

By 1515, rumors were circulating in Tenochtitlan, the Aztec capital, of strange occurrences. Descriptions came back to Motecuhzoma II from the coast that great floating temples or mountains had been seen on the sea. Evil omens were studied. In 1509, a bright comet had alarmed Motecuhzoma, and during the last ten years of his reign he surrounded himself with soothsayers. According to some sources, a sense of gloom prevailed in Central Mexico, particularly in the mind of the ruler. Was the Fifth Sun about to collapse in violent cataclysm, provoking the end of this cycle of life? The melancholic poetry of the king of neighboring Texcoco suggested the transience of life.

> *I, Nezahualcoyotl, ask this:*
> *Is it true one really lives on the earth?*
> *Not forever on earth,*
> *only a little while here.*
> *Though it be jade it falls apart,*
> *though it be gold it wears away,*
> *though it be quetzal plumage it is torn asunder.*
> *Not forever on earth,*
> *only a little while here.*
> (León-Portilla, *Fifteen Poets of the Aztec World*, p. 80)

The Aztecs were the last of the great native Mesoamerican civilizations. Theirs was still a young culture at the time of the Spanish Conquest, and, despite the difficulties that Motecuhzoma II had in suppressing insurrection, they would probably have endured for a century or so had Hernando Cortés and his men not arrived when they did. For the Spanish, Tenochtitlan was the fulfillment of a fantasy, the sort of place they had heard of in the late medieval romances of Amadís de Gaula. Years later, when Bernal Díaz del Castillo, a soldier with Cortés, wrote a chronicle of the Conquest, he could still recall his excited first impressions of the Aztec capital:

When we saw so many cities and villages built both on the water and on dry land, and this straight, level causeway, we couldn't resist

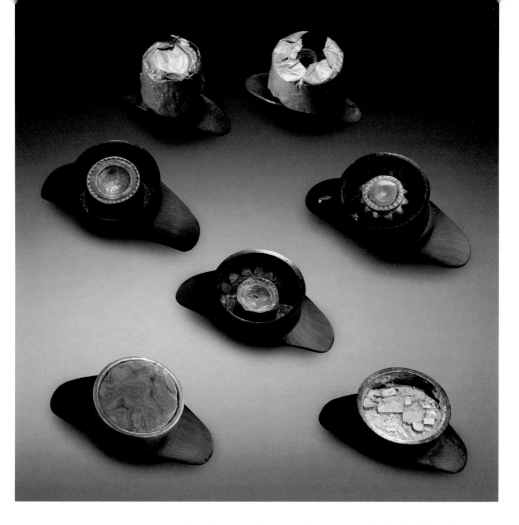

213 Aztec nobles wore labrets, often of precious materials, in the lower lip. These examples were formed of obsidian, worked to transparency, and finished with jade, turquoise and gold foil.

our admiration. It was like the enchantments in the book of Amadís, because of the high towers, cues [pyramids] and other buildings, all of masonry, which rose from the water. Some of our soldiers asked if what we saw was not a dream.
(The Discovery and Conquest of Mexico, trans. A. P. Maudslay, New York 1906)

Aztec history

According to early chronicles Tenochtitlan was founded in 1345. Before that the Aztecs scraped out a mean living on the old volcanic beds south of Lake Texcoco, near the present site of the National University. (The term Aztec, referring to the dominant people of Central Mexico, became current only in the nineteenth century, but it is convenient and will be used here. They knew themselves as the Mexica.) The Aztecs served as mercenary soldiers for more successful groups. In the early fourteenth century, before they moved to Tenochtitlan, they asked their neighbors and overlords in Culhuacan for a royal bride, in order to establish a ruling lineage. The city offered the ruler's daughter. Having accepted, the Aztecs invited the Culhuacan ruler to visit. When he attended the shrine of what was reputed to be a new deity, he found instead an Aztec priest wearing the flayed skin of his daughter. In response to this obscene offense the Aztecs were driven from their settlement. Some fled into Lake Texcoco and made their way to an island, where they founded Tenochtitlan, which is now Mexico City [214, 215].

Such acts characterized the early history of the Aztecs, who claimed to be nomadic barbarians, from the mythical place Aztlan, supposedly in northwest Mexico. It is in fact possible that these Nahuatl-speakers were already in Central Mexico before they embarked on their search for the new home described to them by Huitzilopochtli, their cult god, a war and hunting deity. By the time of the fall of Tula, in any case, the Aztecs had Central Mexican connections, and were perhaps accomplices in the Toltec downfall. The birth, or possibly rebirth, of Huitzilopochtli took place on a hill near Tula, according to Aztec legend. The god promised to lead them to an island in a lake, where an eagle would sit in a cactus. Tenochtitlan was that home.

During the fourteenth century the Aztecs were vassals to more powerful cities around the lake, such as Azcapotzalco to the west. With the accession of Itzcoatl in 1426, however, the situation changed dramatically. Under his leadership, and with the aid of his second-in-command, a military adviser who bore the title of Cihuacoatl, or 'Woman Snake,' the Aztecs crushed their former masters and began to

214 The Valley of Mexico in Aztec times.

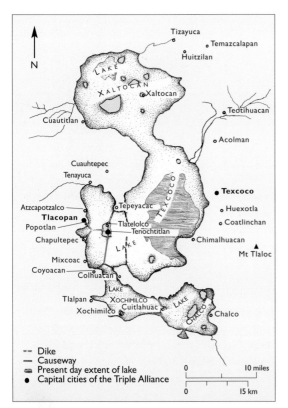

Tizayuca
Temazcalapan
Huitzilan
N
LAKE
XALTOCAN
Xaltocan
Cuautitlan
Teotihuacan
Acolman
Cuauhtepec
Tenayuca
● Texcoco
Atzcapotzalco
Tepeyacac
Huexotla
Tlacopan
Coatlinchan
Popotlan
Tlatelolco
Chapultepec
Tenochtitlan
Chimalhuacan
Mixcoac
Mt Tlaloc
Coyoacan
Colhuacan
LAKE
Tlalpan
XOCHIMILCO
Cuitlahuac
Xochimilco
Chalco

LAKE TEXCOCO
LAKE CHALCO

== Dike
— Causeway
Present day extent of lake
● Capital cities of the Triple Alliance

0   10 miles
0   15 km

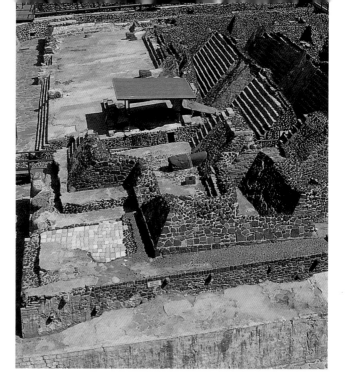

215 Seen from above in 1981, Templo Mayor reveals its layered set backs, all of which lay within the final version of the temple destroyed by the Spanish during their invasion of Mexico. Divided in two, the temple's Huitzilopochtli side is closer to the viewer here, with the Coyolxauhqui stone visible at the center.

consolidate the lake cities under their direction. Their military might made them greatly feared. They formed the Triple Alliance of Texcoco, Tenochtitlan, and Tlacopan, with control east and west of the lake. Under Motecuhzoma I (1440–1468), the empire grew considerably, particularly to the south. Major waterworks and causeways were built, and *chinampa* agriculture (often called 'floating gardens' but in fact a type of raised-field farming) expanded. However, mid-fifteenth century crop failures and other disasters (a snowstorm sank *chinampas* and caused thatched roofs to collapse) afflicted Motecuhzoma's reign. Then a successful New Fire ceremony was held in 1455 to commemorate the end of the 52-year cycle (see Chapter Three), and almost miraculously, we are told, the natural disasters ceased. To prevent food shortages from occurring in the future Motecuhzoma began a new campaign of conquest to the east, particularly in the Huastec region, where agricultural bounty was more certain. Under his administration the Aztecs also began what was known as 'flowery war,' or perpetual warfare for the purpose of gaining and offering sacrificial victims, often in gladiatorial combat. The main target of such warfare was Tlaxcala, a state to the east of the Aztecs and, by the later fifteenth century, largely surrounded by them.

Axayacatl and Tizoc, the rulers to succeed Motecuhzoma I, were less successful on the battlefield. Much energy was expended simply in controlling the dominion already established, and forays to the west brought the Aztecs into unsuccessful combat with the Tarascans, who had the benefit of metal weapons. Perhaps because he was jealous of its commercial success, Axayacatl brought the northern part of Tenochtitlan's island, Tlatelolco – known for its wealthy merchants – firmly under Aztec control. The last ruler of the fifteenth century, Ahuitzotl (1486–1501), was a great soldier who stepped up the pace of both conquest and sacrifice, which made the Aztecs' economic power equal to their military might. Parts of Guatemala, Oaxaca, and even El Salvador were incorporated into the Aztec realm. These last three rulers of the fifteenth century were half-brothers, grandsons of Motecuhzoma I.

Motecuhzoma II, a son of Axayacatl and destined to be the last independent ruler of the Aztecs, was installed as *tlatoani*, literally 'speaker,' in 1502. (The Spaniards equated the title with emperor, but the word suggests 'he who speaks for the people.') By this time, the population of the island had grown to about 200,000. Known more for his religious preoccupations than his military skills, Motecuhzoma presided over troubled times in Aztec history, even before the landing of the Spanish. There were ominous portents, and Motecuhzoma could not be reassured. Perhaps a larger problem was the nature of the Aztec 'empire' itself. The Aztecs kept no standing armies. Following an initial subjugation, they depended on local rulers, sometimes puppets, to carry out their administration, particularly in the fulfillment of tribute and the worship of the Aztec cult god, Huitzilopochtli. By the late fifteenth century, the Aztecs were overextended. More and more, distant provinces rebelled and Aztec might had to be wielded to restore control. The 'flowery war' with Tlaxcala became more than a military exercise, and other parts of the realm grew restless. In the end the very fierceness of Aztec retaliation was their undoing, for their enemies eagerly joined forces with the Spanish. Without the Tlaxcala warriors, the Spanish Conquest of Mexico would have been delayed many years.

Even at their first sighting of the Mesoamerican mainland, Spanish explorers knew they had discovered cultures far more sophisticated than any they had encountered in all the twenty-five prior years of their dominion in the Caribbean. At first they reconnoitered the coast of Yucatan, but their progress was impeded by hostile Maya, some of whom may have learned of the Spanish long before they attempted to invade. The Spanish found them living in small cities, with 'idols' kept in temples. The 'idols' offended and disgusted the Conquistadores, who therefore had no scruples about stripping these cult images of the gold and copper that adorned them. The metal wealth of the Postclassic Maya was negligible, however, and under the leadership of Cortés in 1519 attention was turned directly to the Valley of Mexico, to the people that informants of the time called 'Culhua' or 'Culhua-Mexica.' What drew Cortés to Tenochtitlan was not only the lure of gold; Cortés also perceived a great unknown kingdom, from which, if he could conquer it (with only 500 Spaniards and fewer than twenty horses in his original army), he would gain great power and prestige.

In the summer of 1519 Cortés founded Veracruz (the 'true cross') on the Gulf Coast of Mexico. With the aid of his translators – Jerónimo de Aguilar, a devout Christian captured by the Maya years before and eager to serve his king, and Doña Marina, a noble native woman later given this name who spoke both a Maya language and Nahuatl, the Aztec tongue – Cortés quickly perceived the fragility of the Aztec hegemony. Motecuhzoma commissioned a painting of the invasion that Bernal Díaz was able to recall years later. The presence of Marina may have been the most alarming feature to the Aztec lord, particularly if she was perceived to be the angry goddess thought to be preparing to destroy the world by means of earthquake. Known as Malinche in Spanish, she may also have been recognized as Malinaxochitl, one of Huitzilopochtli's half-sisters, and a known threat to Aztec sovereignty. Cortés and Marina lived together and devised the military campaign together. In mid-August Cortés began his march inland. He convinced local administrators that they no longer needed to fear the Aztecs, and he began to build a reservoir of support. In Tlaxcala, he gained his most important allies. Motecuhzoma tried to dissuade the Spanish from advancing by sending gifts, but this only whetted their appetites. By 8 November 1519, Cortés and his men were able to march into Tenochtitlan. Motecuhzoma did not prevent their entry. Unfortunately for him, however, the Spanish soon made him a hostage to guard their own security, and placed him under house arrest. There is no reason to think that Motecuhzoma perceived Cortés to be the returning Quetzalcoatl, but native accounts describe the way that Cortés stroked Motecuhzoma's hair, a gesture that would have horrified his subjects.

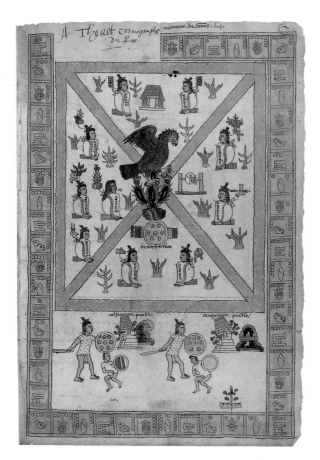

216 Folio 2, Codex Mendoza. Made in the mid-sixteenth century for the viceroy of New Spain, the Codex Mendoza is a record of history, tribute, and customs of the Aztecs. French pirates delivered the book to the court of Francis I, whose 'cosmographe' signed it at top. The central motif of the frontispiece shown here appears on the Mexican flag today.

Meanwhile, Spanish enemies of Cortés had arrived in Veracruz, and Cortés had to hurry back to the coast. In Tenochtitlan, the Spaniards grew uneasy and restless. In a reckless move, they attacked a religious ceremony (that involved human sacrifice) at the temple precinct. Insurrection broke out, and in desperation the Spaniards persuaded Motecuhzoma to try to appease the people. As he urged them not to fight he was struck on the head by a stone and killed. When Cortés returned a few days later, he found the remaining Spaniards under siege, and they fled the city on what is now called the 'Noche Triste,' 30 June 1520. Many men, horses, and much gold were lost. Nine months later, bolstered by thousands of Tlaxcalans and reinforcements and supplies from Cuba, Cortés laid siege to Tenochtitlan. Racked by deprivation and weakened by European disease, the Aztecs under the leadership of Cuauhtemoc at last yielded to the Spanish invaders on 13 August 1521.

Cortés wrote a series of letters to Charles V, recounting events and justifying his behavior. By means of these letters Cortés became the first Western historian and art historian of Mesoamerica. Other important Renaissance figures also commented with enthusiasm on the splendor of New World treasures. Albrecht Durer, for example, visited Brussels at the arrival of the first Royal Fifth, that is, one-fifth of the riches collected by Cortés. Many curiosities were sent: perhaps the Dresden Codex and the marvelous costume elements delivered to Cortés by Motecuhzoma's emissaries were among them. Durer, the son of a fine goldsmith, was particularly impressed by the metalwork:

Also I saw the things which were brought to the King from the New Golden Land: a sun entirely of gold, a whole fathom broad; likewise, a moon, entirely of silver, just as big; likewise, sundry curiosities from their weapons, armor, and missiles; very odd clothing, bedding, and all sorts of strange articles for human use, all of which is fairer to see than marvels. These things were all so precious that they were valued at a hundred thousand guilders. But I have never seen in all my days that which so rejoiced my heart, as these things. For I saw among them amazing artistic objects, and I marveled over the subtle ingenuity of the men in these distant lands. Indeed I cannot say enough about the things which were there before me.

Unfortunately, the same gold that merited Dürer's accolades and dazzled the Old World drove the Spanish to sack and destroy both structures and art in their search for the precious metal. The treasures that Dürer saw were melted down, their value as currency far exceeding their interest as works of art from the New World.

As a result, although the Aztecs made many fine objects of gold and silver, almost none survive. Nor were the buildings that housed these ancient treasures spared. Tenochtitlan – ransacked and subsequently transformed into the Colonial capital of New Spain – suffered more than any other major Precolumbian city. Nevertheless, thanks to the wealth of documentation of Aztec life, art, and 'idolatrous' customs in sixteenth-century chronicles, we still know more about the art and architecture of Tenochtitlan than we do about any other Mesoamerican city. Recently, major excavations at the heart of the ceremonial precinct, as well as minor excavations along expanding subway lines, have revealed yet more of the material evidence for Aztec art.

Architecture and city planning

Bernal Díaz compared the general plan of Tenochtitlan to Venice, and the city was indeed crisscrossed by a web of intersecting canals, laid out on a grid. Four main residential quadrants radiated from the walled ceremonial precinct. Just outside the walls stood the royal palaces. The frontispiece of the mid-sixteenth-century manuscript, the Codex Mendoza, can be read in many ways, but one is as a map of Tenochtitlan [216]. At the center is the eagle in a cactus, the place symbol for Tenochtitlan and used on the Mexican flag today. As the frontispiece shows, the city was divided by water into four sections. The page can also be read as a plan of the walled ceremonial precinct. On Mesoamerican maps (and on

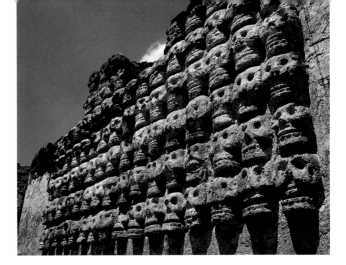

217 The temple precinct included several skull racks, some permanently adorned with skull sculptures.

218 In the mid-sixteenth century, this plan of the center of the ancient Aztec capital was drawn up for Father Sahagún in a manuscript known today as the Primeros Memoriales. The twin pyramid of Huitzilopochtli and Tlaloc is at the center of the drawing. Beneath Quetzalcoatl, in white, are the skull rack and ballcourt. Only three doorways granted access to the precinct.

some European maps as well), east was at the top of the plan. Here we find a house, probably a reference to the great twin pyramid. It is set in opposition to the *tzompantli*, or skull rack, which was also a prominent feature of the ritual precinct [217]. Fifty-one year names run as a border round the page (2 Reed is marked as the year of the Conquest), placing the scene within the cyclical calendar. In the lower margin are two principal conquests of the Aztecs and, as on a Maya stela, captives, the symbols of dominion, lie beneath the heads of state, who are also represented above. For Tenochtitlan, the definition of the city was bound to its position in both space and time.

Another sixteenth-century manuscript, the Primeros Memoriales, also shows the plan of the ceremonial precinct [218]. In this illustration the twin pyramid lies at the top or east; a penitent in white garb stands in front. This is the benevolent – one might say white-washed – Postconquest view of Quetzalcoatl. Beneath him lie the *tzompantli* and I-shaped ballcourt.

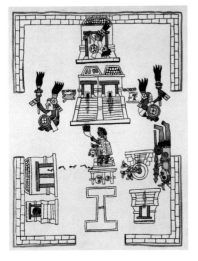

In 1978 a chance discovery by workers digging in the vicinity of the ceremonial precinct helped initiate the most important archaeological excavations in Mexico City of the twentieth century, a project that continues apace. Among many remarkable finds were entire chambers of offerings, some with shells, sand and marine life, locating the temple at the center of the world, along with unusual sculptures of high quality that fundamentally alter our knowledge of Aztec art. Given the combined information that we now have from sixteenth-century manuscripts and recent archaeology, we can at last begin to understand many of the principles underlying the layout of the ceremonial center. The capacity of Aztec artists to work in many different styles at once continues to amaze modern observers.

Excavations have shown that some sort of ceremonial architecture preceded Aztec construction in the ceremonial precinct. Over the nearly 200 years of Aztec domination, the Templo Mayor (as the entire complex is often known) was rebuilt several times [215]. Each successive phase of construction was marked by caches and deposits before the new structures completely encased their predecessors [220, 221]. In 1487 the final building program was completed, and it was this version of the precinct that Cortés and his soldiers saw. Father Durán's history of the Aztecs describes the rededication ceremony of 1487. Sacrificial victims were led in long processions from the Huastec region, some individuals tied together with ropes through their pierced noses. Thousands of sacrifices were offered, and blood ran in the streets and canals.

This city and temple plan, as might be expected, drew on precedents in the Valley of Mexico, from Tula and Teotihuacan to small cities along the lake. The twin pyramid appears to have been a Late Postclassic invention, known at Tenayuca among other places. It offered an equality between the two deities venerated in the shrines at the summit. It also provided the means for retaining a local deity while introducing a new one. For the Aztecs, such a structure facilitated the ready introduction of Huitzilopochtli wherever they made their impact felt. The canals laid out along a grid at Tenochtitlan were probably modeled on the rigid grid at Teotihuacan [68, 69].

Again, as at Teotihuacan, the overall plan of Tenochtitlan took advantage of the natural topography of the Valley of Mexico. The twin pyramid was framed by the volcanoes Ixtaccihuatl and Popocatepetl to the east, recalling the positioning of the Pyramid of the Moon with Cerro Gordo at Teotihuacan [70]. The ceremonial precinct was also laid out to acknowledge the movement of heavenly bodies. During the wetter season, appropriate for agriculture, the sun rose every day behind the blue Temple of Tlaloc, the ancient rain and earth god; in the drier months, the sun emerged from the red Temple of Huitzilopochtli, whose associations with warfare, hunting, and fire were appropriate for this season. On the mornings of the two annual equinoxes, however, the sun rose between these two temples and faced the Temple of Quetzalcoatl.

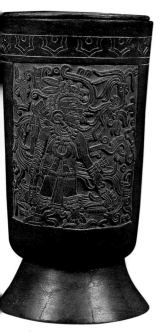

219 Archaeologists found several handsome, carved urns on the Huitzilopochtli side of the temple; they may have held funerary ashes.

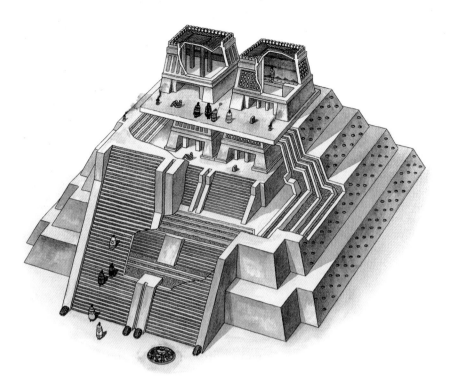

220 Almost constantly in a state of renovation and expansion, the Templo Mayor was rebuilt time and again, hiding within it chambers and caches of offerings, buried sculptures and funerary ashes, and making of it a sacred mountain.

221 Supplicants placed corals, seaweed, and the saw of a sawfish under the small sculpture of a seated deity. Stones carved to represent hand-held drums and leaf-shaped flints formed the uppermost level.

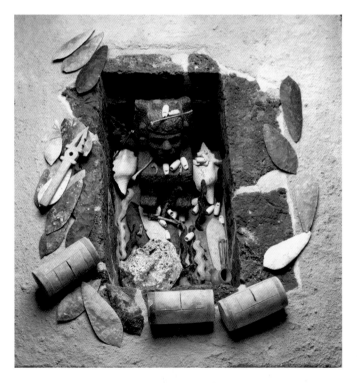

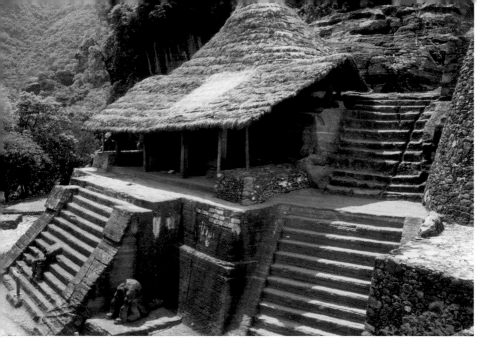

222 At Malinalco, west of Tenochtitlan, a mountainside was carved in Aztec times to set temples into the living rock. The thatched roof is a modern restoration.

In the union between Tlaloc and Huitzilopochtli on the Templo Mayor, the old established deity of the Toltecs and perhaps Teotihuacan gave legitimacy to the new cult of the Aztecs. The two seasons of the tropical world, wet and dry, were also thus united. The Templo suggests too the expression *atltlachinolli*, literally 'water-conflagration,' used by the Aztecs to mean warfare, especially sacred war. In the very pairing of Tlaloc and Huitzilopochtli they made this metaphor the center of Aztec religion.

The Aztecs therefore echoed and recreated within the ceremonial precinct the natural topographic features surrounding Tenochtitlan. At other sites around the Valley of Mexico, however, they carved the mountains themselves, transforming natural forms into manmade ones. At Texcotzingo, a hill east of Lake Texcoco, baths and shrines were worked directly into the cliffside, making it a pleasure garden. Shrines were constructed at the summits of many other mountains in the Valley of Mexico too. At Tepeyacac, Tonantzin, an earth and mother goddess, received offerings at what would become the site of the Virgin of Guadalupe, Mexico's patron saint. To the east, the Tlaloque, or rain gods, dwelt atop Mount Tlaloc: to the Aztecs, it was the gods' raucous parties and the hurling of pots of water that led to thunderous rainstorms. At Malinalco, a ceremonial precinct was built into a mountainside [222]. The most important building there is a round structure carved out of the living rock. To enter the inner chamber one steps through an open pair of monster jaws and onto a giant tongue. A circular bench with jaguars and eagles carved as seats curves round the interior, and a deep hole of narrow diameter at the center of the floor enters the heart of the mountain. The jaguar and eagle pelts suggest that this was a chamber for the military orders of Jaguar and Eagle Knights, who may have conducted penitential rites here, perhaps offering their own blood directly into the earth.

Sculpture

The Aztec word that comes closest to the European concept of a god is *teotl*, which even sounded to Spanish ears like a corruption of *dios*. But the Aztec concept of *teotl* is different from the European concept of god, and although Huitzilopochtli may have been a solar deity, he was not Apollo. Rather, *teotl* called up a series of natural forces, like the Polynesian *mana*. The Aztecs captured the representation of gods in stone and wooden images, but the sacred force dwelled in sacred bundles kept separately inside shrines and temples. Huitzilopochtli's power lived in the bundle carried by the Aztecs on their long migration and then kept at the Templo Mayor, although the Spanish saw the sculptural representation as the force of idolatry.

The ability of human blood to sustain ancestors and to nourish gods is embedded in many Aztec works of art. These references are not metaphorical: one Spanish soldier, Andrés de Tapia, described the experience of seeing a large and terrifying sculpture encrusted with jewels, gold, and human blood. That sculpture may have been similar to the great Coatlicue, or 'she of the serpent skirt,' a depiction so fearsome that it was systematically re-interred at various times after its accidental discovery in 1790 in excavations near the Cathedral, within the old ceremonial precinct. It is probably the greatest of known Aztec sculptures [223].

The Coatlicue is both a two-dimensional work, intricately patterned, and a great three-dimensional portrait. Interestingly, it was once part of a series, one of what may have been a set of four, as Elizabeth Boone has argued. As a multiple, its power would have been even greater, the full force of female terror unleashed. Like many Aztec sculptures, it is also carved on its underside with an earth monster — indeed some early students therefore erroneously imagined that it was meant to be suspended in the air. The bulky figure leans forward, pressing upon viewers and enveloping them in shadow. Particularly in profile, she also

223 Rediscovered in the late eighteenth century, this sculpture of the goddess Coatlicue was so fearsome that it was reburied for some years. Two serpents form her head, and she wears a necklace of hands and hearts.

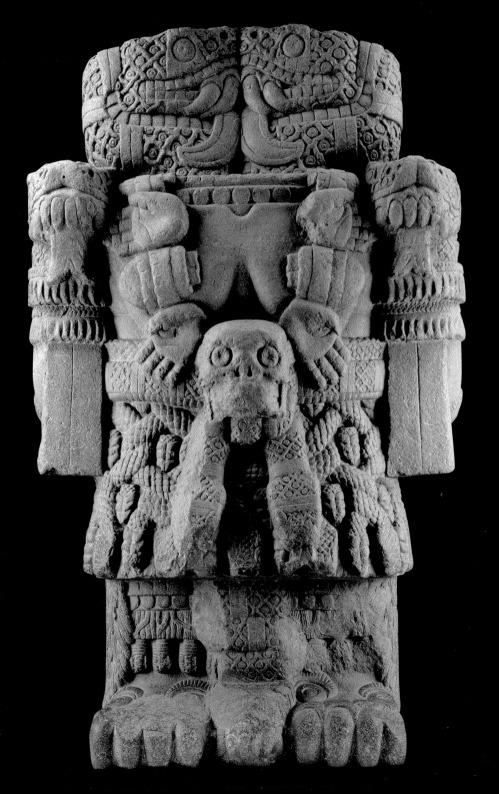

resembles the great twin pyramid. The head is severed and replaced by two snakes, symbolic of flowing blood. Another snake descends from her groin, suggesting both menses and penis. Her hands and feet have been transformed into claws, and she wears a necklace of severed hands and extruded hearts. It is a nightmare cast within female form. It is also a powerful, imaginative sculpture, representative of the superb work created in Tenochtitlan in the last fifty years of Aztec dominion, in what has been termed the 'metropolitan' style by George Kubler.

The goddess known as Coatlicue figures prominently in the story of Huitzilopochtli's parthenogenesis. According to legend, Coatlicue kept a temple shrine on a hill near Tula called Coatepec, or 'hill of snakes.' After tucking a ball of down feathers in her bosom, she became pregnant with Huitzilopochtli. Repelled by her condition, her children, especially her daughter Coyolxauhqui, plotted her death. When Coatlicue's enemies attacked her and sliced off her head, Huitzilopochtli rose from her severed trunk fully grown and armed. He banished the attackers and mutilated his evil sister, severing her extremities, so that she collapsed at the base of the shrine.

The myth was permanently commemorated at the twin pyramid. Serpents lined the base, as if to suggest Coatepec, 'snake mountain'. Within the Huitzilopochtli shrine was a sculpture of that deity, probably made of wood and now lost, like the rest of his images; the deity's representation survives only in manuscripts. The recent excavations in the Templo Mayor have revealed a great round stone of Coyolxauhqui at the foot of the pyramid, mutilated and humiliated, a permanent record of conquest and probably the place of much subsequent sacrifice [224]. Coyolxauhqui was also understood to be the moon and Huitzilopochtli the sun, so the myth repeats the dominance of the greater heavenly body over the lesser, even the three-dimensional over the two-dimensional. In their positioning, we should also recall the Codex Mendoza frontispiece, with defeated figures at the bottom of the page.

Such extraordinary Aztec sculptures reveal the energy given over to the new, imperial style. As parvenus in Mesoamerica, however, the Aztecs had many established sources upon which to draw. Enclaves of foreign artists, particularly from Oaxaca, lived in Tenochtitlan, bringing their own styles and techniques to the metropolis. The Aztecs returned to Tula, Hidalgo, to sack the site, and brought back Toltec sculptures – perhaps *chacmools* and warrior figures – to their own capital. They also derived

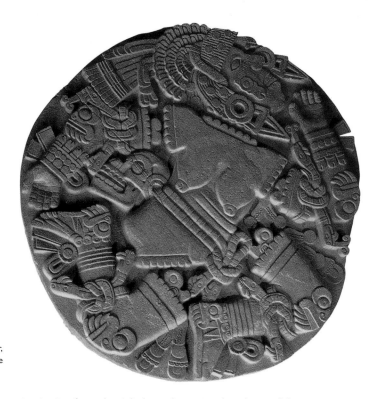

224 Dismembered limbs fly from the body of the goddess Coyolxauhqui on this massive stone that lay at the base of Huitzilopochtli's temple. Discovered by workmen excavating the cellar of a bookstore in 1978, this sculpture sparked renewed interest in the remains of the Aztec sacred center, subsequently the focus of extensive excavation.

inspiration from the rich three-dimensional tradition of the Huastec region of the Gulf Coast, particularly after conquering much of the area in the mid-fifteenth century. And, almost like archaeologists, the Aztecs were continually uncovering elements of the past. Recent excavations in the Templo Mayor precinct have revealed caches of objects, particularly of antiquities even in Aztec times. Olmec, Teotihuacan, and West Mexican stone pieces have been found as offerings. Whether through tribute, looting, or the collection of heirlooms, the Aztecs were the recipients of many works of art that they studied, cherished, buried again, or incorporated into their own visual imagery.

The Stone of Tizoc is essentially a historical monument, worked in the conventionalized, stiff-figured manner characteristic of manuscript painting, particularly in Oaxaca, where historical screenfold writings had long been made [225]. Like a Roman emperor depicted as Hercules, the minor Aztec ruler Tizoc is shown in the garb of Tezcatlipoca, a principal late Central Mexican deity known by his smoking mirror and serpent foot (like K'awiil of the Maya), and in this role he takes a captive. This image appears fifteen times on the Stone, confirming the prowess of Tizoc (in

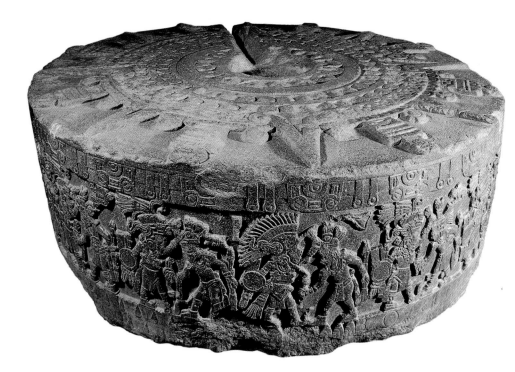

225 The Stone of Tizoc commemorates the brief reign of this minor fifteenth-century ruler. Victorious warriors hold captives by the hair, as do the victors in ill. 43. A solar disk is carved on the upper surface.

fact he was a failure as a military strategist), but set within a cosmic scheme: a solar disk defines the upper surface of the stone; gnawing schematized earth monsters with reptilian skin lie under the protagonists' feet. From such a depiction, we can probably assume that the *tlatoani* was perceived to be the divine perpetuator of the sun by this time. Motecuhzoma II, we know, was thought of as a god during his lifetime.

No single image of ancient Mesoamerica is better known than the great Calendar Stone [226]: it is reproduced on ashtrays, keychains, liquor labels, and is popular both in and outside Mexico. Like the Stone of Tizoc and the Coatlicue, the stone was saved from being recycled as building material late in the eighteenth century when it was found near the Cathedral. Despite its name, the Calendar Stone does not function as any sort of useful calendar but works rather as a record of calendrical cataclysm. It represents an expanded cosmic scheme related to the one recorded on the Stone of Tizoc. The basic representation is of a solar diadem, borne by encircling fire serpents and framing the twenty day names. At the center is the outline of the day sign, Ollin, or Movement, within which are described four dates. These

254

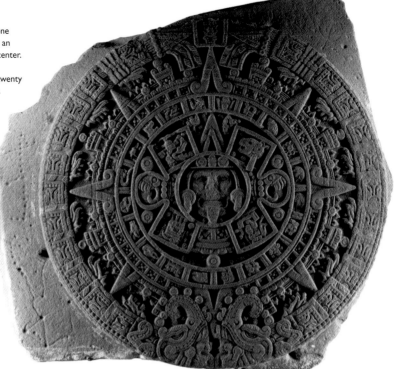

226 The great Calendar Stone features a solar diadem with an earth monster within at its center. Although not a functioning calendar by any means, the twenty day signs appear on the disk.

commemorate the Four Suns, or previous eras, known by the day names on which their destruction took place. On Four Wind, for example (upper left), the world and its inhabitants were destroyed by great winds. According to the Aztecs, the current world would end in cataclysm on Four Movement, the larger date inscribed. At the very center of the stone is a frontal face bordered by clawed extremities that grasp human hearts. Although long identified as the sun god, the face belongs to the female earth monster, Tlaltecuhtli, [227] usually found on the hidden underside of other monuments, and whose monumental depiction came to light recently. The image thus created is of the sun fallen on earth, the cataclysm complete, the Aztec world ended. On the Stone of Tizoc, the sun and earth were kept apart by rulership and captive sacrifice. The Calendar Stone is exhibited and reproduced as a wall panel today, but it was probably set on the ground, with blood offerings anointed on the earth monster. When recovered in the eighteenth century, the stone had been placed face down, to keep further apocalypse at bay. Although the Aztec world did not end in earthquakes, as predicted, it ended in cultural cataclysm, perhaps a metaphorical earthquake.

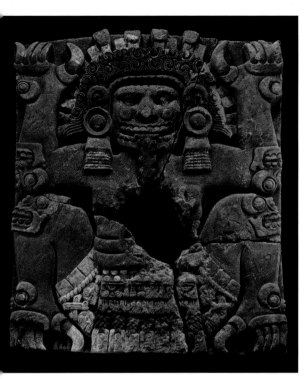

At the Templo Mayor, further understanding of this powerful deity came when Leonardo Lopez Luján and his team discovered a 13-ton monolith under the remnants of a buried Early Colonial house and its gracious European columns in October 2006. The vast but simple representation was designed to be seen from the top of the completed temple, making it possible to perceive the scale of the compound. Skeletal here, like the central face of the Calendar Stone, this massive Tlaltecuhtli is in the posture of parturition, while a stream of blood flows upward to her mouth. The work's distinctive yellow body paint emphasizes the disturbing imagery, with details added in shades or red, brown, white, and black. According to Aztec belief, Tlaltecuhtli drank the sun every day at dusk, regurgitating it at dawn; her destroyed navel may have been the setting for grand rituals, even funereal ones: grasped in the claws of her right foot is the date 10 Rabbit, a reference to the year 1502, when Motecuhzoma's predecessor Ahuitzotl had died. Excavations continue, and chambers underneath and adjacent to the sculpture continue to yield treasures from the known Aztec world, including exotic birds, turquoise, and a canine wearing gold anklets.

Many small cult images are known from shrines throughout Central Mexico. Most common among these are female maize deities, generally standing figures with headdresses like temple roofcombs [229]. Provincial figures are flat and blocky, without the skilled execution of imperial works but also lacking the more horrifying Aztec imagery. The potters of the period also produced a great many deity figures, some braziers designed to be carried like modern-day saints. In provincial works, emphasis thus fell on more beneficient images of fertility.

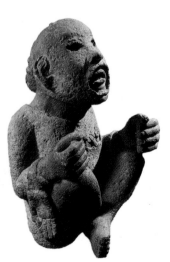

Another common fertility figure, this time male, was Xipe Totec, 'our lord the flayed one' [228]. Xipe Totec was a god of planting, and his ritual imitated the observed natural life of the maize

Opposite top:
227 The recently discovered Tlaltecuhtli squats, as if in parturition; the skulls and crossbones that adorn her skirt are typical of goddesses of childbirth across Mesoamerica. The deity grasps an Aztec calendar date in a clawed foot; polished bones adorn her hair, like those worn by the Tikal ruler on Stela 31 (ill. 122).

Opposite below:
228 The impersonator of Xipe Totec, 'our lord the flayed one,' wears the skin of a flayed human. By the end of a twenty-day ritual in honor of Xipe, the skin would have rotted. An imitation of a plant life cycle, Xipe Totec was a god of springtime. Note the extra set of hands that dangle limply.

Right:
229 Discovered in 100s of pieces in 1996, this large ceramic devotional image (3 ft 6 in, 106 cm in height) represents Chicmecoatl, goddess of maize, who holds the ripe ears of grain. Part of a matching set, she was found with three other fertility deities, all made in the same workshop.

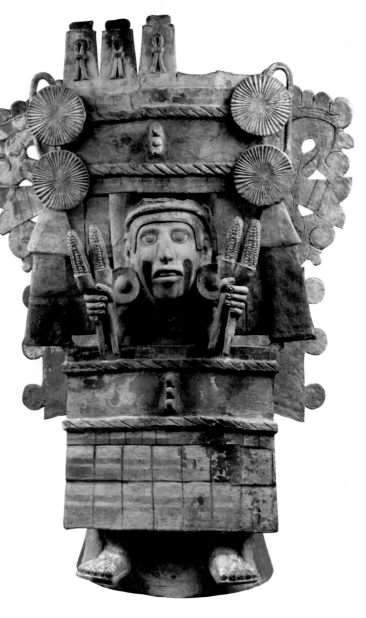

kernel. A human skin was flayed, and a young man wore it until it rotted off (one dreads to think of the stench), allowing the new, clean youth to emerge, like a sprout from the husk of the old seed. Xipe's cult was at first celebrated most along the Gulf Coast, especially among the Huastecs, but with Aztec domination, the cult spread in Central Mexico. Many ceramic and stone images of Xipe are known, and the flayed skin is often shown with almost loving detail. Unlike the female maize deities, the Xipe figures were also executed in rich three-dimensional forms. Three-dimensional sculpture had a sustained life along the Gulf Coast, from Olmec times to the Spanish Conquest, and the sensual, rounded shapes of Xipe sculptures probably derive from this tradition.

The Gulf Coast also gave rise to a tradition of large, hollow ceramic sculptures. The recent excavations in the ceremonial precinct have produced the finest such specimen ever to be found in the Valley of Mexico. Made in four separate pieces, the sculpture represents a life-sized eagle warrior, poised just as if to take flight [230]. Bits of stucco show that he was probably once covered with feathers. One of a pair who flanked a doorway, the warrior is reminiscent of the eagle jamb figure painted at Cacaxtla some centuries before. The beauty and natural proportions of this figure reach out across the centuries, transcending cultural boundaries. It is difficult to believe that the same culture that made the Coatlicue would also create this Eagle Knight. What we find, nevertheless, is a pluralism of aesthetic ideals rarely matched in history, and perhaps best compared with our own era. In some cases such disparate works may have been produced in a single workshop: a pair of death gods was produced using similar technique, to be adorned with human hair. Naturalism was enshrined at the same time as abstraction; beauty and terror both inspired awe. We know relatively little from the Aztecs of the conceptual ideals of their sculpture, but we do have a description of what a beautiful young male sacrificial victim should be:

[He was] like something smoothed, like a tomato, or like a pebble, as if hewn of wood. [He did] not [have] curly hair, [but] straight, long hair; [he had] no scabs, pustules, or boils...not with a gross face, nor a downcast one; not flat-nosed nor with wide nostrils, nor with an arched...nose nor a bulbous nose, nor bent nor twisted nor crooked – but his nose should be well-placed, straight... [he should be] not emaciated, nor fat, nor big-bellied, nor of prominent, hatchet-shaped navel, nor of wrinkled stomach...nor of flabby buttocks or thighs...
(Florentine Codex, Book 4, Sixth Chapter,
trans. Dibble and Anderson)

In the face of the Eagle Knight, we see that perfection.

Naturalism also inspired Aztec artists to make precious works of small scale, including squashes, cacti, and shells. A red carnelite grasshopper refers to Chapultepec [231], the 'hill of the grasshopper,' where Aztec rulers also had their portraits carved, as can be seen in an early colonial watercolour.

Other Aztec sculptures also served as temple or palace furnishings. *Chacmools* had probably long been used as receptacles for human hearts, and a number of Aztec ones have been found. The earliest known Aztec *chacmool* was discovered *in situ* on the Tlaloc side of the twin pyramid, in an early context. It may even have been brought from Tula, with other looted treasures. It is the only *chacmool* to survive with bright polychrome, but most Aztec sculptures were probably painted. In fact, given modern taste, we might be unpleasantly surprised if we were to see them in their original condition. Another very sensuously carved *chacmool* excavated in 1943 outside the ceremonial precinct could have been moved away from the temple compound at the time of the Conquest [232]. The recumbent figure wears a Tlaloc mask and bears a *cuauhxicalli*, a vessel for sacrificed human hearts, on his chest. Tlaloc insignia are inscribed on the vessel's upper surface. The underside of the whole sculpture is worked with a Tlaloc among other aquatic motifs, as if the monument were floating in a liminal state. Like the dead and dying figures at Cacaxtla, this *chacmool* wears a jade plaque from an earlier culture (it would appear to be a Zapotec or Maya piece), as if to associate the antique form of the sculpture with an antique culture. The *chacmool* seems very likely therefore to have come from the Tlaloc side of the twin pyramid, which bore other symbols of antiquity as well.

The Temple Stone was found near the palace of Motecuhzoma II in 1831, and probably functioned as his throne, although it has been called the 'Monument of Sacred War' [233]. It records the date in 1507 of the last New Fire ceremony, normally celebrated at the completion of a 52-year cycle. On the sides, seated deities draw blood from their loins, and this blood drawn in penance supports the legitimate ruler. These seated deities all carry the symbol for stone, or *tetl*, on their backs. making the gods themselves the founders of the temple. Above, Motecuhzoma would be seated on an earth monster, with the solar disk at his back. In this way, he bore the sun; he also prevented it from collapsing onto the earth. The *tlatoani* was thus the conduit of order, the figure whose very essence keeps the upperworld and underworld in place.

Overleaf:
230 Life-sized, this idealized young eagle warrior is poised as if to take flight. Gulf Coast sculptors, skilled in firing such large terracotta works, came to Tenochtitlan.

231 This large red carnelite grasshopper, or *chapulin* in Nahuatl, probably refers to Chapultepec, or 'hill of the grasshopper,' just west of Lake Texcoco. It is 1ft 6 in (45 cm) in length.

232 The recumbent figure of this rain god *chacmool* wears a Tlaloc mask and a pendant with an archaistic motif, as if to refer to antiquity in general. The underside of the monument is worked with aquatic motifs.

233 The Temple Stone. Also known as the 'Monument of Sacred War,' this miniature temple was probably a throne in Motecuhzoma II's palace. When the lord was seated, he would appear to carry the sun on his back.

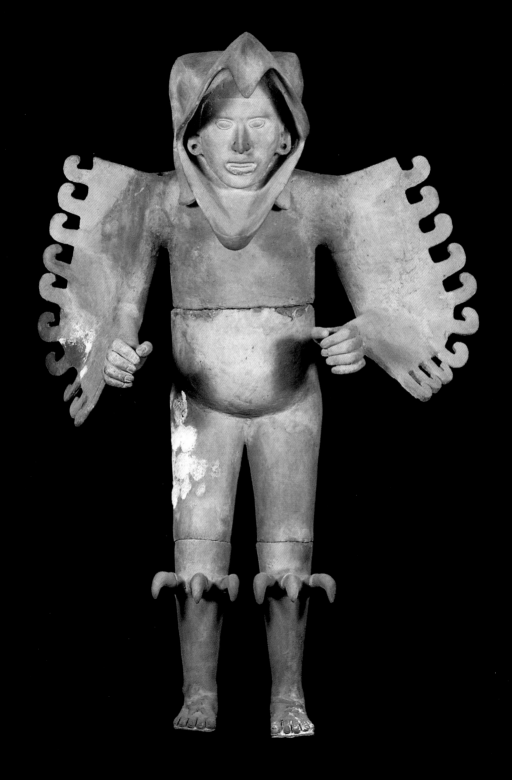

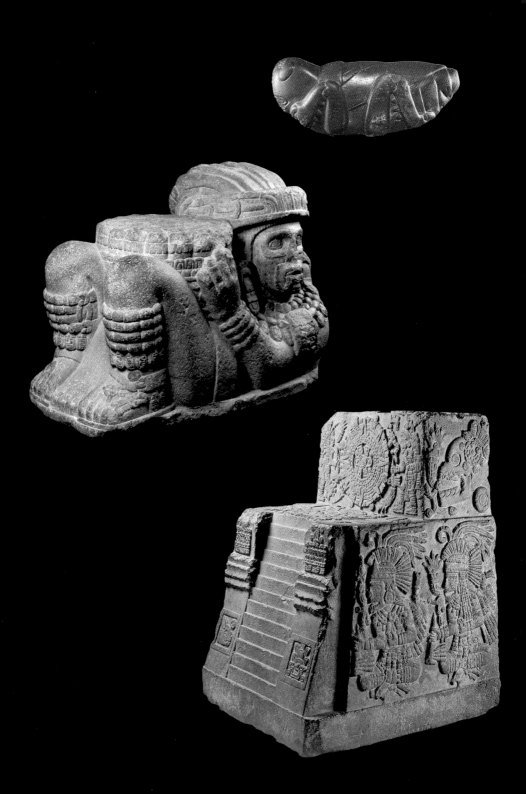

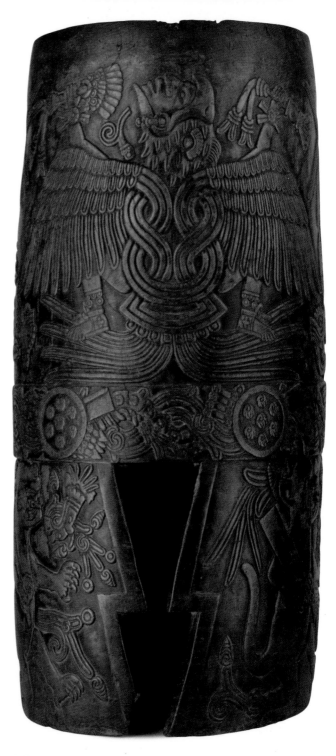

234 A *huehuetl*, or large upright drum, reportedly from Malinalco (ill. 215). Deerhide would have been stretched across the top of the cylinder, and the drum was played with the hand. The *teponaztli*, a longitudinal drum, was played with drumsticks.

Minor arts

Many musical instruments were worked with designs that indicate their importance in Aztec ritual life. A number of *teponaztlis*, the higher-toned, longitudinal drums, and *huehuetls*, the deeper, upright drums, have survived from prehispanic times. A fine *huehuetl*, reputedly from Malinalco, may have been associated with the orders of Jaguar and Eagle Knights there and might even have been used to accompany rites in the Malinalco chambers [234]. The drum carries the date of the destruction of the Fifth Sun, Four Movement. Jaguars and eagles dance ecstatically around the instrument, and all emit speech scrolls of the twined *atltlachinolli*, 'water-fire,' or warfare symbols. They also carry banners to indicate that they are sacrificial victims, as if perhaps to pronounce their willingness to be sacrificed to sustain the Fifth Sun, and such sacrificial events were probably accompanied by music.

Other fine Aztec works were made of feathers or covered with feather mosaic, turquoise mosaic [235], and gold. Little of the goldwork survives, thanks to the destructive lust of the invaders. Virtually the only pieces for us to study and admire are of Mixtec manufacture, discovered in Oaxaca during the 1930s. In Tenochtitlan, the Mixtecs were recognized as the greatest metalworkers of the era, and an enclave lived there to practice their craft. Such craftsmen manipulated many materials, including obsidian, which they worked to translucency to make fine adornments [213]. Oaxaca, the region of the Zapotecs and Mixtecs, was spared much of the violent destruction of the Conquest, In 1932 Alfonso Caso excavated a royal tomb on Monte Alban that had been re-used in the fifteenth century. He discovered a superb cache there of over a hundred gold objects, along with fine artifacts of silver, pearl, jade, rock crystal, obsidian, and bone. At last the skills that earned Durer's accolades became evident to the twentieth century. The most spectacular object is the large pectoral of a skeletal deity, probably female, and made by working filigree atop a lost-wax casting [236].

The malleability, color, and inert nature of gold have always made it an appealing raw material, although the Aztecs valued jade more highly. They referred to gold as *teocuicatl*, or 'excrement of the gods.' Given the destruction of the Conquest, we will probably never know the nature of Aztec goldwork to any greater extent.

High-quality Aztec feather painting (a mosaic technique, really, of finely cut exotic bird feathers) has also not survived, although

Overleaf:
235 The Aztec worked turquoise, much of it from the American Southwest, into fine tesserae and assembled masks and costume elements of it. This exquisite double-headed serpent probably once served as part of a deity's regalia and would have been worn across the chest.

236 A large gold pectoral from Tomb 7, Monte Alban. Filigree maize tassels and headdress adorn the lost-wax skeletal head of a female deity. A day sign, left, is set within a Mixtec year, right.

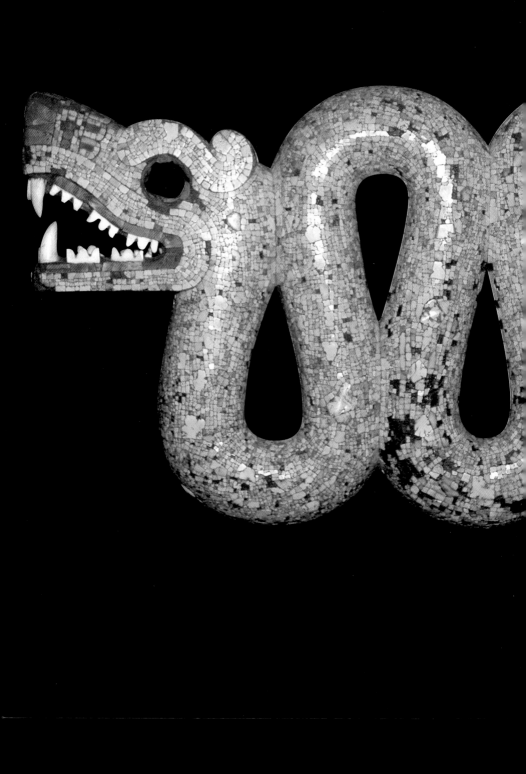

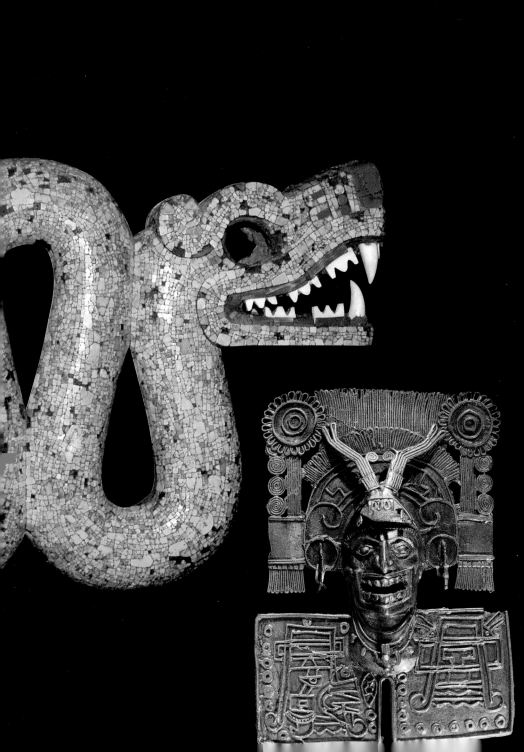

detailed feather paintings are known with Christian imagery. Aztec headdresses and shields, on the other hand, have endured. At an 1890 conference in Paris, Zelia Nuttall first suggested that the fine featherwork preserved in Vienna might be Motecuhzoma's headdress. To prove its wearability, she made and wore a reconstruction. With its extraordinary green quetzal and blue cotinga feathers, gold, and beads, the original headdress certainly may have been a royal garment, but there is no evidence that it was the property of Motecuhzoma II in particular [238]. Illustrations in the chapter on featherworking in the Florentine Codex, the sixteenth-century encyclopedia (see below), show the making of a similar headdress [249]. Skilled craftsmen worked Christian designs in finely applied feathers throughout the Colonial era, the dazzling material adapted to new purposes.

Motecuhzoma II sent Cortés a chest containing turquoise mosaic masks and feather costumes of various deities in 1519. Guided by Doña Marina, Cortés may have given the calculated impression that he impersonated a god when he donned a costume and mask. These curiosities were sent to Europe, but it is no longer certain which ones were in Motecuhzoma's gift. One of the masks in the British Museum is of the deity Tezcatlipoca, with black obsidian bands set against a bright blue face [239]. Pyrites form the eyes. Unlike many of the other masks, this mosaic is built over a human skull, and its wearer would have been unable to see.

Bernal Díaz described the sumptuous meals prepared for Motecuhzoma II. Tens of dishes would be served up for the king's pleasure, including turkey, boar, venison, rabbit, quail, duck, pigeon, and human flesh. Motecuhzoma would sit and eat behind a screen, alone. Díaz informs us that Motecuhzoma ate only from Cholula pottery (so named although it was made at various places in the Valley of Puebla). With their rich polychrome slip design over fine, thin pottery, Cholula wares were far superior to the Aztec product [237]. Many designs and color patterns can be related to the Borgia group of manuscripts (see below), which may also have been made in the Cholula region.

Some unusual ceramics have been recovered from the Templo Mayor excavations. Fine vessels were found on the Huitzilopochtli side that were made in an archaizing fashion, imitating Toltec work, and the cremated remains they contained were perhaps those of Motecuhzoma I. Remarkable bright blue pigment was preserved on a Tlaloc effigy vessel, found on the Tlaloc side of the temple [240]. Like many fifteenth- and sixteenth-century Aztec

237 Ceramic cup from Cholula, with decoration of three jaguars. Bright polychrome slip was used by Cholula potters to draw intricate patterns and figural scenes. The pottery was in demand throughout the Valley of Mexico at the time of the Conquest.

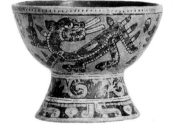

Tlaloc images, the deity has the braided twist over his nose that characterizes the Maya Jaguar God of the Underworld, and may link ancient concepts of war to water.

Rocker stamps and roller stamps, used from earliest times for body decoration, may also have been used in Aztec times to mark paper and fabric with geometric designs, many of which resemble those achieved in weaving [241].

Manuscripts

Shortly after his accession to power in 1426, Itzcoatl collected and destroyed manuscripts, making way for a new record of official Aztec history and religion. Nevertheless, it is obvious from the variety of historical and mythic information later written down in the Roman alphabet that a great diversity of religious and historical ideas continued long after Itzcoatl's edict. The supremacy of Huitzilopochtli as a cult god was contested throughout the region, and in fact Tezcatlipoca seems to have remained the supreme deity among those claiming Toltec descent.

Sadly the Spanish invasion was more effective than Itzcoatl's purge, and, even though books were common among the Aztecs, no manuscript survives that can be attributed to Preconquest Tenochtitlan. Examples from other regions remained intact, however, and various schools of manuscript painting thrived for fifty years after the Conquest. Books served many purposes for the Aztecs: genealogies were kept, 260-day ritual calendars were consulted, and religious esoterica were guarded in screenfold manuscripts. For generations after the Conquest, Mixtec screenfolds were brought to Colonial courts to document testimony in land disputes. Painted in thin stucco on deer hide, these manuscripts were sometimes scraped and re-used; for sixteenth- and seventeenth-century purposes, 'idolatrous' lore might be purged in order to allow legal use of the genealogical records. The Codex Selden relates the genealogy of one prominent Mixtec family [242]. Red guidelines indicate the boustrophedon, or back-and-forth, reading order of the manuscript, and we can observe the highly conventionalized nature of representation. In the section illustrated here, which reads from bottom to top, the heroine 6 Monkey heeds her advisers. Footprints indicate travel or movement: at the bottom of the page, 6 Monkey and her betrothed bathe together. Subsequently she fights the battles that will regain her kingdom for her. She can be identified by her name glyph, which appears like a cartoon balloon above her.

Overleaf:

Above left:
238 Perhaps sent to Charles V by Cortés, this exotic Aztec feather headdress has been preserved in Vienna since the Conquest. Some scholars have speculated that Motecuhzoma II himself might have worn it.

Below left:
239 Probably part of a whole costume of the deity Tezcatlipoca, this mask is made of turquoise mosaic, obsidian, and gold pyrites over a human skull. The jaw is moveable.

Above right:
240 Hundreds of Tlaloc effigies were unearthed from the Tlaloc side of the Templo Mayor. This unusual ceramic effigy vessel was painted bright blue after firing.

Below right:
241 Mesoamericans used stamps and seals to decorate their bodies from the earliest times. This Aztec example features textile-like patterns.

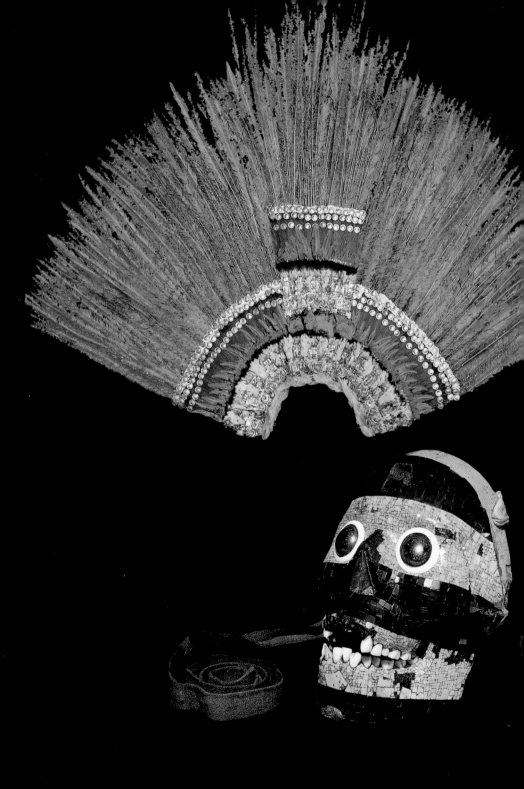

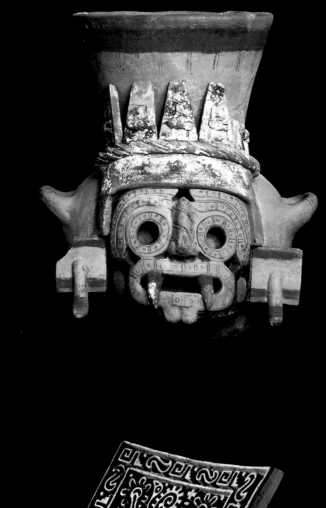

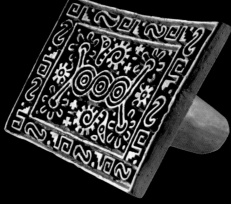

There are many surviving Mixtec genealogies, and although they are embedded within a context of mythic origins (some families derive from trees, others from stones), they are essentially historical. They are also not without interesting contradictions: the heroic 8 Deer of one narration can be revealed as a villainous assassin in another, according to some scholars. The complexity of such interlocked families and narratives gives modern scholars a better view of ancient life and political organization.

Another collection of manuscripts to survive is known as the Borgia Group, so named after the largest and most complex of these screenfolds, now in Rome. Of these, the Borgia, Cospi, and Vaticanus B manuscripts may share a common origin in Puebla or Tlaxcala. Most of the Borgia manuscripts incorporate divining almanacs of the 260-day calendar with other religious material [244]. No histories are known. Calendrical and cosmic concerns are expressed together on the front page of the Féjerváry-Mayer, and the page has the character of a medieval carpet page [243]. Two-hundred-and-sixty dots are laid out in the form of a Maltese cross, recalling the Maya completion sign. Radiating in four

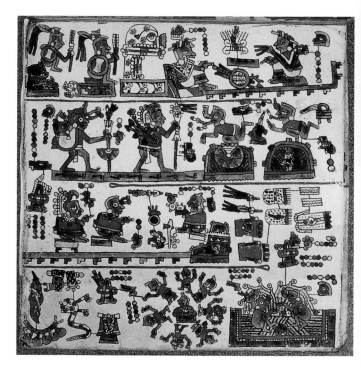

242 Page 7, Codex Selden. Although additions were made after the Spanish invasion to this Mixtec manuscript on deerskin, most of the pages were completed in Prehispanic times. A young woman named 6 Monkey is the heroine of this portion of the genealogy. The story reads from bottom to top, following the red guidelines. In the lowest register visible here, 6 Monkey takes a pre-wedding bath with her fiancé and receives wedding gifts. In the third register up, 6 Monkey rides in a backpack on a visit to enemies who speak with 'flinty tongues.'

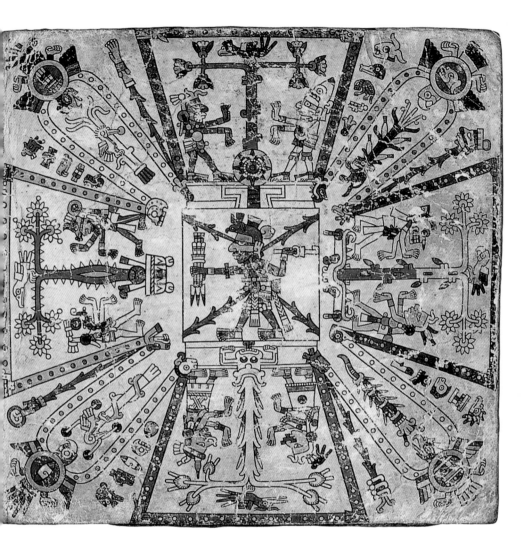

243 Folio I, Codex Féjerváry-Mayer. The cover page of this Prehispanic manuscript presents concepts of the world order: the four cardinal points are associated with particular colors, birds, and trees with a Maltese-cross frame of 260 dots, referring to the calendar round and its completion.

directions from the image of the sacrificed body of Xiutecuhtli, the young fire god, are four world trees surmounted by four directional birds. Such a picture conveys notions of world creation and world order within the frame of the calendar.

The Borgia manuscript is the single most complex surviving Mesoamerican book. The Venus pages in the center of the manuscript contain the travels of Quetzalcoatl in the underworld in imagery that continues to defy intepretation. The divination pages of the 260-day calendar are framed by paired deities, who bookend the calendar. The opposition of Mictlantecuhtli, the chief

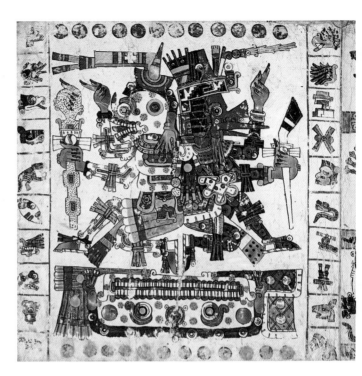

244 Page 56, Codex Borgia. Framing one end of a divination cycle are these paired deities, Mictlantecuhtli and Quetzalcoatl in the guise of Ehecatl, the wind god. They stand over an open-mouthed earth monster, and the twenty day names run along the sides of the page.

death god, with Ehecatl, an aspect of Quetzalcoatl, emphasizes the principle of duality in Mesoamerican thought, for Quetzalcoatl was also perceived to be a creator god.

The early Postconquest era

After the Conquest, the production of indigenous art and architecture slowly ceased, except for personal residences and attire. Temples were dismantled and their stones used to build the churches, civic buildings, and houses of the conquerors. Disease, strife, and despair all took their toll, as did forced labor in mines. In the sixteenth-century history of New Spain, the only light for the native population was the arrival of mendicant preaching friars, charged by Charles V with the mission. They came in groups of twelve, emulating the Apostles, and among their number were educated, enlightened individuals, instilled with ideas of the Renaissance. Just as Europe was in the throes of the Reformation, the new souls for conversion presented the Catholic church with another and different sort of challenge. Millions were converted and they needed schools and churches. This gave rise to one of the most energetic building programs in the history of the world, and even the waterworks, such as the newly rediscovered 'Caja de Agua,' a walk-in well at Santiago Tlatelolco, featured didactic instruction in Christianity. Hundreds of monastic complexes were constructed with native labor under the direction of friars who rarely had any knowledge of architectural principles. The Franciscans arrived first and built establishments throughout the Valley of Mexico; Dominicans came next and entered Oaxaca. The Augustinians, who arrived last, led the conversion to the north.

The predominant type of church constructed was the open-air chapel, a medieval form revived to meet the needs of the Mesoamerican population, who were unused to large interior spaces. The architecture was Christian, but Precolumbian imagery persisted in both obvious and subtle ways as Mesoamerican ideas, formats, or styles were used to convey the new teachings. At the Augustinian establishment at Ixmiquilpan, the paintings that line the nave show Eagle and Jaguar Knights doing battle with villainous centaurs [245]. On one level, we can understand this to show a converted indigenous population in native armor fighting the pagan Chichimecs of the north. The Spaniards, however, were interpreted at first by native Mesoamericans to be combinations

245 Battle of Eagle Knights and centaurs, Postconquest wall painting, Ixmiquilpan, Hidalgo. Under the guidance of Augustinian friars, native artists incorporated European and Precolumbian motifs in several sixteenth-century programs of decoration.

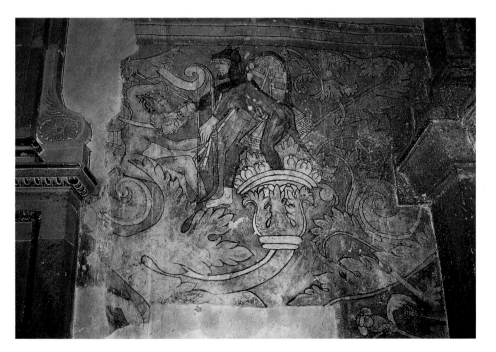

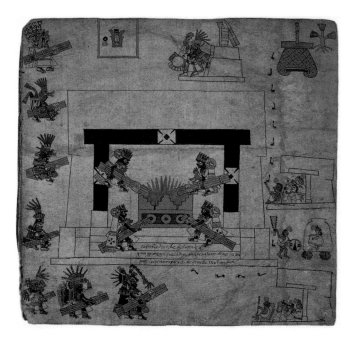

246 Folio 34, Codex Borbonicus. Calendar priests feed the flames during a New Fire ceremony. Aztec deities are drawn along the left-hand side of the page: at the right, a masked, pregnant woman is shown sequestered within doors, as prescribed by the ceremony.

of man-horse, like centaurs. By the eighteenth century, such ambiguity of interpretation would earn these paintings a thick coat of whitewash.

Much of the architectural sculpture associated with the monastic establishments was worked in very low relief, a technique typical of Aztec ornament but one which also came about when woodcut images were transferred to three-dimensional forms. Many of the large atrium crosses, however, had obsidian embedded in them, recalling an earlier practice of incorporating an obsidian heart into many sculptures.

The two prehispanic art forms that succeeded above all others in the early Colonial era were manuscript making and feather painting. Native scribes recorded histories, divinatory almanacs, and religious tracts, generally under the guidance of Franciscan priests. The earliest manuscript of the early Colonial period, the Codex Borbonicus, was long thought to pre-date the Conquest, but it has now been shown that throughout this screenfold on native paper, spaces were left for romanized glosses [246]. The first part of the manuscript is a divinatory guide of the 260 days, with auguries and patrons. The two center pages relate complex notions of calendar and time, and the last pages chart the 365-day cycle and the feasts of the months. The European influence is

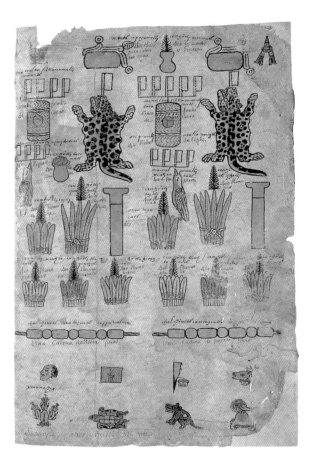

247 Tribute from the Province of Tepecoacuilco, Matricula de Tributos. Strings of amber, tubes of gold, jaguar pelts and fancy bird feathers flowed to the capital from distant provinces, in this case far to the south, from near what is today the Mexico-Guatemala border.

most obvious in this last section. In the rendering of a New Fire ceremony, the priests bear tied bundles of wood whose bindings are angled, as if informed by knowledge of perspective.

European paper soon replaced native fig paper; the screenfold gave way to the bound book. But indigenous painting traditions and conventions survived for some time, perhaps inspired by prehispanic books still available for consultation. The frontispiece of the Codex Mendoza may have its roots in a carpet page such as page I of the Féjerváry-Mayer [216, 244]. The luxurious tribute list of the Mendoza must have been copied directly from a similar record kept by Motecuhzoma, but – as Donald Robertson has pointed out – transferred from screenfold to bound book form, to describe the riches of New Spain for the Spanish Crown [247]. In its third section, the Mendoza accounted for human life, from infancy to old age, with family elders depicted at the book's end

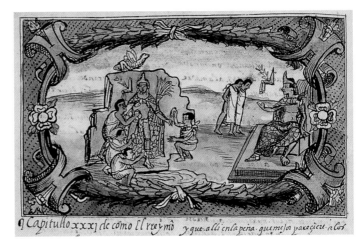

248 Dominican Diego Durán compiled important histories and ritual books. Here a page from his *History of the Indies* shows Motecuhzoma II directing the carving of his portrait at Chapultepec. Motecuhzoma poses for his portrait at right as if a Roman emperor; the results, center, follow an Aztec formula.

¶ *Capitullo xxxj de cõmo El rrey mõ y que alli enla peña. quemeſa pareçieſe alor*

249 Florentine Codex. Father Sahagún's scribes recorded the preparation of fancy feather goods, including the headdress that looks very much like the one shown in ill. 238. This may have been a very standard noble headdress.

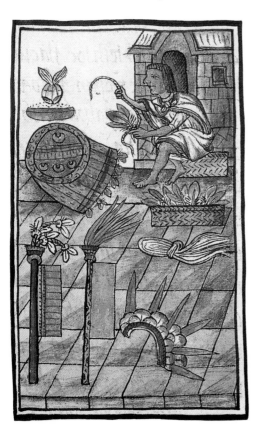

as tipplers to be attended to by the young. Father Diego Durán compiled histories of the Indies and New Spain, with lively hybridic illustrations that draw on both European and Aztec models [248].

The aim of the friars was to understand indigenous religion in order to extirpate it, but in the Florentine Codex, *The General History of the Things of New Spain* (c. 1566–77; 1585) – a twelve-book encyclopedia organized along the lines of a medieval compendium such as that of Bartholomaeus Anglicus – one senses that Father Bernardino de Sahagún's goals exceeded mere religious needs. His interest in the New World was truly catholic and he sought to understand history, religion, and the natural world. His bilingual Nahuatl/Spanish record, written and illustrated by many native scribes, is the single most important document of Aztec life. Father Sahagún's manuscript went through several drafts; illustrations for an early version show stronger Precolumbian traditions, and less concern for shading and landscape, both of which interest the illustrators of the later Florentine Codex. One volume of the comprehensive later work features information on metalwork and feather painting, lavishly illustrated, and a headdress like the one in Vienna today is shown [249]. The most unusual volume is the twelfth, which tells the story of the Spanish invasion from the indigenous viewpoint. Diana Magaloni has revealed the way indigenous scribes manipulated the new visual language of Christianity, using it to tell the story of their recent past, where the seizing of Motecuhzoma by Spanish soldiers is likened to the taking of Christ by Romans. The words to the right also echo the Gospels, naming Motecuhzoma's supporters as abandoning him, like the apostles who abandoned Jesus. Whose past was it?

The Mexican past took on new forms both in Mexico and Europe, drawing, in some cases, on forms that likened it to a safely 'past' Roman antiquity. The benign representation of Tlaloc in the Codex Ixtlilxochitl, [250] for example, would seem to bear a genealogical relationship to the Apollo Belvedere, perhaps based in Marcantonio Raimondi's widely circulated print of the Roman sculpture excavated on Rome's Palatine Hill in 1489, and thus making of Tlaloc an acceptable god of a distant and now extinct belief system.

This manuscript tradition was the final stage of Mesoamerican art and architecture. By the end of the sixteenth century the intellectual friars had been supplanted by parish priests who took less interest in their native flocks. The ravaged indigenous population had shrunk from what might have been 20 million on the eve of the Conquest to a mere million. Perhaps not quite the cosmic cataclysm predicted by the Aztecs, it was, along with the entire demographic disaster of the hemisphere, the worst catastrophe in history. The great art and architecture of Mesoamerica vanished under modern buildings or encroaching wild growth, or in other instances was simply destroyed. Not until the end of the eighteenth century would modern people begin the serious investigation of Mesoamerican antiquities.

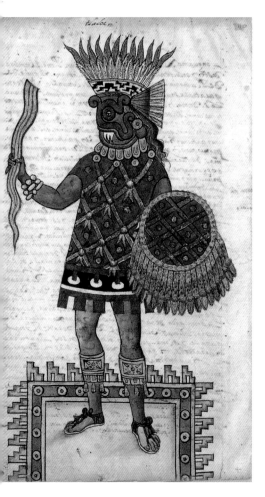

250 The work of an indigenous artist familiar with European prints, this page of the Ixtlilxochitl shows Tlaloc gently lifting a thunderbolt and standing in *contrapposto*; subtle shadows at the deity's feet suggest a European-style play of light.

Select Bibliography

Abbreviations

AA *American Anthropologist*
AM *Arqueología mexicana*
AncM *Ancient Mesoamerica*
BAEB Bureau of American Ethnology, Bulletin
CIW Carnegie Institution of Washington
HMAI *Handbook of Middle American Indians*
FINAH Instituto Nacional de Antropología e Historia
LACMA Los Angeles County Museum of Art
MARI Middle American Research Institute, Tulane University
PARI Pre-Columbian Art Research Institute, San Francisco
PMM Peabody Museum, Harvard University, Memoirs
PMP Peabody Museum, Harvard University, Papers
PNAS Proceedings of the National Academy of Sciences
RRAMW Research Reports on Ancient Maya Writing
UNAM Universidad Nacional Autónoma de México

Chapter 1 Introduction

For general sources students almost always start with a digital search. In this field of study, the outcomes of such searches are often homogenized, repetitious, and inaccurate; Wikipedia tends to be the most informative, but provides no novel or unique study. There are excellent, specialized digital resources: mesoweb.com, famsi.org, ARTstor.org, archaeology.org, nationalgeographic.com, arqueomex.com, and INAH.gob.mx, among them. Many journals are available online and through university libraries and through JSTOR.org, but much of what is published and has been published in this field is to be found in books, in English and Spanish, and they will require visits to libraries. The bibliographic search tool at www.famsi.org indexes articles, as well as books; it's the best tool to use for research in Mesoamerica in both English and Spanish.

For an alternative survey in English of Mesoamerican Precolumbian art and archaeology, one might turn to G. Kubler, *Art and Architecture of Ancient America*, 3rd edition (Pelican), 1984 (it also includes the art and architecture of Central and South America). The 16 vols and 6 supplements of the *Handbook of Middle American Indians*, ed. R. Wauchope *et al.* (Univ. Texas), 1964–2000, and typically found in library reference collections, offer consideration of Mesoamerica but with little attention to art. Valuable archaeological surveys that encompass the entire Mesoamerican region include S. Evans' *Ancient Mexico and Central America: Archaeology and Culture History*, 3rd edition (Thames & Hudson), forthcoming 2013; and M. Coe's paired volumes, *Mexico*, 6th edition (now co-authored with R. Koontz; Thames & Hudson), 2008, and *The Maya*, 8th edition (Thames & Hudson), 2011. Many older art historical surveys have sharp insights into particular works of art, even if some of the archaeological data is now out of date: P. Kelemen, *Medieval American Art* (Macmillan), 1943; E. Easby and J. Scott, *Before Cortés: Sculpture of Middle America* (Metropolitan Museum of Art), 1970; M. Covarrubias, *Indian Art of Mexico and Central America* (Knopf), 1957; J. Pijoán, *Historia del arte precolombino* (Summa Artis X), (Espasa-Calpe), 1952; Ignacio Marquina, *Arquitectura Prehispánica* (INAH), 1951; E. Seler, *Gesammelte Abhandlungen*, Berlin, 1902–23. Journals, among them *RES*, *Mexikon*, *Latin American Antiquity*, and *Ancient Mesoamerica*, serve as up-to-the-minute sources, as does the lavishly illustrated *National Geographic Magazine*. Smart perceptions have been filed at the International Congress of Americanists, held since 1875, resulting in what are often, unfortunately, recondite publications. Since 1993, *Arqueología mexicana* has transformed the publication of Mesoamerican materials, publishing both recent discoveries and thoughtful considerations of well-known materials, all with excellent photographs and line drawings. The new catalogues of collections at Dumbarton Oaks are masterful assemblages of current thinking on a wide range of topics.

Of great value are two encyclopedias, both issued in 2001: D. Carrasco, *The Oxford Encyclopedia of Mesoamerican Cultures: The Civilizations of Mexico and Central America*, and S. Evans and D. Webster's *Archaeology of Ancient Mexico and Central America, An Encyclopedia* (Garland). For religion, see M. Graulich, *Myths of Ancient Mexico* (Oklahoma), 1997; D. Carrasco, *Religions of Mesoamerica* (Waveland), 1998; and M. Miller and K. Taube's *Gods and Symbols of Ancient Mexico and the Maya* (Thames & Hudson), 1993.

The term 'Mesoamerica' has been in use since the mid-twentieth century (P. Kirchhoff, 'Mesoamerica,' *Acta Americana* 1, 1943: 92–107). A *Pre-Columbian World* (Dumbarton Oaks), 2006, ed. J. Quilter and M. Miller, questions the boundaries of Mesoamerica, looking both north and south, and evidence continues to grow: 'Evidence of Cacao Use in the Prehispanic American Southwest,' P. L. Crown and W. J. Hurst, PNAS, 2009, 106(7). N. Davies re-examined and evaluated diffusionist thought in a highly readable book: *Voyagers to the New World* (W. Morrow), 1979. G. Early tackles Afrocentrism, 'Adventures in the Colored Museum,' AA, 1999. Bernal Díaz wrote the most comprehensive and lucid eye-witness report of the Conquest; various abridgments are available today but the 5-vol. translation of A. P. Maudslay (1908–16) remains invaluable. Of all early travelers who looked at ancient ruins, John Lloyd Stephens' accounts are the most interesting today: *Incidents of Travel in Central America, Chiapas, and Yucatán*, 2 vols (Harper), 1841. Bernardino de Sahagún's *Florentine Codex, A General History of the Things of New Spain*, trans. A. J. O. Anderson and C. Dibble, in 13 books (School of American Research and University of Utah), 1950–82, is an encyclopedia of prehispanic life in Central Mexico. Long bounded chronologically as well as geographically, Mesoamerica can now be productively understood to incorporate art-making that extends well into the sixteenth century, if not beyond.

G. Kubler's last book, *Esthetic Recognition of Ancient Amerindian Art* (Yale), 1991, looks at the reception of Precolumbian art. A Dumbarton Oaks conference volume, *Collecting the Pre-Columbian Past*, ed. E. H. Boone, 1993, considers the collection and exhibition of these works. *Mesoamerican Architecture as a Cultural Symbol*, ed. J. K. Kowalski (Oxford), 1999, provides intelligent consideration of architectural history. *Pre-Columbian Architecture of Mesoamerica*, ed. M. T. Uriarte (Abbeville), 2010, provides a new comprehensive survey (available in multiple languages). I have found E. Pasztory's *Thinking with Things* to open useful perspectives (Univ. Texas), 2005.

Chapter 2 The Olmecs

The 2010 exhibition *Olmec: Colossal Masterworks of Ancient Mexico*, ed. K. Berrin and V. Fields (Yale), brought exceptional works and new excavation data together at US museums, as did *Olmec Art of Ancient Mexico*, ed. E. P. Benson and B. de la Fuente (National Gallery of Art), 1996, and *The Olmec World: Ritual and Rulership* (Art Museum, Princeton), 1995; and two additional edited volumes, *Olmec Art and Archaeology in Mesoamerica*, ed. J. E. Clark and M. E. Pye (Yale), 2000, and *Los Olmecas en Mesoamerica*, ed. J. E. Clark (Citibank), 1994, have made Olmec archaeology, research and new discoveries widely available. R. Diehl's study, *The Olmecs: America's First Civilization* (Thames & Hudson), 2004, is worth reading alongside M. Coe's 1968 book of the same title.

Studies of Olmec art continue to ask new questions. C. Tate's new book, *Reconsidering Olmec Visual Culture* (Univ. Texas), 2012, makes a sweeping reassessment of Olmec art, with attention to fetal imagery. Attacks on the authenticity of the 'Wrestler' sculpture have been countered: A. Cyphers, A. Lopez Cisneros, 'El Luchador: Historia Antigua y reciente,' AM 15(88), 2007, 47–71; and M. Coe and M. Miller, 'The Olmec Wrestler: A Masterpiece of the Ancient Gulf Coast,' *Minerva* 2004 16(1): 18–19.

See also K. Reilly, 'The Shaman in Transformation Pose: A Study of the Theme of Rulership in Olmec Art,' *Record of the Art Museum, Princeton University*, 1990. The theory of 'recycled' monuments has been articulated by J. Porter, 'Olmec Colossal Heads as Recarved Thrones,' *RES* 17/18, 1989: 22–29. Painting and petroglyphs are discussed by D. C. Grove, 'The Olmec Paintings of Oxtotitlan Cave,' *Dumbarton Oaks Studies in Pre-Columbian Art and Archaeology* no. 6, 1970; and Grove, *Chalcatzingo: Excavations on the Olmec Frontier* (Thames & Hudson), 1984; see also D. C. Grove and S. D. Gillespie, 'People of the Cerro: Landscape, Settlement, and Art at Middle Formative Period Chalcatzingo,' in *The Art of Urbanism*, ed. W. L. Fash and L. Lopez Luján, (Dumbarton Oaks), 2009, 53–76. A. Pohorilenko addresses 'A Formalistic Approach to Olmec Representation' in *Acercarse y mirar: homenaje a Beatriz de la Fuente*, ed. M. T. Uriarte, L. Staines Cicero (UNAM), 2004. J. Blomster asks 'What and Where is Olmec Style? Regional Perspectives on Hollow Figurines in Early Formative Mesoamerica,' AncM 13.02 (2003): 171–95.

Chapter 3 The Late Formative

The San Bartolo wall paintings have been partly published in *National Geographic*, with more to come: W. A. Saturno, K. A. Taube, and D. Stuart, 'The Murals of San Bartolo, El Petén, Guatemala. Part 1:The North Wall,' *Ancient America* 7, 2005. Many Late Formative works were freshly interpreted in the exhibition at the Los Angeles County Art Museum, and in the catalogue of the same name, V. Fields and D. Reents-Budet, *The Lords of Creation* (LACMA), 2005. See also F. Winfield Capitaine, 'La Estela 1 de La Mojarra, Veracruz, Mexico,' RRAMW 16, 1988; M. Stirling, 'An Initial Series from Tres Zapotes, Vera Cruz, Mexico,' *National Geographic Society, Contributed Technical Papers*, 1:1 1940. For the earliest inscriptions, see the essays in S. D. Houston, ed., *The First Writing* (Cambridge), 2004, which included the controversial Cascajal block. A. Caso, *Los calendarios prehispánicos* (UNAM), 1967, remains a major resource; Houston, O. Chinchilla, and D. Stuart collected key articles that led to *The Decipherment of Ancient Maya Writing* (Oklahoma), 2001. *Research Reports on Ancient Maya Writing*, published since 1986

[Center for Maya Research], offer a steady diet of new hieroglyphic readings. D. Stuart's 'Ten Phonetic Syllables,' RRAMW 14, 1987, is a model of carefully argued decipherment. M. Coe's *Breaking the Maya Code* (Thames & Hudson), 3rd edition, 2012, offers insights into the foibles and successes of decipherment.

For Oaxaca, one might start with *Zapotec Civilization* by J. Marcus and K. Flannery (Thames & Hudson), 1996. For specific problems and sites, readers might turn to 'Zapotec Hieroglyphic Writing,' J. Urcid, *Dumbarton Oaks Studies in Pre-Columbian Art and Archaeology* no. 34, 2001; J. Scott, 'The Danzantes of Monte Alban,' 2 vols, *Dumbarton Oaks Studies in Pre-Columbian Art and Archaeology* no. 22, 1980; I. Bernal, 'The Ball Players of Dainzu,' *Archaeology*, 21, 1968.

Archaeoastronomical principles in ancient American art and architecture are discussed in Anthony F. Aveni, *Skywatchers of Ancient Mexico* (Univ. Texas), 1981. D. M. Earle and D. R. Snow, 'The Origin of the 260-day Calendar: The Gestation Hypothesis Reconsidered in Light of its Use among the Quiche-Maya,' in *Fifth Palenque Round Table*, 1985, 241–44.

Exciting archaeological reports and fresh interpretations of ancient West Mexican art are all included in *Ancient West Mexico*, ed. R. F. Townsend (Thames & Hudson), 1998, the catalogue of a major exhibition organized by the Art Institute of Chicago. See also P. Furst, 'West Mexican Tomb Sculpture as Evidence for Shamanism in Prehispanic Mesoamerica,' *Antropológica*, 15, 1965; H. von Winning and O. Hammer, *Anecdotal Sculpture of West Mexico*, (Ethnic Arts Council of Los Angeles), 1972. Catalogues by M. Kan et al., *Sculpture of Ancient West Mexico*, 2nd edition (LACMA), 1985, and J. Gallagher, *Companions of the Dead* (Los Angeles County Natural History Museum), 1983, provide both clear interpretations and excellent illustrations.

A compelling picture of early Maya civilization and religious formation has been drawn by D. Freidel, L. Schele, and J. Parker in *Maya Cosmos* (W. Morrow), 1993. For Izapa, Takalik Abaj, and Kaminaljuyu, see also J. Guernsey, J. Clark, and B. Arroyo, eds, *The Place of Stone Monuments: Context, Use, and Meaning in Mesoamerica's Preclassic Transition* (Dumbarton Oaks), 2010, and J. Guernsey, *Ritual and Power in Stone: The Performance of Rulership in Mesoamerican Izapan Style Art* (Univ. Texas), 2006; A. V. Kidder, J. D. Jennings, and E. Shook, *Excavations at Kaminaljuyu* (CIW), 1946; and J. Kaplan and M. Love, *The Southern Maya in the Late Preclassic: The Rise and Fall of an Early Mesoamerican Civilization* (Colorado), 2011. F. Estrada-Belli's *The First Maya Civilization: Ritual and Power Before the Classic Period* (Routledge), 2010, adds to the conversation.

Chapter 4 Teotihuacan

The journal *Ancient Mesoamerica* featured a special section on the latest excavations at the Moon pyramid in 2007 (18:2), and the exhibition catalogue, S. Sugiyama, *Voyage to the Center of the Moon Pyramid: Recent Discoveries in Teotihuacan* (INAH), 2004, brought these to public attention in Mexico. The gripping story of destruction in the Xalla complex is recounted in L. Lopez Luján, L. Nadal, B. Fash, W. Fash, 'The Destruction of Images in Teotihuacan: Anthropomorphic Sculpture, Elite Cults, and the End of a Civilization,' *RES*, 2006. Warfare and sacrifice are at the heart of Sugiyama's *Human Sacrifice, Militarism, and Rulership: Materialization of State Ideology at the Feathered Serpent Pyramid, Teotihuacan* (Cambridge), 2006.

R. Millon's archaeological 2-vol. report, *Urbanization at Teotihuacan, Mexico* (Univ. Texas), 1974, remains useful, as do some of the ideas floated by Laurette Séjourné in *Un palacio en la ciudad delos dioses* (INAH), 1959. K. Taube's 'The Teotihuacan Spider Woman,' *Journal of Latin American Lore* 9:2, 1983, 107–89, initiated new thinking about the female cults at the site. The 'goddess' concept has been critiqued in A. Paulinyi, 'The "Great Goddess" of Teotihuacan: Fiction or Reality?', AncM 17 (2006). Also bear in mind J. Berlo, ed., *Art, Ideology, and the City of Teotihuacan* (Dumbarton Oaks), 1992; K. Berrin and E. Pasztory, eds, *Teotihuacan: Art from the City of the Gods* (The Fine Arts Museums of San Francisco, Thames & Hudson), 1993; and K. Berrin, ed., *Feathered Serpents and Flowering Trees* (The Fine Arts Museums of San Francisco), 1988. The Pintura Mural project of B. de la Fuente has now provided complete records of paintings at *Teotihuacan* (UNAM), 1995, 2 vols, and *Bonampak*, 1998, 2 vols. The Museo Nacional de Antropologia organized a major exhibition, with catalogue, in 2008: *Teotihuacan: Ciudad de los dioses* (INAH).

Chapter 5 Monte Alban, Veracruz and Cotzumalhuapa
On Monte Alban, see sources under Chapter 3; see also: A. Miller, *Painted Tombs of Oaxaca, Mexico: Living with the Dead* (Cambridge), 1995; R. E. Blanton, *Monte Albán: Settlement Patterns at the Ancient Zapotec Capital* (Academic Press), 1978; also J. Paddock, ed., *Ancient Oaxaca* (Stanford), 1966; A. Caso and I. Bernal studied the urns of Oaxaca, *Urnas de Oaxaca*, INAH *Memorias* 2, 1952; J. Marcus considers the urns in *The Cloud People* (see Chapter 8).
On Veracruz sculpture, see M. Goldstein, ed., *Ceremonial Sculpture of Ancient Veracruz* (Long Island University), 1988. Recent archaeology is treated in B. Stark, ed., *Settlement Archaeology of Cerro de las Mesas, Veracruz, Mexico* (Institute of Archaeology, UCLA), 1991. Cherra Wyllie has published the Las Remojadas excavations, 'The Mural Paintings of El Zapotal, Veracruz, Mexico,' AncM 21:2, 209–27.
For El Tajin, see R. Koontz, *Lightning Gods and Feathered Serpents: The Public Sculpture of El Tajin* (Univ. Texas), 2009, and A. Pascual Soto, *El Tajín: en busca de los orígenes de una civilización* (UNAM), 2006. O. Chinchilla Mazariegos has both excavated at Cotzumalhuapa and addressed the sculptures abroad: 'Peor es nada: el origen de las esculturas de Cotzumalguapa en el Museum für Völkerkunde, Berlin,' *Baessler Archiv* 44, 1996.
For the Mesoamerican ballgame, one might start with M. Whittington's *The Sport of Life and Death: The Mesoamerican Ballgame* (Thames & Hudson), 2001; T. Leyenaar and L. A. Parsons, *Ulama: the Ballgame of the Mayas and Aztecs, 2000 BC–AD 2000* (Leiden), 1988; M. Miller and S. Houston, 'The Classic Maya Ballgame and its Architectural Setting: A Study of Relations between Text and Image,' RES 14, 1987, 46–65.

Chapters 6 and 7 The Early and Late Classic Maya
Several important books have dramatically changed the history of Maya art and archaeology since the first edition of this book was released. Chief among these are: L. Schele and M. Miller, *The Blood of Kings: Ritual and Dynasty in Maya Art* (Kimbell Art Museum and Thames & Hudson), 1986 and 1992; L. Schele and D. Freidel, *A Forest of Kings: The Untold Story of the Ancient Maya* (W. Morrow), 1990; and L. Schele and P. Mathews, *Code of Kings* (Scribner), 1999. S. Houston and D. Stuart's article, 'The Ancient Maya Self: Personhood

and Portraiture in the Classic Period,' RES: 33 (1998), has been influential.
Major new additions to the bookshelf include M. Miller and S. Martin, *Courtly Art of the Ancient Maya* (Thames & Hudson), 2004; S. Martin and N. Grube, *Chronicle of the Maya Kings and Queens* (Thames & Hudson), 2008; D. Finamore and S. Houston, eds, *The Fiery Pool* (Yale), 2010; M. Miller, *Maya Art and Architecture* (Thames & Hudson), 1999; S. Houston and T. Inomata, *The Classic Maya* (Cambridge), 2009; *I Maya*, the catalogue of the vast Venice exhibition, curated by P. Schmidt, M. de La Garza, and E. Nalda; also published in English as *Maya* (Rizzoli), 1998; A. Stone and M. Zender, *Reading Maya Art: A Hieroglyphic Guide to Ancient Maya Painting and Sculpture* (Thames & Hudson), 2011; S. Houston, D. Stuart, and K. Taube, *The Memory of Bones: Body, Being, and Experience among the Classic Maya* (Univ. Texas), 2006. Particularly innovative is the treatment of color in S. Houston *et al.*, *Veiled Brightness: A History of Ancient Maya Color* (Univ. Texas), 2009. R. Sharer and L. Traxler now write *The Ancient Maya*, 6th edition (Stanford), 2005, the most encyclopedic archaeological resource on the Maya.
Every reader can learn something from the four volumes of the first keen observer of Maya art and architecture, J. L. Stephens: *Incidents of Travel in Central America, Chiapas, and Yucatán* (Harper), 1841, and *Incidents of Travel in Yucatán*, 1843. C. Baudez and S. Picasso, *Lost Cities of the Maya* (Abrams/Thames & Hudson), 1992, offer a good, brief historiography.
Both Early and Late Classic sculptures are discussed and illustrated in S. G. Morley, *Inscriptions of Petén*, 5 vols, CIW Pub. 437, 1937–38; A. P. Maudslay, *Biologia Centrali-Americana: Archaeology*, 5 vols, London 1899–1902; *Corpus of Maya Hieroglyphic Inscriptions*, vols 1–9 (Peabody Museum, Harvard University), 1977–. T. Proskouriakoff's *Classic Maya Sculpture*, CIW Pub. 593, 1950, retains key insights.
On Palenque: M. Greene Robertson, *The Sculpture of Palenque*, 4 vols, *The Temple of Inscriptions* (Princeton), 1983–92; D. Stuart and G. Stuart, *Palenque, Eternal City of the Maya* (Thames & Hudson), 2009. E. Barnhart's dissertation, 'The Palenque Mapping Project: Settlement and Urbanism at an Ancient Maya City,' (2001, Univ. Texas; unpublished) has provided a new baseline for studying ancient waterways and settlement. See also K. D. French, *Palenque Hydro-Archaeology Project, 2006–2007 Season Report* (2008), at famsi.org.
On Belize: D. Pendergast, *Altun Ha, British Honduras (Belize): The Sun God's Tomb*, Royal Ontario Museum of Art and Archaeology, Occasional Paper 19, Toronto, 1969; A. F. Chase and D. Z. Chase, *Investigations at the Classic Maya City of Caracol, Belize: 1985–87* (PARI), 1987.
For Bonampak: M. Miller, 'Maya Masterpiece Revealed at Bonampak,' *National Geographic Magazine*, February 1995, 50–69; M. Miller, 'The Willfulness of Art: The Case of Bonampak,' RES 42 (2002); M. Miller and C. Brittenham, *The Spectacle of the Late Maya Court: Reflections on the Paintings of Bonampak* (Univ. Texas), 2012, and de la Fuente, as listed under Chapter 4.
On Piedras Negras: A. Stone, 'Disconnection, Foreign Insignia, and Political Expansion: Teotihuacan and the Warrior Stelae of Piedras Negras,' in *Mesoamerica after the Decline of Teotihuacan AD 700–900*, eds R. Diehl and J. Berlo (Dumbarton Oaks), 1989, 153–72; F. Clancy, *The Monuments of Piedras Negras, an Ancient Maya City* (New Mexico), 2009; M. O'Neil, *Engaging Ancient Maya Sculpture at Piedras Negras, Guatemala* (Oklahoma), 2012.

For Copan and Quirigua, see E. Boone and G. Willey, eds, *The Southeast Classic Maya Zone* (Dumbarton Oaks), 1988, 149–94; W. Fash, *Scribes, Warriors, and Kings: The City of Copán and the Ancient Maya* (Thames & Hudson), 2nd edition, 2001; D. Webster, ed., *The House of the Bacabs* (Dumbarton Oaks), 1989; E. Schortman and P. Urban, eds, *Quiriguá Reports II*, Papers 6–14 (University Museum, Philadelphia), 1983; S. G. Morley, *Inscriptions at Copán*, CIW Pub. 219, 1920; *Introducción a la Arqueología de Copán, Honduras*, 3 vols, Proyecto Arqueológico de Copan, Tegucigalpa, Honduras, 1983; M. Looper, *Lightning Warrior: Maya Art and Kingship at Quirigua* (Univ. Texas), 2003. A. Herring's 'A Borderland Colloquy: Altar Q, Copan, Honduras,' *Art Bulletin* 87:2 (2005), offers keen insights.

On Yucatan: J. Kowalski, *The House of the Governor* (Univ. Oklahoma), 1986; Harry Pollock, *The Puuc* (PMM), 1980; V. Miller, *The Frieze of the Palace of the Stuccoes, Acanceh, Yucatán, Mexico* (Dumbarton Oaks), 1991.

For Yaxchilan: C. Tate, *Yaxchilán: Design of a Maya Ceremonial Center* (Univ. Texas), 1992.

For religious iconography, see K. Taube, *The Major Gods of Ancient Yucatán* (Dumbarton Oaks), 1992; E. Benson and G. Griffin, eds, *Maya Iconography* (Princeton), 1988; M. G. Robertson, ed., *Mesa Redonda de Palenque* (Palenque Round Table) (R. L. Stevenson School, Univ. Texas, PARI), vols 1–10, 1973–93.

For figurines, see M. Miller, *Jaina Figurines* (Art Museum, Princeton), 1975; R. Piña Chan, *Jaina, la casa en el agua* (INAH), 1968; L. Schele, *Hidden Faces of the Maya*, 1998.

On Maya jades, A. L. Smith and A. V. Kidder, *Excavations at Nebaj, Guatemala*, CIW Pub. 594, 1951; Tatiana Proskouriakoff, *Jades from the Cenote of Sacrifice, Chichen Itzá, Yucatán*, PMM 10:1, 1974.

The chronology and terminology for Maya ceramics derives from the Uaxactun excavations: R. E. Smith, *Ceramic Sequence at Uaxactún, Guatemala*, 2 vols, MARI Pub. 20, 1955. M. D. Coe transformed the study of ceramics in *The Maya Scribe and His World* (Grolier Club), 1973; *Lords of the Underworld* (Art Museum, Princeton), 1978; R. E. W. Adams, *The Ceramics of Altar de Sacrificios*, PMM 63:1, 1971. For the Early Classic, see N. Hellmuth, *Mönster und Menschen* (Graz), 1987. J. Kerr published much of the complete corpus, *The Maya Vase Book*, vols 1–7, 1989–; and continued at www.mayavase.com. Further studies are D. Reents-Budet, *Painting the Maya Universe* (Duke), 1994, and M. Coe and J. Kerr, *The Art of the Maya Scribe* (Abrams/Thames & Hudson), 1998. A. Herring, *Art and Writing in the Maya Cities, AD 600–800: A Poetics of Line* (Cambridge), 2005, treats the relationship between line and thought.

Architecture receives its due in *Royal Courts of the Ancient Maya*, ed. T. Inomata and S. Houston (Westview), 2001; and *Function and Meaning in Classic Maya Architecture*, ed. S. Houston (Dumbarton Oaks), 1998. T. Proskouriakoff based her careful reconstructions on such archaeological reports (*An Album of Maya Architecture*, CIW Pub. 558, 1946). For technical observations on Maya architecture, see L. Roys, 'The Engineering Knowledge of the Maya,' CIW Contributions, II (1934).

Chapter 8 Mesoamerica after the fall of Classic cities
The best book to read in association with this chapter is *Mesoamerica after the Decline of Teotihuacan*, eds R. Diehl and J. Berlo (Dumbarton Oaks), 1989.

On Xochicalco, see B. de la Fuente *et al.*, *La Acrópolis de Xochicalco* (Instituto de Cultura de Morelos), 1995, and K. Hirth, *Archaeological Research at Xochicalco* (Univ. of Utah), 2000.

A flurry of publications accompanied the discovery of the Cacaxtla paintings, including D. McVicker, 'The Mayanized Mexicans,' *American Antiquity* 50:1, 1985, 82–101. See also Marta Foncerrada de Molina, 'La pintura mural de Cacaxtla, Tlaxcala,' *Anales del IIE, UNAM* 46, 1976, 5–20. C. Brittenham, 'Style and Substance, or Why the Cacaxtla Paintings Were Buried,' *RES*: 55/56 (2009): 135–55, is part of a new wave of interpretations of the paintings.

Articles in K. V. Flannery and J. Marcus, eds, *The Cloud People: Divergent Evolution of the Zapotec and Mixtec Civilizations* (Academic Press), 1983, consider the Early Postclassic in Oaxaca. The volume is also valuable for earlier eras in Oaxaca.

On Tula and Chichen Itza: various reports summarize the many years of excavations by the Carnegie Institution of Washington at Chichen Itza. The most important studies: K. Ruppert, *Chichen Itzá*, CIW Pub. 595, 1952; A. M. Tozzer, *Chichen Itzá and its Cenote of Sacrifice*, PMM 12, 1957; E. Morris, J. Charlot, and A. Morris, *The Temple of the Warriors at Chichen Itzá, Yucatán*, 2 vols, CIW Pub. 406, 1931, documented a vast program that remains of keen interest. On Toltec art forms at Chichen Itza, see G. Kubler, 'Serpent and Atlantean Columns: Symbols of Maya-Toltec Polity,' *Journal of the Society of Architectural Historians*, 41, 1982; M. Miller, 'A Re-examination of the Mesoamerican Chacmool,' *Art Bulletin*, 67:1, 1985, 7–17; C. Coggins and O. Shane, eds, *Cenote of Sacrifice: Maya Treasures from the Sacred Well at Chichen Itzá* (Univ. Texas), 1984. J. Kowalski, C. Kristan-Graham, and G. Bey, eds, *Twin Tollans: Chichén Itzá, Tula, and the Epiclassic to Early Postclassic Mesoamerican World* (Dumbarton Oaks), 2008, provides a fresh look at the assumptions that have shaped all Chichen work. On the Toltecs, see A. G. Mastache, R. Cobean, D. Healan, *Ancient Tollan: Tula and the Toltec Heartland* (Colorado), 2002; R. Diehl, *Tula: the Toltec Capital of Ancient Mexico* (Thames & Hudson), 1983; N. Davies, *The Toltecs until the Fall of Tula* (Univ. Oklahoma), 1977; also, *The Toltec Heritage from the Fall of Tula to the Rise of Tenochtitlan* (Univ. Oklahoma), 1980; J. Acosta, 'Resumen de las exploraciones arqueológicas en Tula, Hidalgo, durante los VI, VII y VIII temporadas 1946–1950,' *INAH Anales* 8, 1956, 37–116. D. Charnay first noted the resemblances between Tula and Chichen Itza: *Ancient Cities of the New World* (New York), 1888. See also B. de la Fuente, S. Trejo and N. Gutiérrez Solana, *Escultura en Piedra de Tula* (UNAM), 1988.

The final Carnegie project was carried out at Mayapan: H. E. D. Pollock, T. Proskouriakoff, and E. Shook, *Mayapán*, CIW Pub. 619, 1962. For Tulum, see S. K. Lothrop, *Tulum: An Archaeological Study of the East Coast of Yucatán*, CIW Pub. 335, 1924; also, particularly for the copies of the murals there, A. Miller, *On the Edge of the Sea: Mural Painting at Tancah-Tulum, Quintana Roo, Mexico* (Dumbarton Oaks), 1982. T. Gann visited Santa Rita and published the murals there: 'Mounds in Northern Honduras,' BAEB, 19th Annual Report, 1900. A. L. Smith, *Archaeological Reconnaissance in Central Guatemala*, CIW Pub. 608, 1955, presents Postclassic architecture of the Guatemalan highlands.

On Maya pre- and post-Conquest books: J. E. S. Thompson, *The Dresden Codex* (American Philosophical Society), 1972; J. A. Villacorta and C. A. Villacorta, *Codices*

Maya, (Tipografía Nacional), 1930; the Grolier Codex is illustrated in Coe, *The Maya Scribe* (see Chapter 7 above). The *Popol Vuh* has been translated many times, and the new translation by A. Christensen, *Popol Vuh* (Oklahoma), 2007, is recommended, as is M. S. Edmonson, *The Book of Counsel: The Popol Vuh of the Quiché Maya of Guatemala*, MARI Pub. 35, 1971; see also *Popol Vuh*, trans. D. Tedlock (Simon & Schuster), 1985. A. M. Tozzer published a heavily annotated version of Bishop Landa's account of Yucatan (*Landa's Relación de las cosas de Yucatán*, PMP 18, 1941); also useful is the W. Gates translation, *Yucatán Before and After the Conquest* (Baltimore), 1937, reprinted by Dover, 1978. On religious practice at the time of the Conquest, I. Clendinnen, *Ambivalent Conquests: Maya and Spaniard in Yucatán, 1517–1570* (Cambridge), 1987.

Chapter 9 The Aztecs

Major exhibitions of Aztec materials in London (2003; 2009), New York (2004), and elsewhere refocused modern attention on their art. See particularly *Aztecs*, ed. E. Matos M. and F. Solís O. (Royal Academy), 2003; and *The Aztec Empire*, ed. F. Solís O. (Guggenheim), 2004; C. McEwan, L. Lopez Luján, eds, *Moctezuma: Aztec Ruler* (British Museum Press), 2009.

Other books to consider include E. Pasztory, *Aztec Art* (Oklahoma), 2000; R. Townsend, *The Aztecs* (Thames & Hudson), 3rd edition, 2010; E. Boone, *The Aztec World* (Smithsonian), 1994. R. Townsend's 'State and Cosmos in the Art of Tenochtitlan,' *Dumbarton Oaks Studies in Pre-Columbian Art and Archaeology* no. 20, 1979, is a fine examination of a few major sculptures. See also H. B. Nicholson and E. Q. Keber, *Art of Aztec Mexico: Treasures of Tenochtitlan* (National Gallery, Washington), 1983.

M. Miller and K. Villela have recently assembled every major study of the most famous Aztec monument, *The Aztec Calendar Stone* (Getty), 2010. J. Fernandez treated the Coatlicue with equal attention through the mid-twentieth century, *Coatlícue, estética del arte indígena antigua* (Mexico City), 1954. For precious metals, see A. Emmerich: *Sweat of the Sun and Tears of the Moon: Gold and Silver in Pre-Columbian Art* (Univ. Washington), 1965; Mixtec goldwork is discussed by A. Caso, *El Tesoro de Monte Albán* (INAH), 1969. For featherwork, see T. Castelló Yturbide, *El Arte Plumaria en México* (Banamex), 1993. Many aspects of Aztec life are documented in B. de Sahagún, *Florentine Codex* (see Chapter 1); see also M. Leon-Portilla, *Aztec Thought and Culture* (Univ. Oklahoma), 1963. For music, see R. Stevenson, *Music in Aztec and Inca Territory* (Univ. California), 1968.

On excavations at the Templo Mayor: J. Broda, D. Carrasco, and E. Matos Moctezuma, *The Great Temple of Tenochtitlan: Center and Periphery in the Aztec World* (Univ. California), 1987; E. Boone, ed., *The Aztec Templo Mayor* (Dumbarton Oaks), 1987. The latest work, including the excavation of the Tlaltecuhtli, is being conducted by L. Lopez Luján, *Offerings of the Templo Mayor of Tenochtitlan* (Colorado), 1994; E. Matos Moctezuma and L. Lopez Luján, 'La diosa Tlaltecuhtli de la casa de Ajaracas y el rey Ahuitzotl,' AM 14 (83), 2007. D. Carrasco's *City of Sacrifice* (Beacon), 2000, is an influential summary.

The manuscripts mentioned in this chapter are all available in facsimile editions and increasingly available online. *Codex Selden*, commentary by A. Caso, glosses by M. E. Smith (Sociedad Mexicana de Antropologia), 1966; *Codex Féjerváry-Mayer* (Akademische Druck u. Verlagsanstalt), 1971; *Codex Borgia*, commentary by Eduard Seler (Fondo de Cultura Económica), 1963; E. Boone, *The Codex Magliabechiano* (Univ. California), 1985; F. Berdan and P. Anawalt, eds, *The Codex Mendoza* (Univ. California), 1992; Serge Gruzinski, *Painting the Conquest* (UNESCO), 1992; *Codex Borbonicus*, Graz (Akademische Druck u. Verlagsanstalt), 1974; *Matrícula de Tributos*, Graz, 1980. The Postconquest manuscripts are described by D. Robertson, *Mexican Manuscript Painting of the Early Colonial Period: The Metropolitan Schools* (Yale), 1959, and E. Boone, *Stories in Red and Black* (Univ. Texas), 2000 and *Cycles of Time and Meaning in the Mexican Books of Fate* (Univ. Texas), 2007.

The most readable history of the Aztecs is N. Davies, *The Aztecs* (Macmillan), 1973, and (Univ. Oklahoma), 1980; he follows fairly closely the information from Father D. Duran's *Historia de las Indias de Nueva España*. For the Conquest of Mexico, see B. Díaz del Castillo (see Chapter 1) and Hernando Cortés, *Letters from Mexico*, trans./ed. A. R. Pagden (Yale), 1986. I. Clendinnen's *Aztecs: An Interpretation* (Cambridge), 1991, provides an engaging social history; S. Gruzinski, *The Conquest of Mexico* (Cambridge), 1992, offers the freshest take on the Mesoamerican mind since T. Todorov, *The Conquest of Mexico* (Harper), 1981, first raised the possibility of entering it.

F. Columbus wrote his father's biography, and reported the great canoes of the Maya in *The Life of the Admiral Christopher Columbus by his Son Ferdinand*, trans./ed. B. Keen, (Rutgers), 1959. J. de Grijalva, as recorded in *The Discovery of New Spain in 1518*, trans./ed. H. R. Wagner (Cortés Society), 1942, collected exotic objects from the Maya.

Early Postconquest life and art are examined in R. Ricard, the *Spiritual Conquest of Mexico* (Univ. California), 1966; C. Reyes, *Arte Indocristiano* (INAH), 1981; M. Toussaint, *Colonial Art of Mexico*, rev. and trans. E. Wilder Weismann (Univ. Texas), 1967; G. Kubler, *Sixteenth-Century Architecture of Mexico* (Yale), 1948; J. McAndrew, *Sixteenth-Century Mexico: Atrios, Posas, Open Chapels, and Other Studies* (Harvard), 1965; S. Gruzinski, *Conquest of Mexico: The Incorporation of Indian Societies into the Western World, 16th–18th Centuries* (Blackwell), 1993. J. Schwaller, *Sahagún at 500: Essays on the Quincentenary of the Birth of Fr. Bernardino de Sahagún* (Academy of American Franciscans), 2003. *Reframing the Renaissance: Visual Culture in Europe and Latin America 1450–1650*, ed. C. Farago (Yale), 1995, posed many questions; some have been answered in B. Mundy, *Mapping New Spain* (Chicago), 2000; E. Wake, *Framing the Sacred* (Oklahoma), 2010; and in others, in what is a quickly emerging field of study.

List of Illustrations

Unless otherwise indicated, photographs are by the author and site plans by Martin Lubikowski. Measurements are given in centimeters (and inches): H = height, L = length, D = diameter.

Abbreviations
AMNH American Museum of Natural History, New York
INAH Instituto Nacional de Antropologia e Historia
JK © Justin Kerr
MNA Museo Nacional de Antropologia, Mexico
MZ © Michel Zabé
NGS National Geographic Society
UM University Museum, University of Pennsylvania
YUAG Yale University Art Gallery

1 North Wall, San Bartolo. Drawing Heather Hurst; **2** Mask of the 'Red Queen', MNA. Photo Jorge Pérez de Lara; **3** Chaco vessel. YUAG; **4** Chaco vessel. Catalog no. 3225, courtesy Division of Anthropology, AMNH; **5** Gold disk. Drawing T. Proskouriakoff; **6** Mesoamerica, drawing Philip Winton; **7** Jade standing figure holding supernatural effigy. H 21.9 (8 10/16). Brooklyn Museum, New York. Photo JK – K4838; **8** Maize god from Copan, Honduras. H 89.7 (35 5/16). British Museum, London. Photo JK – K2889; **9** Wooden Aztec mask with turquoise mosaic and shell. 16.5 x 15.2 (6½ x 6). British Museum, London; **10** Frederick Catherwood, portion of a building in the Nunnery complex at Uxmal, 1844; **11** Olmec Colossal Head 8, San Lorenzo. Museo Arquelógico de Xalapa, Veracruz, Mexico. Photo Colin McEwan; **12** Kunz Axe. H 28 (11). AMNH; **13** Axe with footprint, El Manati. INAH; **14** Crocodile, Guatemala, Pacific Coast. Greenstone and shell. 15 x 16 x 48 (6 x 6⅜ x 19). Museo de Arte Precolumbino y Vidrio Moderno, Antigua, Guatamala. Photo Jorge Pérez de Lara; **15** Excavations at the 'Red Palace', San Lorenzo. Photo Ann Cyphers; **16** Wooden figures from El Manati. Proyecto Manati; **17** Colossal Head 5, San Lorenzo. H 186 (73¼). Drawing F. Dávalos, from Coe and Diehl, 1990; **18** Colossal Head 10, San Lorenzo Museum. © David Hilbert/Alamy; **19** Wrestler. H 66 (26). Consejo Nacional para la Cultura y las Artes/INAH. Photo Jorge Pérez de Lara; **20, 21** Hero Twin figures, San Lorenzo. Photo Kent Reilly; **22** Complex A, La Venta. From M. D. Coe 1984; **23** Mosaic mask, La Venta. 457 x 762 (180 x 300). Photo R. Heizer and NGS; **24** Colossal Head 1, La Venta. Photo David C. Grove; **25** Altar 4, La Venta. H 160 (63). Photo Nick Saunders; **26** Altar 5, La Venta. AMNH; **27** Stela 3, La Venta. H 430 (169). NGS – Smithsonian Institution, Washington, D.C.; **28** Offering 4, La Venta. H 16–18 (6¼–7). MNA. Photo M. D. Coe; **29** Las Limas sculpture. H 55 (21⅝). Museo Regional de Veracruz. Photo Irmgard Groth-Kimball, © Thames & Hudson Ltd; **30** Young Lord, El Salvador/Guatemala, Pacific Coast. 65.5 x 11 x 5.4 (25 13/16 x 4 5/16 x 2⅛). Photograph © John Bigelow Taylor, NYC; **31** Greenstone Olmec head. © YUAG, gift of Peggy and Richard Danziger, LL.B 1963; **32** Olmec jade figure. © YUAG, lent by Thomas T. Solley, BA, 1950; **33** Xochipala, Guerrero Matron. Photo David Joralemon; **34** Teopantecuanitlan sculpture. Photo Gillett G. Griffin; **35** Las Bocas 'baby'. H 83.4 (34). Metropolitan Museum of Art, New York, The Michael C. Rockefeller Memorial Collection, Bequest of Nelson A. Rockefeller 1979 (1979.206.1134); **36** Petroglyph I ('El Rey'), Chalcatzingo. H 275 (108). Photo David C. Grove; **37** Oxtotitlan Mural C-1. Courtesy New World Archaeological Foundation, Provo. Drawing Ayax Moreno; used courtesy John Clarke; **38** Olmec petroglyph, Xoc, Chiapas. Drawing Linda Schele; **39** Calendar after J. E. S. Thompson; **40** Number glyphs. Drawing Stephen D. Houston; **41** La Mojarra stela. H 66 (26). Drawing George Stuart; **42** Emblem glyphs. Drawing Stephen D. Houston; **43** Lintel 8, Yaxchilan. H 78 (30¾). Drawing I. Graham 1977; **44** Emiliano Zapata panel. Photo MZ; **45** Codex Reese. [left half], Aztec land map, c. 1565. Western Americana Collection, Beinecke Rare Books and Manuscript Library, Yale University, New Haven; **46** Danzantes at Monte Alban. Photo Irmgard Groth-Kimball, © Thames & Hudson Ltd; **47** Mound J, Monte Alban. Photo ffotograff © Jill Ranford; **48** Hieroglyph showing upside-down head, Mound J, Monte Alban. Drawing P. Gallagher; **49** Hollow tomb figure. The Art Archive /MNA/Dagli Orti; **50** Puma with scarf, Monte Alban II. Photo Irmgard Groth-Kimball, © Thames & Hudson Ltd; **51** Jade bat assemblage. H 19 (7⅜). Photo Scala; **52** Colima dog. H 20.9 (8¼). MNA. Photo Jorge Pérez de Lara; **53, 54** Nayarit couple. H 60 and 58.4 (23⅝ and 23). © YUAG, Stephen Carlton Clark BA 1903 Fund; **55** Ballcourt. © YUAG 2001; **56** Mezcala temple model. H 12 (4¾). MNA. Photo JK – K6728; **57** Structure 5, Cerros. Photo D. Freidel; **58** Stela 1, Nakbe. Drawing Richard D. Hansen UCLA RAINPEG Project; **59** Structure 1, San Bartolo. Reconstruction Heather Hurst; **60** West Wall, San Bartolo. William Saturno; **61** North Wall, San Bartolo. Reconstruction Heather Hurst; **62** Stela 1, Izapa. H 193 (76). Photo courtesy Matthew W. Stirling and NGS; **63** Stela 11, Kaminaljuyu. H 182.8 (72). Photo Jorge Pérez de Lara; **64** Kaminaljuyu Monument 65, H 290 (114 3/16), Photo MZ; **65** Later copy of 16th- century Map of San Francisco Mazapan; **66** Jose Maria Velasco, Pyramid of the Sun, Teotihuacan, Mexico, 1878. © The Art Archive/Alamy; **67** *Talud-tablero*, after Marquina; **68** Aerial view of Temple of the Moon. © Yann Arthus-Bertrand/ CORBIS; **69** Isometric view of Teotihuacan, after G. Kubler; **70** Pyramid of the Moon, Teotihuacan; **71** Pyramid of the Sun at Teotihuacan. Photo Nick Saunders; **72** Pyramid of the Sun, Teotihuacan, seen from a hot air balloon. © Henry Romero/Reuters/Corbis; **73** Isometric view of Zacuala compound, after L. Séjourné; **74** Great Goddess, Pyramid of the Moon, Teotihuacan. H 320 (126). MNA; **75** Tlaloc sculpture, Teotihuacan. H 136 (53 9/16). MNA; **76** Seated figure from Pyramid of the Moon, Burial 5, Teotihuacan. Photo Saburo Sugiyama; **77** Xalla figure. Teotihuacan. H 128 (50⅜). MNA-INAH. Photo Martirene Alcantara; **78** 'La Ventilla Stela', ballcourt marker. H 215 (84⅝). MNA-INAH; **79** Teotihuacan greenstone mask. Consejo Nacional para la Cultura y las Artes/INAH. Photo Jorge Pérez de Lara; **80** (Left) Ceramic standing portrait figurine. H 10 (4). Natural History Museum of Los Angeles County, Gift of the Stendhal Gallery, 4964. (Center and right) Ceramic standing portrait figurines. H 5 and 8 (2 and 3⅛). Los Angeles County Museum of Art. Lent by Mrs. Constance McCormick Fearing, L83.11.1113-.1114; **81** Necklace of teeth, shell and human jawbone. 20 x 20 (8 x 8). INAH. Photo MZ; **82** Mass-produced urn from Late Teotihuacan. The Art Archive/MNA/Dagli Orti; **83** Temple of the Feathered Serpent, Teotihuacan. Photo J. Soustelle; **84** Wall painting from Tetitla. H 72.2 (28¼). MNA. Photo MZ; **85** Agustín Villagra, Copy of Tepantitla painting. MNA; **86** Eagle mural, Palace of Tetitla, Teotihuacan. © Macduff Everton/Corbis; **87** Parrot/quetzal mural, Palace of the Plumed Shells, Teotihuacan. © Charles & Josette Lenars/ Corbis; **88** Tripod vessel with fresco decoration. MNA; **89** Thin orange old god effigy. National Museum of the American Indian, Smithsonian Institution, Washington, D.C.; **90** 'Host' figure inside ceramic tripod vessel. Vessel H 16.5 (6½), figure H 22 (8 11/16). Palace Museum Cantón, Mérida. Photo Jorge Pérez de Lara; **91** Plan, Kaminaljuyu B-4, after Kidder, Jennings and Shook, 1946; **92** Pyramid, Cholula. Photo Philip Baird/www.anthroarcheart.org; **93** Monte Alban. Photo Colin McEwan; **94** Plan, Monte Alban, after Blanton and Kubler; **95** The northeast corner of the South Platform, Monte Alban. Courtesy Joyce Marcus and Kent Flannery, University of Michigan; **96** Stela 4, Monte Alban. H 186 (73). Photo MZ; **97** Tomb 104 façade, Monte Alban. H 91 (35⅞); **98** Tomb 104 painting, Monte Alban, from Caso, 1936–37; **99** Tomb 105 painting, Monte Alban, from Caso, 1936–37; **100** Ceramic urn. H 43.1 (17). YUAG. Stephen Carlton Clark BA 1903 Fund; **101** Zapotec funerary assemblage from Tomb 103, Monte Alban. Photo MZ; **102** Pyramid of the Niches, El Tajin. Photo Joyce Kelly; **103** South Ballcourt, El Tajin; **104** Stela, El Tajin. H 178 (70). Michael E. Kampen; **105** Ballcourt panel 4, El Tajin. H 156 (61⅜). Photo Philip Baird/ www.anthroarcheart.org; **106** Palma. H 58 (22⅞).

MNA; **107** Granite yoke. 13.4 x 38.1 (5¼ x 15). Photo JK – K6517; **108** *Hacha.* H 28 (11). MNA. Photo JK – K6507; **109** 'Smiling face' figure. YUAG, gift Richard Danziger 1986; **110** Wheeled toy. L 17 (6 11/16). Photo JK – K3670; **111** Veracruz *incensario.* H 83 (32 11/16). Photo JK – K3673; **112** Tlaloc effigy, El Zapotal, Veracruz. H 48 (18⅞). Museo de Antropologia de Xalapa, Veracruz; **113** Stela 8, Cerro de las Mesas. NGS. Photo R. Stewart; **114** Stela 3, Santa Lucia Cotzumalhuapa. H 282 (111). Werner Forman Archive/Museum für Volkerkunde, Berlin; **115** Pantaleon head; **116** E-VII-sub, Uaxactun. Photo AMNH; **117** A–V, Uaxactun. Drawing after G. Kubler; **118** North Acropolis, Tikal; **119** Rosalila structure, Copan. Christopher A. Klein/National Geographic Image Collection; **120** Stela 29, Tikal. H 205 (80¾). Drawing W. R. Coe; **121** Stela 4, Tikal. H 230 (90½). UM; **122** Stela 31. Tikal. H 230 (90½). UM; **123** 'Po' Panel. H 44.5 (17½). Photo Benjamin Watkins; **124** Leiden Plaque. H 21.6 (8½). Rijksmuseum voor Volkenkunde, Leiden. Photo JK – K909a, K909b; **125** Río Azul tomb painting. Photo I. Graham; **126** Uaxactun: Structure B-XIII, Room 7. Photo Harvard University, Peabody Museum 50-1-20/22982; **127** Lidded tripod vessel with carved decoration. Copan, Honduras, Structure 16, Hunal Tomb. 21.2 x 21.5 (8 ⅜ x 8 7/16). Photo Jorge Perez de Lara. INAH, Centro Regional de Investigaciones Arquelógicas, Copan, Honduras (CPN-C-1796); **128** Old God effigy, Tikal. Photo JK – K4884; **129** Lidded vessel with figure of canoer. Maya area, Central Lowlands. Dallas Museum of Art, The Roberta Coke Camp Fund (1988.82A-B); **130** Quadruped vessel with bird. H 26 (10¼). New Orleans Museum of Art. Photo JK – K2866; **131** Cache Urn. H 47.5 (18 11/16). Photo MZ; **132** Monkey Scribe on lid of vessel at El Zotz. Courtesy El Zotz Archaeological Project. Photo Jorge Pérez de Lara; **133** Plan, Palenque, after Stierlin, 1964; **134** Palenque Palace; **135** Temple of the Cross, after Marquina; **136** East Court, Palenque Palace; **137** Temple of the Inscriptions. Drawing Philip Winton; **138** Temple of the Inscriptions, Palenque; **139** Yaxchilan Lintel 16. British Museum; **140** Structure 33, Yaxchilan; **141** West Acropolis, Piedras Negras. Drawing T. Proskouriakoff; **142** Plan, Tikal, after Morley and Brainerd; **143** Sarcophagus lid, Palenque. L 372 (146½). Photo M. G. Robertson; **144** Twin pyramid complex. Drawing by M. Lubikowski after W. R. Coe; **145** Central acropolis, Tikal. Photo Linda Schele; **146** Temple 1, Tikal. Photo Nicholas Hellmuth; **147** Main acropolis and the Main Plaza, Copan. Drawing T. Proskouriakoff; **148** Structure 22, Copan. Drawing A. P. Maudslay; **149** Structure 22, Copan. Photo Linda Schele; **150** Structure 22a, Copan. Photo E. Theodore; **151** Copan ballcourt; **152** Hieroglyphic stairway, Copan. Drawing T. Proskouriakoff; **153** Chicanna. Photo James Terry; **154** Structure 1, Xpuhil. Drawing T. Proskouriakoff; **155** Pyramid of the magician, Uxmal. Photo J. Sabloff; **156** Nunnery quadrangle, Uxmal. Photo Irmgard Groth-Kimball, © Thames & Hudson Ltd; **157** House of the Governor, Uxmal. Photo G. Kubler; **158** Great Arch, Kabah; **159** Palace Tablet, Palenque. © Merle Greene Robertson, 1976; **160** Panel from Temple 19, Palenque. Photo Jean-Pierre Courau/Bridgeman Art Library; **161** Captive figure, Tonina. © Moyses Zuniga/epa/Corbis; **162** Lintel 25, Yaxchilan. H 127 (50). British Museum, London. Photo JK; **163** Stela 11, Yaxchilan. H 358 (141). Photo T. Maler. Courtesy of the Peabody Museum, Harvard University; **164** Stela 14, Piedras Negras. H 282 (111). UM; **165** Stela 12, Piedras Negras. H 313 (123). Museo Nacional de Arqueologia, Guatemala City. Photo T. Maler, courtesy of the Peabody Museum, Harvard University, Cambridge; **166** Stela 16, Tikal. H 352 (138½). Drawing W. R. Coe; **167** Lintel 3, Tikal. Museum für Volkerkunde, Basel; **168** Altar Q, Copan. Photo YUAG; **169** Stela F, Quirigua. H 732 (288). Drawing A. Hunter, in A. P. Maudslay, 1899–1902; **170** Zoomorph P, Quirigua. H 221 (87). British Museum, London. Photo A. P. Maudslay; **171** Jade mosaic vessel, Tikal. Photo JK – K4887; **172** Gann jade. H 14 (5½). British Museum, London; **173** Bone, Burial 116, Tikal, after A. Trik; **174** Eccentric flint, H 24.8 (9 ¾). Dallas Museum of Art, The Eugene and Margaret McDermott Fund in honor of Mrs Alex Spence. Photo JK – K2822; **175** Jaina carved shell. H 8 (3⅛). Dumbarton Oaks Research Library and Collection, Washington D.C. Photo JK – K2881; **176** Male/female Jaina pair. H 24.8 (9¾). Detroit Institute of Arts, Founders Society purchase, Katherine Margaret Kay Bequest Fund and New Endowment Fund. Photo JK – K2881; **177** Figurines, Waka. Photo Ricky López; **178** Codex-style pot. Rollout photo. Metropolitan Museum of Art, New York. Photo JK – K521; **179** Altar de Sacrificios vase. H 25.5 (10). Museo Nacional de Arqueologia y Etnologia, Guatemala City. Photo T. Grieder; **180** Bonampak mural; **181** Bonampak reconstruction painting. Bonampak Documentation Project. Heather Hurst with Leonard Ashby; **182** Bonampak reconstruction painting. Bonampak Documentation Project. Heather Hurst; **183** Mural, Calakmul. Photo Jorge Pérez de Lara; **184** Stela 1, Seibal. H 237 (93); **185** Battle Mural, Cacaxtla; **186** Structure A, Cacaxtla; **187** God L, Red Temple, Cacaxtla. Photo D. Magaloni; **188** Pyramid of the Feathered Serpent, Xochicalco. Drawing Adela Breton. Courtesy City of Bristol Museum and Art Gallery; **189** Hall of the Columns, Mitla. Photo Antonio Attini/Archivo White Star; **190** 'Apotheosis' sculpture. H 158 (62½). Brooklyn Museum, Henry L. Batterman and Frank S. Benson Funds; **191** Pyramid B, Tula. Photo W. Bray; **192** Atlantean columns, Tula. Photo Nick Saunders; **193** *Chacmool* sculpture, Palacio Quemado, Tula. Photo Robert Cobean; **194** Plumbate vessel. H 16 (6¼). YUAG. Gift of Mr and Mrs Fred Olsen. Photo Joseph Szaszfai. Audio Visual Center, Yale; **195** Warrior shirt, Tula. South American Pictures; **196** Stela, Tula. H 122 (48). © Interfoto /Alamy; **197** Plan, Chichen Itza, after Morley and Brainerd; **198** Sacred cenote. Photo Jorge Pérez de Lara; **199** Caracol, Chichen Itza; **200** Section, Caracol. AMNH; **201** Castillo, Chichen Itza; **202** Temple of the Warriors, Chichen Itza. Photo Colin McEwan; **203** The Great Ballcourt, Chichen Itza; **204** Great Ballcourt relief, from Marquina; **205** *Chacmool*, Chichen Itza. MNA; **206** Wall painting, Temple of the Warriors. Ann Axtell Morris, Carnegie Institution of Washington; **207** Mayapan Stela 1. Drawing T. Proskouriakoff; **208** Castillo of Tulum. Massimo Borchi/Archivio White Star; **209** Tulum mural, after copy by M.A. Fernández 1939–40. Anales del INAH; **210** Dresden Codex. Sächsische Landesbibliothek, Dresden; **211** Pyramidal platforms, Iximche. Photo Philip Baird/www.anthroarcheart.org; **212** Book of Chilam Balam. Firestone Library, Princeton University, Princeton; **213** Aztec labrets. Courtesy MAS – Museum aan de Stroom. Photo Hugo Maertens, Bruges; **214** The Valley of Mexico, after Coe, 1984. Drawing P. Gallagher; **215** Templo Mayor excavations, 1981. Photo Great Temple Project; **216** Codex Mendoza. Bodleian Library, Oxford, MS Arch. Selden A1; **217** Skull rack, Templo Mayor precinct. Photo Great Temple Project; **218** Primeros Memoriales; **219** Tenochtitlan ceramic funerary urn. H 32.9 (12 15/16). Photo Great Temple Project; **220** Reconstruction of Templo Mayor. Drawing Philip Winton; **221** Offering 106. Museo del Templo Mayor, Mexico City. Photo MZ; **222** Malinalco. Photo James Terry; **223** Coatlicue. H 257 (101). MNA. Photo MZ; **224** Coyolxauhqui stone. H 340 (134). Photo Smithsonian Institution, Washington, D.C.; **225** Stone of Tizoc. D 275 (104½). MNA; **226** Calendar stone. D 360 (142). MNA. Photo MZ; **227** Goddess Tlaltecuhtli. © Kenneth Garrett/ NGS/Corbis; **228** Xipe Totec. Museum für Volkerkunde, Basel; **229** Votive vessel with an image of Chicomecoatl. H 106 (48¾). MNA. Photo MZ; **230** Eagle warrior. H 190 (75). Photo Great Temple Project; **231** Carnelite grasshopper. L 45.7 (18). Photo Irmgard Groth-Kimball, © Thames & Hudson Ltd; **232** Rain god *chacmool.* H 73.6 (29). MNA. Photo MZ; **233** Temple Stone. H 123 (48⅜). MNA. Photo MZ; **234** *Huehuetl.* H 115 (45¼). Photo MZ; **235** Turquoise serpent. British Museum, London. Photo Nick Saunders; **236** Gold pectoral. H 12.2 (4⅞). The Art Archive/Museo Regional de Oaxaca Mexico/Dagli Orti; **237** Cholula pottery cup. H 12 (4¾). Metropolitan Museum of Art, New York; **238** Feather headdress. H over 124 (49). Museum für Völkerkunde, Vienna; **239** Skull mask. British Museum, London; **240** Tlaloc effigy vessel. H 35 (13¾). Templo Mayor collection; **241** Stamp. MNA. Photo MZ; **242** Codex Selden. Courtesy Visual Resource Collection, Yale University; **243** Codex Féjerváry-Mayer. Board of Trustees of the National Museums on Merseyside; **244** Codex Borgia, Vatican Library; **245** Wall painting, Ixmiquilpan; **246** Codex Borbonicus. Bibliothèque de l'Assemblée Nationale, Paris; **247** Matricula de Tributos. Biblioteca del MNA; **248** Codex Durán Diego Durán, *Historia de las Indias de Nueva España e Islas de Tierra Firme*, 1579–81. Biblioteca Nacional, Madrid; **249** Florentine Codex. Facsimile published by Archivo General, Mexico, 1982; **250** Tlaloc depicted in Codex Ixtlilxochitl. Bibliothèque Nationale, Paris.

Index